# CHOPIN

*Profiles of the man and the musician*

Frédéric Chopin
(A daguerreotype taken in 1849, shortly before his death)

# FRÉDÉRIC CHOPIN

## PROFILES OF
## THE MAN AND THE MUSICIAN
## EDITED BY
## ALAN WALKER

PAUL BADURA-SKODA

ARTHUR HUTCHINGS    BERNARD JACOBSON

LENNOX BERKELEY    ALAN RAWSTHORNE

PAUL HAMBURGER    HUMPHREY SEARLE

ROBERT COLLET    ARTHUR HEDLEY

PETER GOULD

BARRIE AND ROCKLIFF
LONDON

© and first published 1966 by
Barrie & Rockliff (Barrie Books Ltd.)
2 Clement's Inn, London WC2
Printed in Great Britain by
W. & J. Mackay & Co Ltd, Chatham

# Contents

2.9196

# Illustrations

*Music examples drawn by Paul Courtenay*

# *Acknowledgements*

I should like to express my thanks
to Mr John M. Thomson, music adviser to Barrie & Rockliff, who gave generously in time and energy on the production of this book and whose personal interest in it I greatly appreciate;
to Mr Arthur Hedley, who offered helpful advice at the proof stage, loaned me photostats, and allowed me to inspect his remarkable collection of Chopin manuscripts;
to Mr Maurice Brown, who kindly checked the proofs of the Chronological Tables and brought them into line with the latest research;
to Mr Christopher Headington, who checked the final proofs of the entire book;
to Mr David Simmons, who checked the Discography;
to Miss Diana Slattery and Mrs Margaret Harrison, who typed the bulk of the script and helped me to deal with a voluminous amount of correspondence;
to Dr Gerald Abraham, who took a fatherly interest in the book from the start and offered many a kind word of encouragement;
to the staffs of the BBC Music Library and the BBC Gramophone Library for loaning me essential materials;
and, finally, to the contributors themselves, who produced their chapters on time and so enabled the book to meet its publication deadline.

A.W.

# Editorial Note

## Capitals

These have been kept down to an absolute minimum. They are invariably used in *particular* cases (e.g. Chopin's Ballade in G minor), but not in *general* cases (e.g. Chopin's ballades are among his longer works).

Where a general case temporarily becomes a particular, it takes a capital (e.g. Chopin's Studies, Op. 25, are similar in style to his Studies, Op. 10).

## Italics

Apart from their normal function of stress, italics are used throughout this volume

(a) for all foreign words not yet assimilated into the English language (e.g. compare *etüdenhaft* with *émigré*);

(b) for all 'descriptive' titles, as opposed to all 'normal' ones (e.g. compare *Les Sylphides* with Nocturne in C minor, Op. 48).

Italics have not been retained for straightforward musical terminology (e.g. Moderato, Allegro, etc.); neither are they used for nick-named compositions, for which quotation marks are used (e.g. 'Revolutionary' Study).

## Opus Numbers

Generally speaking, these have only been retained where the identification of a work would otherwise remain in doubt (e.g. compare Scherzo in C sharp minor with Mazurka in A minor, Op. 17, No. 4).

## Spelling

As far as possible the titles of Chopin's works have been anglicized. Thus 'Study', 'Prelude' and 'Waltz' are preferred to 'Étude', 'Prélude' and 'Valse'.

## Punctuation

This is a stylistic rather than an editorial matter. Consequently, the contributors have exercised some freedom in this respect.

A.W.

# Notes on Contributors

*Paul Badura-Skoda*, internationally known pianist and writer on music, was born in Vienna. He failed in the International Chopin Competition at Warsaw in 1949, but since then has given world-wide concert tours. His recordings of Chopin are frequently broadcast on the Polish radio. With his wife Eva, he has written *Interpreting Mozart on the Keyboard*.

*Lennox Berkeley*, composer, was a pupil of Nadia Boulanger in Paris from 1929–33, and since 1946 has been Professor of Composition at the Royal Academy of Music, London.

*Robert Collett*, pianist, and writer on music, has been a professor of Piano at the Guildhall School of Music, London, since 1952.

*Peter Gould*, pianist, since 1947 has been on the staff of the BBC Music Division, where he is now in charge of the chamber music department.

*Paul Hamburger*, pianist, and writer on music, was born in Vienna. He has toured England and the Continent as soloist, chamber music player and accompanist and since 1962 has been a BBC staff accompanist. A regular broadcaster, he has also contributed essays to books on Mozart and Britten.

*Arthur Hedley*, a leading Chopin authority, is the author of a book on Chopin in the Master Musician Series and editor of the recently published *Selected Correspondence of Chopin*. Since 1949 he has been Vice-Chairman of the Jury of the International Chopin competitions in Warsaw.

*Arthur Hutchings* is Professor of Music in the University of Durham and author of *Mozart's Piano Concertos*, *The Baroque Concerto*, and books on Delius and Schubert.

*Bernard Jacobson*, a writer and critic with a special interest in languages, has written for leading British and American journals. He has made an extensive study of contemporary Dutch music.

*Alan Rawsthorne*, composer, as a young man abandoned the study of dentistry in favour of composition. His extensive output includes many orchestral and chamber works, including several for piano.

*Humphrey Searle*, composer and writer on music, was a pupil of Anton Webern. He has translated Rufer's *Composition with Twelve Notes* into English and has also written *The Music of Liszt* and *Twentieth Century Counterpoint*. From 1964–5 he was Visiting Professor at the University of California.

*Alan Walker* until 1960 was a professor of Harmony and Counterpoint at the Guildhall School of Music, London, and is now in the BBC Music Division. He is also the author of *A Study in Musical Analysis* and a contributor to numerous periodicals.

# Preface

I first conceived the idea of a large-scale symposium on Chopin in 1963. Within a few days, I had secured the publisher's approval. Within a few weeks, my invitations to the various contributors had been despatched. Eighteen months later, the book was written. Not even I, with all my unbounded admiration for the composer, could have anticipated such a swift and overwhelming response to my idea. The very name of Chopin, it seems, was sufficient to stimulate into activity even the most recalcitrant pens.

From the start, I was quite clear about the kind of book I wanted and I set myself three aims:

First: I wanted a book that would concentrate on the music while not necessarily excluding the man. Most books on Chopin do the opposite. All too often, by the time the music is reached, the writer can do little more than hint, apologetically, at what he *could* have said about it if only he was not inhibited by 'lack of space'. In this book, I determined, 'lack of space' would not arise. The result is probably the most comprehensive account of Chopin's music yet to appear. There is hardly a single piece that is not mentioned somewhere; a great many of them receive the most detailed discussion.

Second: I wanted a book written by musicians who understood Chopin from the inside, so to speak, musicians who carried his music in their heads and fingers; in short, I wanted my contributors to consist, as far as possible, of composers and pianists who could write about Chopin, if I may be permitted the phrase, on a basis of loving understanding. I have never grasped the point of writing about a composer on the basis of dislike, the foundation on which many critics nowadays seem to rest their opinions. As for the 'impartial' writer, he is the enemy of us all.

Music is not something you can be impartial about. You either like it, or you do not.

Finally, I wanted a book which was addressed primarily to musicians. Paradoxically, the man in the street has never entertained any doubts that Chopin is a genius of the front rank. The professional musician, on the other hand, sometimes assigns to Chopin a position slightly less than this. His wrong reasons for doing so are, I hope, fully set out and answered in this volume.

Within the limits of their individual briefs, my contributors were free to adopt any approach that they wished. Diversity of approach is no bad thing. Certainly, I do not regard it as a 'built-in defect' of a symposium, a commonplace criticism (though a misconceived one) against books of this kind. Nor have I attempted to conceal the (very) occasional clash of opinion between contributors; indeed, whenever it happens I have drawn attention to it because I believe that the reader finds this kind of thing invigorating.

ALAN WALKER

Hampstead, N.W.3
October, 1965

# CHOPIN

*Profiles of the man and the musician*

ARTHUR HEDLEY

---

# Chopin: The Man

IN a book of this kind it is desirable that, at the outset and before the music itself is submitted to a critical examination, there should be established a trustworthy image of the man behind the music. Such a need would be felt in respect of any serious composer, but with Chopin it is a real prerequisite to any profitable investigation of his work. We have not here the example of a composer being unrecognized and neglected by his contemporaries—a familiar tale in the history of art; it is rather a question of misunderstanding and misrepresentation spread over the decades following Chopin's death in 1849, which caused a diminution of his value and historical importance, notwithstanding the unflagging popularity of his work with the general musical public and the vast piano-playing fraternity. Never was a composer less neglected than Chopin, and it has been well said that during the last hundred years the six letters of his name have accompanied every one of the untold thousands of pianos which have found their way all over the world. His name and some of his more familiar pieces have become household words, yet an image of the man and his music has been fixed in the public mind such as may indeed be sentimentally endearing to music-lovers, but which is, in fact, often degrading (in the exact sense of that word) to an artist who is entitled to the respect as well as the affection of those who play or listen to his compositions.

It has been Chopin's fate that the image of him as a man should have worked in some measure to the detriment of his standing, and that in the age of industrial civilization, of railways and easy communications, a figure of romance should have taken the place of the real man of flesh and blood. The process of viewing him and his art through a kind of distorting lens began almost as soon as he was dead, and went on at ever-quickening pace during the second half of the nineteenth century, reaching its climax perhaps in the years before the First World War. It may seem bold and paradoxical to assert that Chopin was less well understood by the generation that immediately followed him than by that of a later period, yet such is the state of affairs revealed by a close study of his 'posthumous career'. The real Chopin has been obscured by the circumstances in which he has been presented to the world. His life and character have become subject-matter for romantic biography; his own playing has become a topic of fiction, and the interpretation of his music, instead of being an object of serious musicianly consideration, has passed too often into the province of personal whim and caprice, based on nothing more than the vanity of the interpreters or their private attitude towards the Chopin legend. Looking into the origins of that legend, one may distinguish certain factors which must be taken into account.

During his lifetime Chopin came before the world as a somewhat enigmatic figure, an artist known to and heard by comparatively few people, and those few not well fitted to transmit a faithful record of his personality, so that sentimental anecdote and inaccurate generalizations took the place of fact. The 'romantic' circumstances of his short life conspired to falsify the picture. As a French-Pole, exiled from a martyred country whose cause awoke a sympathetic response throughout western Europe, he could not fail to be an object of interest. He appeared on the scene as a distinctive phenomenon in music. His playing and composition gave a 'new look' and certainly fulfilled an emotional need of the restricted society to which his work was addressed. The impact of his personality was not diminished but rather increased by the tantalizing veil of inaccessibility which he threw over his private life. His piquant and (to many people) incomprehensible affair with

George Sand, and finally his tragic death from consumption at the age of 39 set the seal on Chopin as a figure of romance—the real-life counterpart of the 'Poet' whom the world later learned to recognize and sigh over in *Les Sylphides*.

Chopin's extreme reserve where the outside world was concerned is a pre-eminent feature of his psychological make-up, and it is difficult to escape the conviction that as time went on he cultivated it to an almost morbid degree. His attitude towards his work was that of the 'closed book'. Not even to his intimate friends (and they were few, and not musicians) did he reveal what was at the back of his mind, what were the mainsprings of his music. He would deny, indignantly and emphatically, that his work had any literary or picturesque background; and he would have utterly repudiated those 'programmes' which have been the curse of Chopin playing for so many years. Only rarely, in his early Warsaw days, did he give any hints as to the direction of his impulses while composing—for example, in the case of the little D flat major Waltz, op. 70, no. 3 (1829), or the Romance of the E minor Concerto (1830). But once he found himself abroad there was an end to these timid half-openings of the door of his mind. There is practically no trace of such confidences in his letters to his family or friends—only a few threads of conversation with Eugène Delacroix, a painter, not a musician. What he may have said to other sympathetic listeners is lost: George Sand herself has little to offer. That Chopin had looked into his own soul and knew what was to be found there is more than once hinted at (but no more than hinted) in letters to a few very intimate Polish friends: 'It is not my fault if I am like a mushroom which seems edible but which poisons you if you pick it up and taste it, taking it to be something else. I know I have never been of use to anyone—and indeed not much use to myself.'[1] Or he compares himself with 'some old monk who had perhaps more fire in his soul than I have, but stifled it, stifled it and put it out'.[2] Or again, at the end of his life: 'We are the creation of some famous maker, in his way a kind of Stradivarius, who is no longer there to mend us. In clumsy hands we cannot give forth new sounds and we stifle within ourselves all those things which no one will ever draw from us—and all for lack of

[1] Letter to Fontana, 2 March 1839.
[2] Letter to Fontana, 14 December 1838.

someone to mend us.'[3] This recurrent idea of the 'stifling' of feeling and of the need for a self-control which blocks the public display of emotion will seem strange to those who have come to regard Chopin's music as a vehicle *par excellence* for the parade of sentimentality.

How does Chopin emerge as a man in the light of the evidence now available from strictly contemporary documentation, from his own letters and the diaries and correspondence of those who knew him best? It is not possible in a short essay to adduce much of this evidence for an interpretation of his personality: one can but offer a summary of what results from the mass of material that was not available when the commonly accepted picture of Chopin was created by writers at the end of the last century.

One thing is clear from the start: that his music, which contains alongside with softness and charm so much of passion and indeed ferocity, was not the product of the gentle inoffensive creature with whom legend has made the world familiar. There is also in Chopin a note of defiance, of insolence almost, towards the *musical* conventions of his time which forms a striking contrast to his exaggerated respect for the strict *social* conventions of the aristocratic circles in which he moved. Chopin is indeed a bafflingly complex individual, full of contradictions, and it is to his early formative years that one must return to find some key to his character. In his study of Liszt, Ernest Newman has shown how Liszt consciously created for himself a mask, the 'Saint Francis' that met the public eye, under which was hidden a very different man. In another way and on an unconscious level Chopin seems to have assumed a mask in order to defend his inner self against the prying curiosity of outsiders. Some people were not afraid to use the word 'hypocrisy' to define the barrier which he erected between himself and the world—the barrier of a charm and politeness which were equal to every situation. To get behind that barrier is not easy.

Two national strains were blended in him. His father, Nicholas Chopin, was a Frenchman of purely peasant stock who showed unusual enterprise and independence in seeking his fortune in Poland at the age of 16, in the service of a Polish landowner's steward. He remained there and gradually made a respectable situation for himself as a high-school teacher of French. Nicholas Chopin appears to have

[3] Letter to Fontana, 18 August 1848.

had all the best characteristics of his race and type: manly, hard-working and careful. His feet were firmly set on the ground, yet he was broad-minded and in his way a man of modest but earnest cultivation. He was, in short, the country lad who has made good at a social level higher than the one from which he has sprung. It is easy to see how many of his characteristic traits were handed down to his son, modified but not essentially weakened by what the boy inherited from his mother's side and by a life spent in a world very different from what the father had known. There is seen in Frédéric Chopin a basic fund of sound common sense which allowed him to judge persons and events with complete coolness and a profound sense of reality, never really disturbed by a parallel tendency towards romantic day-dreaming away in those 'strange spaces' in which he sometimes found himself wandering. He was far more of his father's son than has been generally realized. From him he inherited his love of order, precision; his quick intelligence and his ironic attitude to mere sentimentality, whatever form it appeared in, whether in the shape of adoring women admirers or the Germanic soulfulness of a Schumann.

What he took from his mother's side was emphasized by the circumstances and the milieu in which he spent his first twenty years—Poland at a time of intense national consciousness and everlasting preoccupation with the themes of patriotism, independence and cultural freedom. Whatever charges of instability might then be brought against the Poles, no one could deny their mental alertness, and the society in which Chopin lived was wide awake to all the movements of current European thought. Warsaw was a veritable beehive buzzing with intellectual activity. In this atmosphere Justyna Chopin was the natural and harmonious counterpart of her husband. His decidedly virile and positive character was balanced by her gentle, pious and unassertive 'romantic' nature. She was the dutiful wife and mother whose only interests lay in her home, her family and her faith. From her Chopin inherited the dreamy, sensitive and poetical side of his nature, and one may study in him the interplay and collisions of the two streams of inheritance, from father and mother, set against the dual background of the early Polish scene and the sophisticated world of aristocratic (and plutocratic!) Paris.

The Chopin household was extremely modest, and but for his

musical talent Frédéric would probably have remained unnoticed by
the higher circles of Warsaw. However, the child's marvellous gifts
soon took him outside his normal sphere. The boy Chopin had a
difficult path to tread, especially when he left infancy behind and
became a fashionable young man, acutely aware of his social situation.
Enjoying the patronage of princes, he ran the risk of being snubbed (as
sometimes happened to young Liszt), but this, so far as one knows,
never happened, thanks to Chopin's early-developed sense of tact, his
delicate perception of limits to be drawn and frontiers that might not
be crossed. In these impressionable years were implanted that exquisite
feeling for what is 'right', that reserved and perfectly correct attitude
towards the outside world which were to become a fundamental and
unalterable part of his character. All this involved no strain of adjust-
ment, since there already existed within him a natural compatibility
between the demands of the society in which the boy genius from an
unpretentious family found himself and his own deep innate tendencies.
Chopin responded so easily to his situation that before he was 20 he
could go anywhere and meet anyone, impeccable in dress, manners and
tone, with his natural ebullience kept in check by restraints which he
readily accepted and soon came to admire and insist on. He was never
subjected to the burden of that inferiority complex which bedevilled
Liszt's early years. He was never a rebel against society, for the simple
reason that he 'fitted in' and was accepted for what he was soon seen
to be.

While laying full stress on Chopin's achievement of perfect social
command of himself one must not diminish or gloss over some other
characteristics which come out in his relations with his friends. Side
by side with his invulnerable 'exterior' went powerful inward forces
and violences of temperament whose existence, even if they had not been
revealed in his intimate correspondence, might easily be deduced from
the nature of much of his music. In unguarded moments he could be
swept by strong waves of anger or contempt, which found expression
in language far removed from that of the elegant salons he frequented
in Warsaw or Paris. His letters (in Polish) show this constantly, as do
the confidences of friends who saw him in some boisterous or passionate
mood. With strangers the lid of the pot had to be firmly held down, and
George Sand for one has described how he sometimes almost choked

in keeping a tight hold over his temper. To release what was inside he had to resort to sarcasm (of which he had a ready fund) or else contemptuous silence. And with this capacity for powerful emotion, whether love or hatred, went a strong instinct to assert his will over others. George Sand experienced this soon after their liaison began—in 1838, when Chopin was 28—and it is a great mistake to assume that it was always she, the masterful woman, who was in charge of the situation. To the casual spectator of their daily life it might appear so, but under the surface a rather different state of affairs prevailed. Chopin undoubtedly had the art of getting his own way, and one can observe in his intimate relationships some of that curious 'tyranny of the weak over the strong' which has puzzled philosophers and psychologists. He had the gift of inspiring absolute devotion in his friends, and yet it cannot be denied that he sometimes made use of them without paying them back in the true coin of perfect trust and sincerity.

How far the asperities and inconsistencies of his character must be attributed to his long-drawn-out physical sufferings is difficult to say. From boyhood he had to take care of his health. Not that he was positively ill or in pain; but it was generally recognized that he was 'not strong'. During the years 1840–9 his life was a long slow decline; and who shall say how far sleepless nights, sensations of breathlessness and choking, overpowering feelings of weakness and frustration, contributed to distort his essentially warm and affectionate nature? Only a perfect angel, which Chopin was not, could have withstood, untouched, all that he was condemned to undergo. He did, it is true, show remarkable powers of recuperation at times when his disease seemed less menacing or actually about to be cured, and at such times he surprised those around him by his tenacious hold on life and his cheerful optimism. And one must admire the courage of a man who, within a year of his death, could face up to the terrors of a London 'season' with all its fatigues, disappointments and demands on nervous resistance. Not only did Chopin confront his destiny; he was able to smile and joke in the midst of his torments.

No one can now claim to be able to fathom the deep inner springs of that rare poetic nature. He was, as was at once recognized, a unique personality, one of those exceptional human beings who exercise over

others a spell that cannot be defined. 'Come,' said Berlioz to an acquaintance whom he wished to introduce to Chopin, 'I am going to show you
something that you have never seen and someone you will never forget.'
It was not necessary for such a man to put himself forward or to assert
himself in any way. By simply being his own modest self, without effort
or pose, he was able to give others the impression that they were in the
presence of a superior. We are told that wherever he went he was
invariably treated 'as a prince'; and this distinction of personality was
carried over into his music, so free from the slightest taint of the
commonplace or obvious. The word 'dandy' has indeed often been
used with respect to Chopin's attitude to life and to his art. The term is
admissible, but it is dandyism with a difference.

The 'dandyism' of a Chopin was something that went far beyond a
mere elegance of dress or behaviour; nor had it anything in common
with the gilded foppishness, often cloaking a gross coarseness of temperament, which is associated with the dandies of the Regency period.
It was the expression of an attitude of *mind*, involving many factors,
among others a rejection of disordered or overexuberant types of
thought and behaviour, and a natural preference for the self-domination
and control which are imposed by reason and will-power. There went
with it the affirmation of the artist's individuality and the supreme
rights of his own sensibility. It acknowledged that the source of all
worth-while creative activity must be an inspired wealth of feeling
and an abundant outflow of poetic impulses arising from the artist's
inner life. For Chopin the primary reality of life was to be found in his
own *self*, and the feeling welling up from the inner depths was to be
subject to the control of the intelligence and the scholarly discipline
without which the inward vision cannot receive a coherent form. Only
exceptional artists can bring these apparent contradictions—the 'classical'
concern for form and the 'romantic' urge of inspiration—into that
creative equilibrium which is found in the highest art, and Chopin
was one of them. A single short example will illustrate what is meant
by this creative 'balance': the Mazurka in C sharp minor, op. 63, no. 3,
the last mazurka published by Chopin two years before his death. Here
the music is stripped of every superfluity. All the composer's feeling is
concentrated into a page or two of deceptively simple-looking music;
and at the end the poetic impression is reinforced by the use of

an academic procedure—a canon at the octave—which, so far from being a mere scholastic curiosity, is a vital factor in the build-up of tension and an added grace of this perfect composition.

The imperious craving for perfection dominated and tormented Chopin's whole life. He could be satisfied with nothing less, whether in composition or playing, love or friendship, clothes, manners, taste . . . everything. And when, in love and friendship, his exacting demands could not be met, in an imperfect world among imperfect people, Chopin would retreat, disillusioned, into himself, and let his music receive what he had failed to give away.

When one sees Chopin, in the daily routine of his life as a quasi-invalid, continually dependent upon others, he may appear as something of a weakling; and it is easy to be misled into imagining that there was something effeminate and fragile in his nature. The world has been too ready to seek and find a correspondence between the slender, frail young man with the air of high breeding and 'graceful cough' and the music he left behind. This is an error, for the correspondence is super-ficial. The man who was forced by ill health to rely on others for help in organizing his existence showed in his art an astonishing degree of self-confidence and independence. Once he had realized what his true direction must be he followed it without hesitation and without allow-ing himself to be turned aside. There is no evidence at all for the state-ments, so often made, that he weakly submitted to the advice of interfering friends and accordingly modified or toned down some of his too boldly original ideas. Even as a boy Chopin had the 'nerve' (for so it must be called at a time when academic correctness counted for so much) to follow his own line and *dare* things which made his contem-poraries' hair stand on end. And this originality was no mere playing with half-digested discoveries or lucky strokes, but was the outcome of a calm and confident exploration of new ways and means. Chopin did not, of course, live in a vacuum: he was subject as much as anyone to the pressures and influences exercised by his environment, and in his early works there may be found obvious echoes of the composers whose music formed part of his ordinary background. But his mind was so constituted that it seems at a relatively early stage to have been closed to impressions from the world around him and to have remained thenceforth impervious to them. He was not a follower but, without

intending it, a leader. By the time he arrived in Paris at the age of 21 his
personality, in all its aspects, was established. It is difficult to detect any
essential change in Chopin over the remaining years of his life: there
was only the expected maturing and the consolidation of territory
already acquired. The process of tightening up, of discarding the less
worthy elements of effective pianistic brilliance which had first attracted
him—one thinks of works like the Grande Polonaise, op. 22, or the sets
of variations—went hand in hand with his serious discovery of Bach, a
revelation which did not occur until after he reached Paris. There is
something quite moving in Chopin's reverent and modest attitude
towards the great man, especially at a period when Bach had not yet
fully recovered his complete stature after a long eclipse. In 1838 Chopin
could not set out on the difficult trip to Majorca, so remote and unknown in those days, without taking his copies of Bach with him.
And in his monastery cell on the island he counts his own Twenty-four
Preludes as mere 'scribblings' when placed side by side on a desk with
the 'Forty-eight'. Later he tells how in his spare moments he is correcting
for himself in the Parisian edition of Bach 'not only the mistakes made
by the engraver but those which are backed by the authority of people
who are supposed to understand Bach—not that I have any pretensions
to a deeper understanding, but I am convinced that I sometimes hit
on the right answer. Oh, you see how I have gone and boasted!'[4] This
was not false modesty put on to impress others: it was the reflection of a
basically modest character.

The nationalistic and patriotic motive behind a large area of Chopin's
work is there for all to see; but it is an exaggeration to suggest, as has
been done, that he did not write a note which did not come from this
unique source of inspiration. Perhaps the fact that he bore a French
name, which might raise a doubt as to his national allegiance, impelled
Chopin (especially when he had left Poland for good) to become 'more
royalist than the king'. He was passionately, but not blindly, devoted
to the land of his birth as a real country which he knew to its very heart,
but even more perhaps as an abstraction: 'Poland'—a spiritualized
conception which existed in his imagination and continually nourished
his emotions. Although he spent one half of his life on the other side of
Europe among a cosmopolitan society in Vienna, Paris or London, his

[4] Letter to Fontana, 8 August 1849.

roots were in Warsaw, and he never identified himself with any background save that of the Polish circles of his early days. He may say that he has learnt to consider the French 'as his own people', but it does not ring true. He remained at heart the home-loving Pole, nostalgically referring all values to the standards set at home. Even in the moments of his most brilliant success he is more concerned to know what his own people will think rather than how the 'outsiders', of whatever nationality, will be impressed. His most intimate relations were exclusively with Polish émigré society in France. His close contacts with the French, as in the affair with George Sand, did nothing to loosen that bond. George Sand herself was always aware that Chopin could not be 'possessed' by anyone outside the restricted circle of his family. She came as near as any outsider, man or woman, ever did to penetrating the barrier, but she never achieved the final result of becoming one with him. His patriotism, as expressed more obviously in the polonaises and mazurkas, springs both from the wide generalized vision of national glory and tragedy cherished by the Poles after the collapse of the 1830 revolt against the Russians and from the narrower, 'provincial' sentiments of the 'boy who has left his heart at home'. In one of his rare flashes of self-revelation Chopin confessed: 'I am a real, blind Mazovian', and who can tell whether his deepest, most concentrated patriotic feelings are not to be found in the phrases of some quiet mazurka rather than in the extrovert splendours of the great A flat major Polonaise?

Chopin comes before us, then, as a man of extremely complex make-up, and there is no easy solution to the problems which his personality and the music through which it was expressed present to his modern interpreter. One can only approach him by sweeping aside the clutter of trivial romantic legend which has accumulated around his name and his works. When all the sentimentality, pathos, patriotic fairy-tales and garbled 'memories' have been cleared away he appears in simple dignity as Thomas Carlyle saw him in 1848—a great artist and 'a noble and much suffering human being'. He was more than any other musician of his period the 'artist' in that word's most absolute sense. His mind was never diverted from its single, absorbing preoccupation by any chasing after will-o'-the wisps in the fields of literature, the visual arts, politics, social questions or abstract theorizing. To some it

will seem a weakness that he should have lived in a world of upheaval
and rapid change without ever allowing himself to be 'committed' or
'engaged', as our modern jargon puts it. Yet it was precisely therein
that his strength lay. He was dedicated to the one task of exploring the
world he knew best—that of his own heart and imagination; and in
giving shape to what he discovered within himself it turns out that he
was embodying in his music those unchanging essentials of feeling
which ordinary inarticulate humanity recognizes but cannot express for
itself. In limiting himself to the piano he in no way crippled or tied down
his genius, for by his natural affinity with his instrument he was provided with a sufficient outlet for the wealth of sensibility with which his
double inheritance had endowed him. Where else will one find in so
confined a space as the few hundred pages of his complete works such a
striking *variety* (to say the least) of musical images of a rare poetic
quality? Chopin is indeed the complete illustration of Goethe's dic-
tum: 'It is when working within limits that mastery reveals itself.'

It is when one studies Chopin as he moves about on his daily course
in Warsaw or Paris that one obtains the truest portrait of the man. None
of those who felt honoured to know him—Berlioz, Mendelssohn,
Meyerbeer, Rossini, Delacroix, the poet Mickiewicz, Heinrich Heine,
George Sand herself (the list comprises everyone of distinction in that
compact world)—were people to tolerate mediocrity of intelligence or
character. And if Chopin occupied a special place among them it was
because they saw in him a happy combination of qualities which go to
make up a sympathetic and likeable personality: lively intelligence, a
generous warmth of feeling, a sense of fun (he was an admirable
mimic) and, over all, that indefinable aura which singles out the natural
aristocrats of this world regardless of birth or fortune. They recognized
in him, too, the uncompromising perfectionist, strict in demanding,
and in his own sphere living up to, the highest standards. Those
standards were part of an attitude to life and a code for civilized living
during an era that has so completely vanished that it is only by an effort
of historical imagination that we can think our way back across the
barrier not only of intervening years but of profound mental and
spiritual change. The gulf separating us from the France of Louis-
Philippe and the elegant and exclusive circles in which Chopin played
and composed on his silvery-toned Pleyel grand is indeed enormous,

but this does not mean that the man and his music are to be treated like some rare museum-piece, kept in a silk-lined case and protected by glass. They have still much to say to the modern world; and music like Chopin's, which has undergone and survived so much violent handling over a hundred years, must possess beneath its delicate skin an inner toughness and vitality which it derived from its creator. One may sometimes see a cast of Chopin's hand, taken on the morning after he died: let it not be forgotten that this small hand had a grip which gave the lie to its fragile look!

### The Interpretation of Chopin

It is now time to turn from the man to the pianist and composer and to consider in general terms what light may be thrown on the interpretation of his music. The question of 'how to interpret Chopin' is one of standing interest, and one can only arrive at some useful conclusions by cutting through a thick undergrowth of spurious tradition which sprang up soon after his death. Side by side with the picture of Chopin the man arose another of Chopin the pianist and interpreter of his own music. The two sets of legend nourished each other.

That Chopin's music can only be understood by reference to his art as a pianist is a fact that needs no emphasis: the music is so absolutely conceived in terms of the piano that it can scarcely be imagined apart from it. This is not to suggest that it is merely the result of casual exploration at the instrument by a skilful executant, although, as is well known, Chopin was himself a brilliant and inventive improviser. A ballade or scherzo is not a piece of music picked out of the keyboard by someone hunting for effective combinations of phrases and figures: it is a completely logical musical structure, but one whose fabric is determined by Chopin's profound understanding of the instrument for which he was writing.

He was, after all, trained as a composer, and it was as a composer rather than as a mere pianist that his first teachers saw him. For them the two functions were separate, and in his apprentice days no one fore-saw that piano playing and composition would be inextricably inter-woven in his approach to music. His teacher Elsner never realized it, and continued to lament Chopin's failure to write operas and orchestral works ('Your genius should not cling to the piano: operas must make you immortal.') But the young man had a clear insight into the nature of his own gifts, and he could answer: 'I have a unique opportunity of realizing the promise that is within me. In Germany there is no one I would take piano lessons from, although a few people have felt that I still lack something. In my view he is a lucky man who can be both composer and executant at the same time'; and he goes on to speak of his 'perhaps too audacious but noble wish and intention to create for myself a new world.'[5] Composer and executant at the same time—that was the point of vantage from which Chopin could reveal himself as the originator of a new style.

How this composer-pianist envisaged and performed his own music is a question that can only be answered by reference to the most *strictly contemporary* and objective accounts; but whether, having inquired how Chopin himself played, the modern interpreter should attempt to give some quasi-historical reproduction of the style—that is another matter. With regard to the later 'memories' of his playing, set down years after Chopin's death, it soon becomes clear that such recollections and the so-called 'traditions' stemming from aged pupils—one active claimant surviving until 1922!—are to be treated with the greatest reserve.[6] The same may be said of what derives from the various 'schools' such as that of Liszt or the Russians.

The factual details of the background of Chopin's career are not to be disputed. His legendary reputation as a pianist was, for his whole life, based on a mere thirty or so genuinely *public* appearances. (One thinks of the scores of times a modern virtuoso may appear in a single year.) Very few were those who had heard Chopin play. His largest single audience was one of twelve hundred at a concert in Manchester, and not more than about six hundred persons, mostly aristocratic music-lovers, heard him during the last ten years of his life in France. He had no luck with his pupils. Apart from one bright genius, the boy Karl Filtsch, who died when he was 15, Chopin's pupils were medio-

[5] Letter to Elsner, 14 December 1831.

[6] It is difficult to make an exception in the case of Carl Mikuli, who published an edition of Chopin which at one time enjoyed a high reputation. There are things in that edition (textual errors, etc.) which make one wonder how far Mikuli was able to speak for Chopin. He could not distinguish Chopin's writing from that of a copyist.

crities—mostly aristocratic young ladies, none of whom made their mark or were able to pass on a positive tradition embodying everything that mattered: tempo, phrasing, pedalling, general dynamics—in a word: style. Leaving aside Liszt for a moment, none of the leading German virtuosi but Clara Schumann was acquainted with Chopin's style from personal experience; and it should be noted that towards the end of the century Clara Schumann's playing of Chopin met with little favour, being considered 'very tame'—this in spite of the fact that Chopin had said: 'She is the only woman in Germany who knows how to play my music.' As for Russia, the great school of pianism which has admittedly produced miracles of virtuosity was principally founded on the teaching of Adolf Henselt, who from 1863 was given, and enjoyed exercising, the powers of a dictator in everything connected with piano teaching in the Russian Empire. Yet Henselt never heard Chopin play a note—a loss which he deeply lamented. And the great Anton Rubinstein himself, whose interpretation of Chopin during his many concert tours had a profound effect in Russia and the rest of Europe (particularly his conception of the B flat minor Sonata),[7] had only the faintest acquaintance with Chopin's playing: he heard him when he was a little boy in Paris in 1841.

The other 'great names' in the piano-playing world from 1850 onwards, too numerous to mention individually, almost without exception took their cue where Chopin was concerned from Liszt—the Liszt of Weimar, whose prestige was enormous and whose master classes, held over a lengthy period, had far-reaching repercussions and in some quarters still hold their ground today. When one turns to Liszt, all in all the principal source of the later tradition and the source, too, of much that was detestable and spurious in the Chopin interpretation of the fifty years up to 1914, one finds little that is reassuring. Liszt, of course, knew Chopin's playing intimately, and Chopin on one single recorded occasion expressed his admiration of Liszt's handling of his Studies. But in the long run it is difficult to avoid the question (without pretending to answer it finally): did Liszt *really* understand Chopin? One need not recount here the story of the hostility between the two men, ending in almost virulent dislike on Chopin's side. Was it possible for Liszt to appreciate absolutely a personality and an art so essentially

[7] See p. 246.

remote from his own? Liszt's public pianistic career, which ended 'officially' just before Chopin's death, was founded on the grandiose, the astounding, the dazzlingly *effective* both in composition and performance, coupled with an equally effective pathos and the heart frankly worn on the sleeve. It was these very elements that caused Chopin's revulsion, especially when he saw, as he did on occasions, Liszt tampering with his music and encouraging others to do so. ('He can't keep his hands off anything' were Chopin's words.) Although Liszt cannot be held personally responsible for the excesses of his pupils, his celebrated 'school' at Weimar between about 1866 and 1886 bore some strange and unpalatable fruit.

Chopin's own playing was the counterpart of his personality. Every characteristic which may be distinguished in the man came out in the pianist—the same precision; the horror of excess and all that is 'sloppy' and uncontrolled; the same good manners and high tone of breeding, combined with poetic warmth and a romantic fervour of expression. No one had ever heard such polished playing, although others could make a more overwhelming impression by their rush and violence. It is a mistake, encouraged by sentimental legend, to believe that Chopin's playing was invariably limited by a delicacy which was equivalent to weakness. The fact is that even in the last stages of consumption he could rally and summon the strength to play (as in Scotland in 1848) works like the F major Ballade with an energy that surprised the audience, who saw in front of them 'a slight, frail-looking person.' At his final public appearance at the Guildhall in November 1848, less than a year before the end, and although he was more dead than alive, he managed to play 'with his usual brilliance'.

'Good taste'—these words are of great significance in Chopin's attitude towards his art, and that taste was in many respects the taste of the late eighteenth century rather than that of the full-blooded Romantics. (In his last days Chopin read Voltaire's *Dictionnaire Philosophipue* instead of the lurid novels and plays of Victor Hugo!) Although inevitably involved in the Romantic movement and sharing some of its enthusiasms, Chopin was in his heart a stranger to those circles which gave the movement its tone in literature, drama, music. He could not really join in the fun of the period 1830–50. He stood aside, a witness of the movement rather than a participant; and one should not imagine that the pianists of the later nineteenth century, the children and grand-children of the movement, could come close to a faithful interpretation of Chopin's music by the fact of being close to him in time. The Germany of Bismark and William II, the France of the Second Empire and Third Republic, the England of late Victorian and Edwardian days, and the America of the first millionaires, all these had nothing in common with Chopin's elegant and exclusive world. As time passed the shadowy tradition of Chopin's playing vanished into thin air. In all its aspects his art as a pianist and composer was overmagnified and coarsened. His warm but restrained poetic sentiment was degraded into luscious sentimentality; his dramatic episodes became sensational melodrama; his moments of exhilarating virtuosity degenerated into vulgar displays of crazy speed and showmanship; and passages to which Chopin had given an added charm by his fanciful but discreet rubato now staggered along under a weight of distorted rhythm and cheap 'effects'.

The process of coarsening naturally extended to Chopin's text. Where, after scrupulous consideration, he had written a light but sufficient accompaniment to a waltz or mazurka, the pianists of a later date did not hesitate to lay on heavy octaves and thickened chords, together with an abundance of extra harmonies and uncalled-for counterpoints ('More nice, more melodious, you know', as Pachmann cheerfully explained.) Every drop of emotion was to be squeezed out of some nocturne or prelude; not a bar but had its programme. And the way was open for 'Revolutionary' Studies, 'Winter Winds', 'Little Dog' or 'Minute' Waltzes, and so forth. Every polonaise had its hidden patriotic and political significance and every ballade its story. The greatest of Liszt's pupils, Karl Tausig, could only conceive of Chopin's Barcarolle as a duet for two lovers in a gondola, with a kiss at bar 78. In extreme cases it was possible for pianists who had made a 'corner' in Chopin to impose a truly fantastic image of the composer on a public already conditioned to receive it, thanks to the mushroom-like growth of a literature that sprang up around Chopin's name: memoirs, stories, legends and traditions of all kinds. A Polish countess was pointed out as the only one of her class in whose arms Chopin had *not* died; while about 1904 a gramophone record was issued of another who claimed to hold the world speed record for a performance of the D flat major Waltz,

C—B

op. 64! It is a sad catalogue; and those who wish to see summed up on a single disc the 'end-product' of eighty years of 'tradition' need go no further than the jubilee record made by Hofmann in 1937, before an enraptured New York audience. Everything that may safely be described as anti-Chopin is there: the insane prestissimos, the shattering thundercrashes of fortissimo, the wild fluctuations of rhythm (otherwise known as rubato)—in a word, the depths have been reached.[8] Without labouring the point one may refer the reader to the literature of the period 1850–1910 and to the recordings left by those whose careers as pianists began during the fifty years after Chopin's death.

One of the explanations offered for the treatment of Chopin's music as if it were little more than a rhapsodical product, not subject to recognized rules and consequently a suitable terrain for a sort of pianistic 'free for all', has been the belief that no one knows what Chopin wanted, that he himself did not know for certain, and that his printed text is little more than an approximate guide to his thought. This pernicious error has received support from the countless editions which have flowed from the press since the original copyrights expired. The existence of all these editions does not mean that they were really needed because of the situation with regard to Chopin's text. The simple commercial fact is that even the smallest music publisher has been tempted to bring out his own edition of Chopin's compact volumes, sure to find a ready sale if some excuse for a new edition could be trumped up. On the face of things it is unlikely that an intelligent and careful worker like Chopin should not have been able to set down what he wanted from his interpreters. Whatever hesitations and uncertainty in his mind may have preceded his final version, once it was given to the world he certainly intended it to be adhered to. Marmontel, who knew him well in Paris, records what everyone in Chopin's circle knew: 'Either from his deep love of art or from an excess of personal conscientiousness Chopin could not bear that the text of his works should be touched. The slightest modification seemed to him a serious fault which he could not forgive his most intimate friends, no exception being made for Liszt . . . the composer considered these alterations as a veritable act of sacrilege.'[9]

[8] I am not suggesting that Hofmann invariably played Chopin like this.
[9] A few specimens of 'improvement' may be chosen at random: Moiseiwitsch

Chopin's manuscripts reveal the care he took to ensure that the definite version he had decided on should prevail over any first thoughts he may have had. He went to quite absurd lengths in obliterating beyond recall the rejected version.[10] He hesitated long before attaching a final indication of tempo or expression, so that no pianist has the right to treat these things as a simple matter of personal preference. The same applies to the metronome marks which he placed on his earliest publications, notably the Studies. They were put there by Chopin himself and undoubtedly represent his own choice of tempo.[11] It is, alas, rare for one to hear the music performed in accordance with the composer's own careful markings. His *allegro* generally becomes a giddy *prestissimo*, and *mezza voce* or *sotto voce* (expressions he was fond of) are usually completely disregarded.

In the matter of tempo Chopin's actual notation is in itself a reliable guide to the method of performance. For instance, he began by writing the F minor Study, op. 25, no. 2, marked *Presto agitato*:

EX. 1

i.e. *presto agitato* in semiquavers; but on consideration he decided on a simple *presto* in quavers, with emphasis on the *molto legato*:

EX. 2

---

preferred to omit eight bars from the Finale of the B minor Sonata, while transposing the end of the E minor Nocturne. Pachmann (on Bülow's suggestion) thought it better to leave out four vital bars in the F sharp major Impromptu while making up for this by inserting about a dozen bars of his own into the B minor Mazurka, op. 33. Paderewski had no hesitation in denaturing the scale in the C sharp minor Waltz . . . and so on: the list is endless. Scores of pianists still play 'nice' quiet endings to works in which the composer and the logic of his music demand a decided *forte*.

[10] See autograph facing p 138. ED.
[11] See p. 128 for further discussion about Chopin's metronome markings. ED.

The key to the interpretation lies in the notation. Similarly the Prelude in F sharp major began as a *lento ma non troppo* in $\frac{6}{8}$ time, but Chopin later chose a plain *lento* in $\frac{6}{4}$. He knew Italian quite well and understood exactly the words he was using. When, in the Prelude in B minor, he crosses out the first indication *largo* and replaces it by *lento assai*, he is simply asking for *very slowly*, an indication which not one pianist in a hundred follows.

In general it may be said that in playing Chopin the tendency has been for pianists, pressed by the insatiable demand for more speed to satisfy jaded and ignorant audiences, to play quick movements faster and faster until it seemed that the limit would never be reached. It is by no means uncommon to hear the C sharp minor Study, op. 10, no. 4, a favourite showpiece of virtuosos, played at twice the speed indicated by Chopin; and in recent years it has been sufficient for a well-known virtuoso to issue a record of the E major Scherzo taken at a vertiginous pace, which makes nonsense of the music, for all the younger pianists to seek to imitate the example given. And so the charming garlands of chords which form one of the beauties of this Scherzo are turned into a senseless chatter of monkeys, and the contours of the running passages vanish in a meaningless torrent of sound.[12]

On the other hand, Chopin's indications of a mere relaxation of tempo are often twisted into a slowing-down to snail's pace which nothing in the music can justify. This usually happens in cases where, after a quick movement, (as in a sonata, ballade or scherzo) Chopin has asked for a modest *più lento*. The range of speed is often enormous and completely foreign to Chopin's general style. By a curious perversity one not infrequently hears the *più lento* of a piece marked vivace scherzando actually taken more quickly than the vivace itself!—e.g. the Study in E minor, op. 25, no. 5.

It is only by remembering that in Chopin all *excess*, in one direction or another, is bad that one can hope to come to satisfactory terms with the music. To a cheeky pupil who ventured to give him a lesson on a Beethoven sonata, complete with exaggerated dynamics and intense 'expressiveness', Chopin mildly retorted: 'Why should one always have to play in such a declamatory manner?'—and there is no doubt

[12] It is satisfactory to note that Rubinstein counteracts this by adopting a rational *presto* which allows the music to be heard.

that in his own playing he avoided such extremes. The true expressiveness of his playing was not found in any sentimental lingering over 'the melody'—in Chopin the melody can usually look after itself—but in the perfect balance of parts and a sensitive distribution of emphasis. Needless to say, he had a horror of what later became a trade-mark with many pianists: the 'splitting' of the hands whereby a fake intensity or heart-throb was produced by delaying a melody note until the left hand had pronounced its corresponding bass note. And he was equally severe on those who did not play the notes of his chords simultaneously (except where he had expressly indicated the arpeggio). On all these points Chopin was out of touch with, and ahead of, the common amateur and professional practice of his day; and one cannot help feeling that if he could have been heard in, say, 1910, many admirers would have been disconcerted by the coolness of his playing, so accustomed had audiences grown to the gushing manner combined with that poetic frenzy so long thought appropriate to an effective 'rendering' of his work.

While for the main body of Chopin's output a modern pianist will be wise to use and respect an edition based on reliable sources and careful scholarship, a note of warning must be sounded with regard to the posthumous works, opp. 66–74, which include some of the most popular pieces. They were published in spite of Chopin's formal command that his unfinished manuscripts should be burnt, and often their text was furbished up from sources of all kinds—bits of manuscript, odd copies and so forth, the whole being flavoured to suit the personal taste of their editor, Chopin's friend, Fontana. (He never saw Chopin after 1841 and had no knowledge of anything composed after that date.) Some striking examples of distortion of Chopin's intentions are to be found among them, and in this region of the composer's work the interpreter has to rely on his grasp of Chopin's style derived from a knowledge of the rest of his work. How far the posthumous texts may differ from what Chopin himself wrote is well illustrated by the so-called Nocturne in C sharp minor, sometimes called the *Lento con gran espressione*, whose published version is based, not on Chopin's autograph, but on a copy made and probably 'adapted' by his sister. The piece contains quotations from the F minor Concerto which are easily recognized. What one always hears is this:

EX. 3

Whereas what young Chopin dared to write, in 1830, was literally

EX. 4

This telescoping of different time-signatures is something that was 'not done' at the time Chopin was writing and is characteristic of his independent attitude of mind.[13] The same independence is seen in his quite uninhibited treatment of the keyboard, in the shape of his pianistic figures, the liberation of the left hand, the fine-spun decorative arabesques—in a word, all those things which come under the easily recognized heading 'Chopinesque'. This useful but often misapplied word ought not to be restricted to a sense which implies a kind of trick or (if one may use a modern term) 'gimmick', for Chopin brought to the piano a genuine revelation of new possibilities. The extent of his originality can be best appreciated when one compares his piano writing with the efforts of other people who enjoyed an equal or even greater contemporary reputation. In the countless *Albums des Pianistes* which flourished during this period one will find Chopin thrown in with the motley crowd of Moscheles, Kalkbrenner, Herz, Henselt, Döhler and the like. In the 1834 Album, for instance, Chopin's Three Nocturnes, op. 15, stand out like an island in a sea of mediocrity and triviality.

In the succeeding pages of this book the reader will be taken on a survey of Chopin's achievement and will realize that here is an artist whose work demands in its interpreters first and foremost *musical intelligence*, not mere cleverness—the nimble fingers, the facile recipes for expressiveness, the general pianistic know-how. It is the intelligence

[13] Compare this passage with the F minor Concerto p. 152, Ex. 13. ED.

which takes in both head and heart, which is modest in its approach to Chopin's immense labours for perfection, and is ready to see his work in a truly historical light, leaping over the 'years in the wilderness' when he was demoted to the rank of little better than a salon-composer. The real interpreter of Chopin will resolutely throw aside all those stories and 'programmes' which have become attached like barnacles to so many of his works, and will give his attention solely to the plain text as the pure, unadulterated *musical* expression of a remarkable personality. There may be those who lament the passing of the old days when a giant of the keyboard would pack the Albert Hall on a Saturday afternoon for a display of fireworks and nonsense at the expense of Chopin's reputation among serious musicians. Such regrets are foolish, at least in my view, for I believe that most young and rising pianists of today acknowledge their respect for Chopin the musician and are fully aware of their duty and responsibility towards his work. There can be little doubt that Chopin would rejoice to see himself clear of the jungle of vulgarity and misrepresentation in which he has come near to being lost. Each new generation of pianists may be expected to rediscover Chopin for itself, while bringing to its image of him the colour of its own mind. Today the anti-Romantic current is running strong, but this need give no cause for criticism if it sweeps away false sentiment, wilful distortion and impudent tampering with a work of art which asks only to be allowed to rely on its own virtues in order to manifest the enduring quality with which its creator has endowed it.

ARTHUR HUTCHINGS

# The Historical Background

WHEN history left any incomplete account of a man or of his music the late Cecil Gray's imagination amplified it with a conviction and gusto that is elicited from more cautious and less colourful writers only by incontrovertible documentary evidence. In his 1928 *History of Music*[1] Gray wrote:

> Neither literature nor any other art played any part in Chopin's mental development or in his music. Not merely had he an instinctive and profound aversion from anything in the nature of 'programme music', but he was never known even to read a book. . . . Nothing in the outside world, neither human relations, feeling for nature, nor appreciation of any art save his own, exercised the slightest influence upon his work either for good or evil. He would seem to have actively disliked the music of his greatest contemporaries. Berlioz, Liszt, and Meyerbeer he particularly detested . . . and in Beethoven he cared only for cantabile passages.

Gray does not mention Chopin's near-adoration of Bach and Mozart, and we may wonder whether his words accurately describe one who

[1] In the series *The History of Civilization*, ed. C. K. Ogden, Kegan Paul, London.

maintained close friendship with Delacroix, enjoyed more than casual acquaintances with Balzac, Musset and Heine, and entered into the closest of human relationships with a writer and novelist, a woman who conceived it her duty to be Egeria to all artistic and literary talents of the romantic movement, including Chopin himself.

Yet suppose that Gray's description is strictly true. Suppose that Chopin's musical ear was attentive to no music but his own, that he 'never opened a book' after the last one prescribed for his education, and that he had no interest in other personalities than his own. Just as bad music as well as good is documentary, so such a creature as Gray imagined was the mirror of others. By attempting to envisage the places and communities in which he lived, or the ideals and ideas with which he came into contact, including those he disliked, we do not necessarily substitute shallow sociology and psychology for the reception of his art by our musical wits. The aim of our exercise is to enhance that reception by comparisons, of which the first should be among his own works.

Chopin's music testifies to three historical 'backgrounds', only one of which calls for amplification in this chapter. The first background is not national but international—that of public concert rooms from Vienna to Edinburgh. In these, after J. C. Bach had established the piano concerto in London, the composer-pianist proved his calibre by performing and directing piano concertos, and therefore young Chopin hoped to secure attention in Warsaw, Dresden, Vienna, Munich and Paris chiefly by playing his First Concerto; yet despite the distinct personality which shines through this work it ranks with his variations and rondos among the pieces which most nearly link him with Hummel, Weber, Cramer, Kalkbrenner and the other composer-pianists who most frequently confronted audiences during Beethoven's last years and the two following decades. From this background Chopin recoiled very early, and from it he receded almost completely in his years of fame. When he played in salons and to an élite, or on rare occasions publicly but still to an élite, his style was utterly unlike that of the popular concert-hall virtuosi. Though his audiences sometimes heard movements (usually the middle ones) from his concertos either with a small supporting ensemble or with a second pianist, they were not rivals to other concertos.

The second background is Poland, more specifically the educated and national-conscious society of Warsaw. To it belong the polonaises, the mazurkas and the rarely heard songs. Since Chopin was an infant when his father took up a teaching appointment and the family moved to the very middle of Warsaw, we stretch imagination by savouring any rural background to his music. None of it is directly evocative of the village on the Skarbeck estate, or of the somewhat dull countryside of Poland. Chopin's father was French; polite society in Russia and Poland conversed in French; and Chopin settled in France while Poland suffered the climax of her struggle and the agony of annexation. The pieces by Chopin which have been called nationalist include no heroic attitudinizing and are not merely the equivalent of feathered caps and scarlet sashes on émigré folk-dancers. Polish nationality may be important in the alchemy of Chopin's melody and harmony—a matter so esoteric that I am glad my task does not involve its analysis. Yet the Polish element in Chopin's music is as urbane as the Hungarian element in Liszt's, and Chopin's Polish background is not of paramount artistic importance. All we can safely declare is that his sympathies with Poland and the deliberately national idioms in his music are none the less sincere for being romantic.

The third background is Paris and her salons, his own elegant rooms and those of his friends, together with the summers spent at Nohant with George Sand. To it belong the waltzes and nocturnes which Wagner stupidly classed as 'lap-dog Chopin', for they contain some of the most original harmonies of 'volatile' pianism and they stand along with Chopin's more impressive pieces as counterparts of romantic verse—both the flamboyant and the introvert kind. To this background also belong the studies, scherzos and preludes. These are not simply 'Produce of France', 'Produce of Poland' or 'International Concert Produce', but produce of a highly original mind, the finest achievements of that unique Chopin of whose backgrounds we are unaware as we listen. Yet they are also produce of an age and society associated chiefly with Paris.

Before amplifying this third and most important background we should be aware of a danger. To be wise after events and 'read into' music the mental and social changes of a composer's lifetime is as mistaken as to regard his collected compositions as the equivalent of his diary. For his beneficiaries his music is certainly like a second diary more interesting than the one he kept in his pocket or his drawer, and it may even prove his real diary to be unintentionally mendacious. Being the diary of his unconscious, his music may show the hidden and less-harnessed part of his personality reacting *against* the declared aspirations of his time and place, and contradicting sentiments known to have come from his lips and to have been implicit in his public behaviour. This fact explains the words 'escapist' and 'revolutionary' applied to at least some works by composer after composer. Musical expression reveals the unconscious to an extent neither possible nor permissible in verbal expression, and therefore music should not be judged according to its susceptibility to verbal description. The point is illustrated by a recent controversy about Mozart's G minor Symphony —whether its first movement could be called 'tragic' or whether its opening rhythm negates the epithet. The word is relevant to discussion, but not to assessment, since the power of that great music and of all fine music lies in its providing experience not only of what may be named—victory, rage, despair, self-pity—but of what can neither be named nor conveyed in prose. If words could convey all that music conveys, then music would be merely ancillary.

Therefore the events, scenes and people known to Chopin while in France are not traced in order to pin-point their specific reflection in his music. To regard one of his pieces chiefly as a musical picture of Majorca, of George Sand, or of the 1830 revolution would be foolish even if the composer had been like Berlioz and specifically advertised these 'programmes'; yet to regard them as utterly irrelevant to the understanding and enjoyment of Chopin would be to flaunt not only modern knowledge but also the perceptions of alert minds as far back in history as Plato, who, in the *Phaedrus*, gave us the first great exegesis of our dual character, conscious and unconscious, which he likened to the harnessing together of two horses, one docile and one wild. During movements called romantic, artists tend to reveal the 'wild horse' to the delight of the young, the adventurous and the less tame spirits of society, and to the public rebuke, with or without private fascination, of the old, the conservative and the domesticated.

Transported by some scena in a Handel opera, or by some pathetic and deeply disturbing passage in a Mozart quartet, we understand

Stendhal's aphorism 'All art is romantic in its own day'. The late Professor Sir Walter Raleigh[2] defined one element of the romantic as the power to transport us mentally in time or space; so a blue gown in a medieval painting, or the blue of distant hills can both induce romantic yearnings. Mild or passionate, these yearnings betoken discontent with present circumstances that is quickly relegated to the unconscious so that daily duty may be performed in disciplined if sometimes insincere contentment. Whatever the pull between conscious and unconscious, the daily control does not necessarily hide romantic rebellion. What is hidden in us may prove as dark and primitive when it is evoked by the gentle melancholy of Chopin (though Chopin is not by any means an entirely gentle artist) or of Fauré as when it is excited by the more explosive rhetoric of Berlioz or Liszt. Chopin and Musset were not less romantic artists than their contemporaries, Berlioz and Hugo.

Romanticism, which has not been an extinct volcano in the most controlled of periods, becomes notably active when the superficial climate is least stormy. Recent eruptions reached their climax not during but after the two great wars of our century, and the most famous eruption of all, which elicited the terms 'romantic' and 'classical' as critical antonyms and inaugurated unspent argument as to the propriety of their opposition, has now a prescriptive place in history as *the* romantic revival or *the* romantic movement. This phenomenon was not fully manifest in the politically revolutionary and Napoleonic epoch, but later, as if in reaction against that externally prosperous and complacent France wherein English travellers were surprised not to see a starved peasantry. Most of the poor were urban. The Quaker, Morris Birkbeck, a Surrey gentleman farmer, wrote in *Notes on a Journey through France* (London, 1814):

> Instead of a ruined country, I see fields highly cultivated, no houses tumbling down or empty, no ragged, wretched-looking people. Everybody assures me that agriculture has been improving rapidly for the last twenty-five years. I see comfort and plenty . . . I ask for the wretched labourers of whom I have heard so much. It seems they have vanished . . . From Dieppe to this place (Montpellier) we have seen scarcely a working animal whose

[2] W. A. Raleigh, *Romance: Two Lectures*, Princeton, 1916.

condition was not excellent . . . We have not seen one such famished, worn out object as may be met among the labouring people in every parish of England, nor a spot of good land that is not industriously cultivated. France, so cultivated, moderately taxed, without paper money, without tithes, without poor rates, almost without poor, with excellent roads, overflowing with corn, wine and oil, must be a rich country.

Here is a striking contrast with Arthur Young's and Doctor Burney's descriptions of rural France! Birkbeck did not like Paris, which seemed like a nation apart; there he saw poverty contrasted with affluence and there he was sorry to see the Bourbon dynasty restored in Charles X. The restoration and the reactionary Government under Polignac did not last long, for a political domination of acquired wealth over titles and pedigree was manifest even before the 1830 revolution set Louis Philippe on the throne. It was during the smug reign of Louis Philippe that Berlioz was constrained *épater le bourgeois* as composer and writer, and during the same reign that the finest music of Chopin, like the poetry of Musset, disturbingly and deliciously 'found' the sentiments and aspirations which its hearers could neither name nor acknowledge. Chopin's art was particularly subtle, since one could rarely justify one's enjoyment of it by calling it 'bizarre'—a favourite critical term during the whole of the nineteenth century.

The romantic movement reached its maximum strength as the nineteenth century approached its prosperous middle years and as belief in material invention and 'progress' was tacitly added to the articles of religion, God helping those who helped themselves. Because the romantic spirit is never wholly crushed it was active during the years of the revolution and war; but common sense tells us that the pompous architectural paintings, grandiose operas and cantatas, vulgar buildings and sculptures of the revolutionary and Napoleonic period, essays in the attitudinizing heroic by such as were not Beethovens, can no more be classed with the dominantly romantic works of artists who were young in the 1820s than can those of Beethoven himself; and it is difficult to recall any period except that of our twentieth-century wars in which literature has been more copiously sterile than during the revolutionary years in France. The romantic novelists, dramatists, poets

and musicians made their decisive conquest and enjoyed their triumph
in the time of Chopin and 'the bourgeois king', whose palace was open
on certain days so that citizens might see the double bed and the table
laid for luncheon at which the King himself carved, approving domestic
appointments like their own and unlike those in the châteaux of the
old régime. Yet the historian Taine, telling us how reactionaries (the
legitimists who wanted the Bourbons back, the republicans, and the
Bonapartists who eventually prevailed) swelled the numbers who over-
threw Louis Philippe and Guizot in 1848, was constrained to say 'La
France s'ennuie'—France is bored and sighs for glory, political and
military glory beyond her frontiers and a little pomp within them.
Thus the romantic spirit unconsciously affected even political destinies.
It was chiefly those who 'had never had it so good', the comfortable
middle and professional classes of France after the revolution, who bred
the romantic poets and novelists and who enjoyed their works overtly
or secretly.

In 1831 any fastidious musician who needed a large capital city to
provide his means of livelihood, any highly civilized man who might
choose where to live, was more likely to settle in Paris than in Rome,
Vienna, Berlin, Leipzig, Munich, London or New York. From 1815 to
about 1822, or even perhaps during the last years of Schubert and
Beethoven, Vienna might have been his choice. Congress Vienna was
'old' Vienna made newly gay, colourful and prosperous, and 'old'
Vienna was more beautiful than 'old' Paris, which Napoleon had
altered but not substantially transformed. Indeed, the Paris we know did
not assume its distinctive and appealing contours until after Chopin's
death, when Haussmann constructed his boulevards and squares under
the aegis of Napoleon III; if before Chopin's time Paris was absolutely
more attractive than other capital cities, no writing known to me, even
by patriotic Frenchmen, declares the fact; on the other hand, plenty of
unprejudiced authors writing between about 1650 and 1820 praise this
and disparage that feature of 'old' Paris without suggesting that, except
during very pleasant weather or when the visitor enjoyed some special
occasion or favour, the city had sufficient charm to make the visitor
quit his own country and settle there. Venice had this charm only from
April to October, but Congress or *Biedermeier* Vienna had its delights
even during severe winters. They were largely superficial delights—the

deer-haunted glades of Schönbrunn, the open spaces and miniature woods or avenues of the Augarten, and then, farther out near the river, the Prater and Leopoldstadt, a village-absorbed-into-city which seemed to the citizens as Vauxhall was to Londoners in Handel's day or as Sadler's Wells, Ranelagh, Cremorne, Hampstead Heath and now Battersea Park became to their succeeding generations. The squares, coffee-houses, small palaces or town houses of the nobility mentioned in Beethoven's dedications, the bandstands, booths, beer-gardens and little dance places set up in these pleasaunces, the many temporary theatres and peep-shows as well as the fine shops and established halls and theatres of the city itself—all these, coupled with the easily assumed and infectious *Gemüthlichkeit*, created 'Vienna, city of my dreams' long before the popularity of Lanner's and then Strauss's waltzes. The Congress pageant made Vienna vaunt her charms, from fireworks to paint and sunblinds, because she badly needed money from her crowd of foreign visitors after a war which had made her poor.

As Metternich and his Congress grandees ceased to hold the European stage (let us say when Chopin passed through Vienna on his way to Paris) the French capital was in most ways as attractive as Vienna and in some ways more so. The nineteenth century beautified Paris and spoilt Vienna. Paris streets were widened and the number of her squares and interesting monuments increased; but with the building of the Ringstrasse, magnificent though it was in itself, Vienna lost her most popular and lovely evening resort for promenaders—the Glacis or circle of wide grass banks which sloped outwards from the old city boundary, the rampart, and provided views over fine houses and estates or pretty villages as far as an outer ring of fortifications. Once the ramparts were removed and spread flatly from the river to the villages in which Beethoven and Schubert sought idyllic retreat, greater Vienna was no more if no less attractive than greater London. Moreover, despite the bourgeois attractions of the Vienna that is idealized in Johann Strauss's operettas and fifty inferior popular entertainments, despite her orchestral and operatic tradition, Vienna ceased to be the supreme musical capital of Europe even before the death of Schubert, 'the last of the giants'. How did she treat Schubert's symphonies? The musical centre of gravity was to swing towards the north German cities associated with Weber, Schumann, Mendelssohn,

Brahms and Wagner; but there was a period before these ascendant
stars reached their zenith in which Paris could claim to be the musical
centre of Europe, her *Opéra* primarily Italian, her *Opéra Comique*
(applying the term to various theatres) primarily French, and her
concert and recital repertory international, with the Viennese classics
and the rising German school as well represented as anywhere. Paris
already outshone Vienna by 1830, having become partly what Venice
had been in the eighteenth century—Europe's chief pleasure city—and
partly what Venice had been in the seventeenth century, the autumn of
her greater artistic glory.

This Paris to which Chopin came in 1830 could not accurately be
described as entirely 'old' Paris of revolution days, nor as the pre-
eminently desirable capital that preened herself for the international
exhibitions of 1855 and 1867. That city was completed after the 1848
revolution, when Baron Georges Haussmann, prefect of the Seine,
located his new boulevards to suit the new city gates, namely the railway
termini. He built his Halles Centrales and his big new cross-roads and
squares, the Places de la République, d'Étoile and de la Nation, completed the Louvre to its present appearance, and replaced the medieval
slums of the *cité* with grand public buildings. He laid out squares in
imitation of those in London and, after the cholera epidemic of 1832,
abolished the old open drains and constructed the vast catacomb of sewers
which is still shown to visitors with pride, or was in 1938, when my guide-
book also featured the morgue and the Villette abattoirs, about which
the commune is now said to have grown squeamish. He also made the
Solferino and Alma bridges and brought the distant water supply.
Haussmann's name is remembered by the Boulevard Haussmann, which
runs from the Chaussée d'Antin, where Chopin lived, behind the opera
and past the wide approaches to St Lazare Station, beyond which it
crosses his Boulevard Malesherbes at a spot marked by one of his big
new and vulgar churches (St Augustin) and becomes a fine avenue as it
reaches Étoile and the nodal Arc de Triomphe.

Haussmann's boulevards altered much of the Paris known to
Chopin—for instance, the Latin Quarter which was almost entirely
inhabited by students and not the prosperous professional classes. Yet
we can still find Chopin's first residence, even though the Rue Soufflot
has since been made south of the Sorbonne. Chopin's generation was

the last to know at least one area of Paris which still kept much of its medieval character, to the delight of Hugo, Sainte-Beuve and other romantics who loved the crumbling gothic of Notre Dame and St Denis before Viollet le Duc's neat restorations, for Paris had changed rapidly in the years after Napoleon's downfall. In his *How to Enjoy Paris* of 1842, Hervé tells us that the city is more 'clean, comfortable and civilized than London', has wider streets, newer and better houses and 'a pride in her embellishments'. The Arc de Triomphe was finished in 1836, Concorde and the Madeleine in 1842, but above all (hence my comparison with eighteenth-century Venice) Paris became as early as 1828 *la ville lumière*—the first city to employ gas lighting, horse-drawn omnibuses, macadamized sidewalks and large plate-glass windows for cafés and shops. Paris was a city to enjoy at night when, even during a reign which history has branded prosaic, her river, her trees and her gaslights could produce a romantic setting for pleasure-seekers.

Did Chopin gravitate to Paris at the age of 21 because most upper- and middle-class Polish emigrants did so? It is hardly likely, although theirs was the first society he cultivated on arrival in France. He was probably more beholden to the émigré aristocracy than to musicians such as Kalkbrenner and Rossini for his initial introduction to the wealthy French families whose salons he was to adorn and whose daughters he was to teach for the topmost fees. His father wrote suggesting England and America as countries likely to be rewarding, but Prince Valentine Radziwill, by introducing him to the Paris Rothschilds, ensured the social and financial success that banished any thought of further emigration. Few of Chopin's compatriots in Paris were as well off as he could be by teaching the daughters of the nobility at 20 francs per lesson, the fee to be placed on the mantelpiece. Having first taken rooms at 27 Boulevard Poissonnière, he moved in 1833 to 38 Rue de la Chaussée d'Antin, the newly developed and fashionable district near the opera and the Madeleine, owned his carriage and employed a manservant.

It was not a peculiarity of Paris to be at all points pleasantly near the country, for when Chopin was alive Kensington, Hampstead and Chelsea were still villages separated from London by fields, although St Martin-in-the-Fields was already St Martin on Trafalgar Square and would soon be St Martin by Charing Cross Station and Hospital. Yet some conception of the green solitude which the well-to-do Parisian could command can be gained from André Maurois's life of Victor Hugo who as a child lived at 12 Impasse des Feuillantines, a house in Montparnasse which had once been a small convent. General Hugo's family went there in 1809 and his famous son remembered that it had a garden

> like a park with a wood, then open country, then an avenue of chestnuts with room for a swing, and a dry quarry in which to play at soldiers . . . all the flowers one could want and what, to a child's eyes, was virgin forest where we were constantly making discoveries . . . leading to the dome of the Val-de-Grâce.

In Chopin's day Montrouge looked like a market-garden area covered with allotments. Beyond the Arc de Triomphe the village of Chaillot was completely separated from the city by many fields, and among the districts favoured by speculative builders were Saint-Lazare, Malesherbes, Grenelle, Batignolles and Austerlitz.

One has heard and read disparaging comments upon artists who chose to live in big cities or whose works do not bear direct witness to their love of what is miscalled wild nature. Among musicians Mozart and Chopin have been cited as 'unresponsive to nature'. This quite unproven and unprovable judgement sometimes accompanies comparisons with other composers (also city dwellers) who invoked flora, fauna and 'natural' phenomena in their titles or programmes; but Vivaldi's or Handel's hailstorms, cuckoos and nightingales never inclined the composers to abandon their wigs or tight hose or to prefer rural solitude to a civilized routine in Venice or London. Beethoven sought temporary retreat to villages near Vienna for convalescence, exercise and the opportunity to think without distraction; but the onomatopoeic effects in his sixth symphony are as irrelevant to its greatness as would be farmyard noises from some flapdoodle invention producing all the sounds in Haydn's toy symphony. The romanticizing of nature began precisely during the industrial revolution, as nature receded from big cities to join other distant objects of yearning; and it was in Germany, England and the inclement northern countries that nature-mysticism became a cult. To exclaim during a visit to Salzburg:

'Why on earth should Mozart want to leave here for Vienna?' is to show crass lack of imagination and ignorance of history; and to suppose that Chopin was unresponsive to natural beauty in Majorca, Nohant or Paris itself is as perverse as to blame an urbane creature for living in a city, close to the means of retreat and relaxation, but in the sophisticated and intelligent society that not only ensures his livelihood but also stimulates his efforts as performer and composer.

Chopin's enormous reputation as a performer cannot have been based solely upon public recitals. The number of his concert-appearances from his arrival in Paris to his death (that is to say between the ages of 21 and 39) was probably not above seven, counting his going to Rouen in 1838 to play his E minor Concerto. To judge by existing documentary evidence only one of these, at Pleyel's rooms in April 1841, was a brilliant success, albeit before an audience consisting almost entirely of Parisian high society along with his pupils and friends. Not only the regular journalists but also Liszt himself had more to say of the 'brilliance' and 'elegance' of the audience than of the music. A letter by Chopin's father mentions his son's disappointment in Liszt's article and approves his remaining superficially friendly with Liszt. To these few public concerts (if they are rightly so described) we must add Chopin's contribution to charity and benefit concerts—for Harriet Smithson, for the Polish refugees, or at Berlioz's concert chiefly intended to launch Berlioz's own music. Most of the glowing tributes to Chopin's playing which we have inherited may have originated at this or that *soirée charmante*, to use a favourite phrase of contemporary Parisian notices. The novel points of Chopin's style, his intimate tone and his use of the sustaining pedal as a veil, were more suited to such a gathering than to a public concert in a big hall. If the fact should incline anybody to think the less of Chopin's art, let him ask if Schubert was a smaller artist than he might have been because the nursery of his songs was a domestic 'Schubertiad' of amateur musicians, minor romantic poets and their lady friends. 'Was there ever anything to compare with those salons in which Chopin played?' asks H. C. Schonberg of the *New York Times*.[3] He continues:

> Paris in the 1830s was the intellectual capital of the world, and
> anybody who was anybody in the world of music, letters, art or

[3] *The Great Pianists*, London, 1964.

science would attend one of the big soirées. Chopin might share the programme with the cellist August Franchomme, or the contralto Maria Malibran, or the tenor Adolphe Nourrit. If Liszt were present there would be four-hand music, Liszt playing the treble, Chopin the bass . . . or some two-piano playing with Mendelssohn or Moscheles at the second piano. Games would be played. Heine might improvise a story to Chopin's accompaniment. Chopin might sit at the piano to imitate the way Liszt played and, not to be outdone, Liszt would return the compliment. Grouped around the piano might be George Sand, the Countess Marie d'Agoult (she, mother of two children, who ran away with Liszt and had a child who married Liszt's pupil, the pianist-conductor Hans von Bülow, *that* child, Cosima, later running away from von Bülow to live with, and eventually marry, Wagner), Balzac, Delacroix, Lamartine, Gautier, Rossini (when he went out; normally people came to *his* house), Viardot-Garcia, Eugène Sue, Meyerbeer.

Chopin's favourite make of pianoforte was a Pleyel, though the 1955 edition of *Grove* shows a photograph of the Broadwood which he used in England. As usual in the history of music, the instrument was ready for the artist, for in 1808 Sébastien Érard had patented his 'repetition action' by which a key could be made to reiterate rapidly without returning fully to its bed. In 1821 he went further by patenting in England his famous 'double escapement'—a lever action which is still basic for all makes of instrument. Admirers claimed that only the player's limitation of control prevented note repetition as rapid as that which a violinist produced by tremolo bowing. Yet Chopin considered Érard's instruments to be 'too insistent', and we can understand what he meant if we recall comments upon his playing that were made by critics who were themselves good players. Moscheles wrote: 'He needs no powerful forte to produce the necessary contrasts. Therefore one never misses the orchestral effects which the German school expects from a pianist.' Alfred Hipkins of Broadwoods, a fine player and historical researcher, tuned pianos for Chopin and mentions left-hand arpeggios which 'swelled or diminished like waves in an ocean of sound'.

This parallels Schumann's comment upon Chopin's playing of the 'harp' study—'an undulation of the A flat major chord . . . the pedalling exquisitely entangled in the harmony. We followed a wonderful melody on the sustained notes while from the middle (of the texture) a tenor voice broke clearly from the chords and joined the main melody.' Hipkins, less fanciful than Schumann, proceeded at once to an account of some of the (then) unorthodox ways by which Chopin secured his perfect cantabile and other effects—using the thumb on black keys, passing it under the little finger, sliding one finger from one key to another, especially black to white, or changing fingers on one key like an organist who must preserve the legato of a phrase. None of these procedures was a makeshift, for Stephen Hiller, describing Chopin's 'slim hands', declares that they could 'suddenly expand and cover a third of the keyboard like a serpent opening its mouth to swallow a rabbit whole'!

These testimonies adequately explain Chopin's choice of an instrument. He knew his limitations. His music, like his nature, was often impassioned, and therefore required the extremes of recognized expression which he was thought to command as a youth despite his light body; as he grew frail and weakened by disease he could make his art explicit only by maintaining the range, but replacing its scale from pianissimo to fortissimo, and during his last years the fortissimo was evidently suggested rather than produced. In many respects therefore, but by no means in all, his playing was in strong contrast with Liszt's. He frequently came into contact with Liszt, who lived so close to him, and we have seen that his mingled respect and dislike for Liszt prevented his maintaining more than a superficial friendship. (His uneasiness with the man Liszt needs no more explanation than his distaste for much of Liszt's music.) Remarkable, therefore, is Chopin's reaction to Liszt's performance of his music. In a letter from Chopin to Hiller there occurs the sentence: 'I should like to steal from him his way of playing my own Études.' To a pupil who apologized for snapping a piano string Chopin is reported to have said: 'If I had your strength and could play that polonaise as it should be played there would be no string left unbroken by the time I had finished!'

There can be no doubt that, as a performer, Chopin made a virtue of necessity to the permanent enrichment of music. The effects of crescendi, contrast and nuance depend as much upon the lower as upon the upper limit of intensity, and by resetting the scale of volume that a pianist would henceforward be expected to control Chopin found the Pleyel instrument nearest to his ideal. A piano that was 'too insistent' might, by a single note, spoil the undulation of an arpeggio, the nuance of a phrase, the ripple of a figure, the near-perfect illusion of cantabile. Though *piano cantabile* had been taught and heard from Mozart's time onwards, Chopin's way of 'making the piano sing' was a unique experience, the point in his technique most frequently reported by those who heard him play. It brings us back to the main subject of this chapter—the background of a particular city. He disliked most music by his contemporaries, even by men for whom he felt the affection or esteem he showed to Berlioz. He also disliked much music by great men before him, including Beethoven, and preserved complete enthusiasm only for Bach and Mozart. Apart from the piano, his chief musical passion was for singing, and no doubt his love of Mozart is partly explained by Abert's phrase that in quartet, wind serenade, piano concerto or orchestral symphony, Mozart makes *singers* of all kinds of instrument. Like Mozart, Chopin loved the lyric stage and *bel canto* singing, and in his time no city was better able to gratify his taste than Paris.

> During the first half of the nineteenth century Paris was virtually the European capital of opera. Not only did many composers of eminence live there, but even those residing elsewhere did not feel that they had arrived until they had had a Paris success.[4]

Furthermore, the employment of the best Italian singers and composers by Paris, together with a reputation for scenic beauty and choral magnificence which had been established when Gluck was first drawn to France, made the French lyric drama an example and a standard as soon as the international Neapolitan *opera seria* was ousted by entertainment in the vernacular, and by the new German romantic opera— the glorified *Singspiel* of Mozart and Weber; for in the 'grand' opera of Paris what had been admired in classical Italian singing was retained and developed. The same authority continues:

[4] D. J. Grout, *A Short History of Opera*, New York, 1947.

It must be acknowledged that the original inspiration of German romantic opera, both for the poetry and for the music, came from France . . . During the 1830s and 40s it seemed almost as if the Italians had been driven from German opera houses only to be replaced by the French.

Chopin made acquaintance with Italian-French opera and developed his great love of *bel canto* singing and the 'decorated' aria long before he settled in Paris, and as Arthur Hedley has wisely warned us in his *Grove* article on Chopin, anything 'Italian' in him had been acquired 'before he made acquaintance with Bellini's music'.

That he should have been fond of Bellini's work was natural: it appealed to a taste already formed, and we may continue by noting that Bellini and Chopin had common stylistic ideals based upon their common admiration of Mozart. In a sense they were among the most conservative of romantics, because they sought a classical clarity and elegance. Bellini (1801–35) also died young. It is unlikely that Chopin heard any of his music until he reached Paris, for Bellini's masterpiece *La Sonnambula* was first produced at Milan in 1831, the year of Chopin's arrival in France, and his other internationally acclaimed pieces, *Norma* and *I Puritani* (this latter commissioned by Paris after he had gone there to live) followed in the next few years. Just as the style of the aria-andantes and buffo-allegros in Mozart's concertos, serenades and other instrumental works owe nothing to one particular composer, but often remind us of Mozart's rivals, Paisiello and Salieri, so the kind of melody found in Chopin's nocturnes, studies and ballades owes much to the Italian operas he heard as a boy in Warsaw (either at the opera, or when accompanying them at the piano or hearing them sung at gatherings), and therefore it is likely that Rossini influenced him more than Bellini. The point is of no more importance than an answer to the question: 'Which pianist more influenced him, Hummel, Weber, Field, Moscheles or Kalkbrenner?' and it is raised only to establish the single fact that no city could have better gratified his tastes than Paris and no city could have influenced him more powerfully by offering what he could judge and reject in music and the arts. Absurd though it seems to us, he even disliked the application of the word 'romantic' to himself, associated as it was with bohemianism and defiance of conventions which upheld the elegant society in which he shone and wished to shine.

And who were his 'society' pupils? A few of their names are saved from sounding like Dickens's 'The Hon. Mrs Wititterley' or 'The Misses Colonel Wugsby'—types of comic vapidity now becoming increasingly pitiful—by being associated with ancestors who were protectors and patrons of genius. Among those who regularly placed 20 francs on the mantelpiece while Chopin looked out of the window were one or two Rothschilds, the Princess de Spuzzo, the Countess d'Apponyi, the Baroness Branicka, the Princess Marcelline Czartoryska, the Princess Elizabeth Czernikeff—one is tempted to invent names, for the list includes not a single one which belonged to a great performer or musician. A young Hungarian, Karl Filtsch, was the only pupil of Chopin to show such great promise that Liszt envisaged his own eclipse, but Filtsch died of tuberculosis at the age of 15. Chopin quite enjoyed giving lessons, although some of the pupils were observed to leave in tears. The rate of remuneration enabled him to accept as few teaching hours as he liked, and his method of sitting at a second piano gave him the pleasure of playing, experimenting and practising himself. The pupils represented their families, not their pianistic prowess. They were his daily assurance of his place among the so-called *crème de la crème*, and while I deride the claim of such creatures to the simile, let me not forget that their masquerade is as old as civilization and continues in every form of society, including that of socialist, communist, and so-called democratic states. The artist can affect to please only himself, but if he does not appeal to duller sensibilities than his own he can either starve in body or become artistically bloodless, interested only in 'method' or 'technique', because he shares no common aspirations or emotions. Artistic vitality needs a background, and not only at the nursery stage. The vitality does not depend upon whether the appeal is to 'the people' (whoever they are) or to 'a society', since all varieties of sensibility and intelligence are represented in both audiences. Chopin may rarely have been conscious of composing (perhaps of playing) for anybody but himself; in fact, few musicians have appealed to a wider audience from salon to slum, and no other musician of his epoch can share Chopin's claim to have maintained the appeal during strong reactions against nineteenth-century style and expression. Few artists have been so limited yet few so powerful, if power is measured by the area over which a spell may be cast. He conquered *both* the audiences we have just mentioned. As Bach in Leipzig, Handel in London, Haydn in Esterház, Mozart when determined to leave Salzburg and play his concertos at his own concerts in Vienna, or Mozart when determined to write a German 'magic' opera, he did so by identifying himself with a *particular* background in a particular city and society.

## List of Sources

Encyclopaedia Britannica:
    *Paris*, article by James Douglas Lambert.
    *George Sand*, article by Robert Baldick.
Hedley, Arthur, *Selected Correspondence of Chopin*, London, 1962.
Pourtalès, Guy de, *Frederick Chopin: A Man of Solitude* (translated from the French), London, 1930.
Raleigh, Sir W. A., *Romance*, two lectures, Princeton, 1916.
Schonberg, Harold C., *The Great Pianists*, New York, 1963.
Vuillermoz, E., *La vie amoureuse de Chopin*, Paris, 1927.

ALAN RAWSTHORNE

# Ballades, Fantasy and Scherzos

## The Ballades

CHOPIN'S four ballades occupy a unique position in his out-put, and, one may surely venture to say, in music. They do not all belong to the same period of his life, the first appearing in 1836 and the last in 1843, and were clearly not conceived as an 'opus'. From some points of view they do not particularly resemble one another; there are many divergences of shape, of formal presentation, and some-times of mood. Indeed, to some musicians they would appear to have hardly any coherent pattern at all; Busoni wrote in a letter to his wife 'the second and third are remarkably badly composed'. But he had just been practising them exhaustively and exhaustingly, and hard work is a great distorter of values. (In another letter he says, 'I have written down my ideas about Chopin.' One would like to know where.) In spite of this seeming waywardness, however, these four pieces have a curious unity of purpose, a unity that pays little attention to uniformity of design, or even of scope, but which saturates their most disparate elements and gives them an unconscious cohesion. They are certainly temperamentally akin, as one sometimes perceives a kinship in families whose features are not superficially alike. They are ballades in as distinctive a sense as the scherzos are scherzos, or the mazurkas are mazurkas, although perhaps one could not answer the question 'What is a ballade?'

Of course, it would be absurd to say that Chopin created a new 'form' in these pieces, either by accident or design. But he did manage to produce in them four works of art which, to say the least, have a family resemblance, and which are of a nature sufficiently idiosyncratic to justify a special title. Of this he must have been aware when he called them 'ballades'. Unquestionably they have a strange unity of style, and it is surely not too fanciful to call this style 'narrative'. It is not the ballad narration of Sir Patrick Spens or Tam Lin, which Chopin's age, like Dr Johnson, would probably have still considered barbarous if it had heard of them. Perhaps its sophisticated ease has more to do with the professionalism of Chaucer or Froissart, though Chopin was concerned with deeper matters, and has only occasionally time to spare for dalliance. The $\frac{6}{4}$ or $\frac{6}{8}$ time in which they all unfold their tale unifies their style in a more obvious way; it gives an easy movement, a flowing and sometimes deceptively gentle persuasiveness to the strange events which present themselves. The first and the last of them are furnished with important introductions, but this is not a feature they have in common; there is a couple of bars' preliminary wooing of the note C at the beginning of the Second Ballade, but it would be frivolous to call this an introduction. The introductory material of the Fourth Ballade, as we shall see, is woven into the texture of the subsequent music, but that of the First, one of the most arresting passages Chopin ever wrote, never reappears, though it has possibly a faint echo in the coda. In these introductions Chopin employs an oblique approach to his subject—an approach which he favours, in varying degrees, elsewhere. (The Mazurkas, op. 24, no. 4 in B flat minor and op. 30, no. 4 in C sharp minor for example.) It is nowhere, I think, so significantly employed as in these two Ballades. Such opening gestures lend immense weight to the subsequent statements; without them, indeed, the statements could hardly be made at all.

These simple observations on introductions involve us immediately in the fundamentals of composition, and we are not wasting our time on the obvious in taking note of them. It is of the highest importance when writing movements of any degree of organization to compose the form at the same time as the music, and this is what Chopin is doing in these pieces. This creative conception of form is one of the (admittedly many) things which make Haydn, for instance, so great a master.

Forms in music differ from those supplied by H.M. Inspector of Taxes; they are not there to be filled in. It may seem superfluous to mention this, but many people, strange as it may seem, do not appear to have considered the matter from this point of view. Even composers sometimes ignore it, and the result is what is usually called 'academic'. The master-touch in musical form is revealed in this: that each musical event sounds inevitable but not predictable. From the climax of the Viennese school we learn the great lesson that form is sensation, and that if the articulations of a musical structure are not so regarded, the formal scheme is dead. These moments must produce their effects of tension, of relaxation, of expectancy or whatever they may be, so that the listener is carried from place to place in the action, and can participate therein. Such facts Chopin knows in his bones, being a born composer.

So it is an important part of the composer's task to devise the various units of his structure in such a way that they sound like what they are. A bridge-passage must sound like a link, and not like important new material. We are on treacherous ground here, since there can be no catalogue of attributes, in a technical sense, which such units must possess, in order that they can fulfil their various functions with success. But we can often tell, upon reflection, whether they are expressive of their place in the general scheme of a composition or not. Sometimes, with this in mind, a composer will have to remove a passage—even, maybe, a passage which he thinks one of his best—because he knows it is not really doing its job in its context. He may even substitute a passage which seems inferior musically in itself, but which he knows will carry the listener more successfully from one moment to another. And this is from no merely 'formalistic' point of view, but because the real composer feels the 'form' in his bones.

One of the most obvious necessities of this kind is, I suppose, to contrive a beginning which really opens the door to the listener. I can never feel, for instance, that Liszt's well-known piece about Saint Francis of Paola walking on the waves, impressive though it is, has a very satisfactory beginning. To me it seems as though the holy man must have been half-way across the Straits of Messina before the piece began; the opening phrase is much too casual a remark to introduce so grandiose a piece, to say nothing of so remarkable a journey, and when we realize in retrospect that this phrase is but one of the phrases which make up the thematic material of most of the work—a more or less random phrase, as it were—the effect is formally amorphous. In the 'Sermon to the Birds' of the saint's namesake from Assisi, however, the reverse is the case, and what we first take to be introductory matter proves, as the music proceeds, to be a substantial and integral part of the work. The birds, in fact, are presumably preaching to Saint Francis, rather than the other way round. Liszt's towering genius is exuberant and comprehensive. He is a much more commanding figure than Chopin. Yet this genius, abundant though it is, does not always penetrate to the roots of the composer's art, as Chopin's almost invariably does. Chopin's instinct rarely errs, and it is instinct conditioned by experience and reflection that will ultimately solve the problems of musical form.

But what, it may be asked, has all this to do with Chopin's ballades? The answer is that it is only within these terms of reference that I feel able to appreciate them. The same kind of aptitude, or rightness, that we demand of an opening phrase or passage is to be sought in every component part. And it is in this connotation that I hope we may differ, with deepest respect, from Busoni, and say that the ballades are well, and not badly composed. We find in these ballades not the invention of a new 'form', but patterns of behaviour which are viable for these pieces alone, and where the emergence of 'form' is as creative an act as the texture of the music itself. The logic is the same logic as drives forward a sonata movement, though the resultant shape may be different. Indeed, the sonata principle is implicit in at least three of these works, insofar as they concern themselves with two musical ideas, and the relation of these ideas to one another. Sometimes this relation is quite elaborately worked out, as in the Third Ballade; sometimes it is inherent, as in the First. But, of course, it would be foolish to regard these pieces from the point of view of sonata movements, in spite of certain resemblances. After all, sonata-form is only a crystallization of certain basic principles, deep-rooted in music itself; to me Chopin's ballades grow out of these principles into shapes as convincing and beautiful as any sonata movement. Perhaps more so than his own.

'In almost every work in the larger forms we find him floundering lamentably,' says Niecks. I take it that this absurd remark applies mainly to sonata movements, in the accepted parlance of the academies. But I also take it that we may regard the G minor Ballade as a large work in terms of Chopin's oeuvre, and that a large work demands a large form. So let us see how Chopin flounders through.

EX. I

The introduction is based on harmony known to the textbooks, for reasons I have never been able to find out, as 'Neapolitan'. Perhaps it was first used by a composer of the school of Naples, by mistake. The point of its employment here is that we do not know, at the outset, that the A flats in the challenging phrase are related to the key of G minor; we accept them as the tonality of the piece. Not until the cadence do we realize where we are, and not until we are fairly launched on the opening subject is our position unequivocally settled. (The E flat in the last bar of the introduction may surely now be taken as authentic.)[1] What an extraordinary range of tension these seven bars take us through! The approach is as oblique emotionally as it is harmonically. The resplendent sweep of the opening phrase, as it ascends, seems to lose its confident swing, and to take on a kind of pathos, till in the sixth bar it is posing an almost agonizing question, in which the once-doubted E flat plays an important role. All this must have been very surprising in 1836, and, to me, still is. Even today, in an age which probably regards Chopin's adventures in Majorca as uncomfortable rather than naughty, we may still react with some kind of *frisson* to a master-stroke such as this. (The German edition of Breitkopf and Härtel gives 'Lento' instead of 'Largo' for this introduction, and there is some reason to suppose that Chopin approved this alteration. I can only hope he didn't!—for 'Largo' it remains to me.)

Now the main subject appears; it is very persuasive and almost confidential, mostly composed of a series of cadences, in the form of arpeggio fragments only suitable to such as used, in Chopin's day, unconventional fingering. Its opening phrase, cadence-wise, is the perfect answer to the question of the introduction's last phrase, and the theme continues to expand and elaborate this material. The section which is to

[1] See Badura-Skoda, p. 269. ED.

lead us to the second subject is built on a short phrase of four notes

which after four bars repeats itself with a difference, thus:

The rests in the second version, after the held octaves, have the effect of little gasps, giving the agitato an added sense of unrest. Subtleties like this only arise from an impeccable ear.

Soon we are conscious of a horn-like motif in the left hand below the arpeggio figures, and this results in what seem to be quite definite preparations for the orthodox relative major—fairly thumping away, indeed, at the dominant of that key. But strangely and very beautifully this chord has changed itself into the supertonic of the new key, and we proceed in E flat major instead of B flat. It has been accomplished so naturally that few will have been conscious of anything unusual. And now we have the second subject proper (bar 58), and an example of thematic unity that is rare, I think, in Chopin's works. For this second theme is a kind of complement to the first, a restatement in the major mode and in a more consolatory mood of the earlier utterance in G minor. Both consist basically of a dominant thirteenth resolving upon the tonic, and both proceed melodically from the mediant to the key-note. One can demonstrate this affinity by playing the second subject as in Ex. 4(a):

Fortunately one does not have to do anything so horrible to grasp the point, but the kinship continues to assert itself in passages such as Ex. 4(b).

Next, the first subject reappears in the remote key of A minor, but that this is only a pause in the journey is clear from the dominant pedal which holds it back; we realize that this passage is a preparation for the triumphant jubilation of the counter-statement, when it arrives, of the second theme in the still more remote key of A major. Such preparation gives this magnificent outburst all the conclusiveness of an immensely elaborated Tierce de Picardie with which eighteenth-century composers liked to clinch their arguments. The music thunders on until the harmony seems to explode and dissolve into a kind of buzz round the dominant of E flat minor at bar 126 (Chopin's dynamics are a little vague at this point) which is a preparation, most unexpectedly, for a waltz-like episode of great charm and vivacity. The aptness of this apparent irrelevance is, in fact, its very quality of being a diversion; it distracts the attention without confusing the issue because it runs so naturally and immediately into the passage-work of the succeeding harmonic complexities. It was necessary for the temperature to be lowered in order to prepare for the next appearance of the second subject, which can now afford to be less strenuously laid out. Still strong and confident, though with considerable differences, it leads us back to the home key of G minor and the first theme. But not with the full effect of a recapitulation, for this version, as in its previous appearance in A minor, is tied down to a dominant pedal, and behaves as though it were again going to lead us to the second theme. But clearly this would not do, and instead it carries us on to an enormous and powerful coda.

Chopin's use of the coda is a very characteristic feature of his forms. In tending to shun, or at any rate modify, orthodox recapitulations he seems to anticipate modern developments.[1a] Thus the sensation of a reprise is often present, as here, but without the finality of a formal restatement, and consequently the coda has a more responsible part to play than usual. It is a facet of Chopin's general conception of creative form, which I have referred to earlier. This coda, as is often the case in his works, has no thematic connexion with preceding material, except for a faint hint at the very end, unless one likes to think of the 'Neapolitan' harmony of the passage beginning at bar 216 as an echo of the introduction. It is pleasant but possibly fanciful to do so. Further reference to the themes would undoubtedly impede the wild rush of the

---

[1a] See pp. 145f. for a further discussion of Chopin's recapitulations. ED.

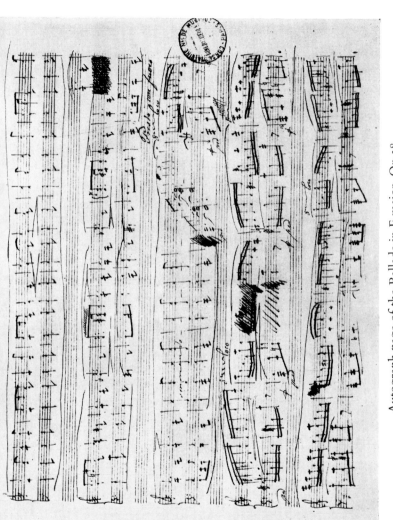

Autograph page of the Ballade in F major, Op.38
(Library of the Paris Conservatoire)

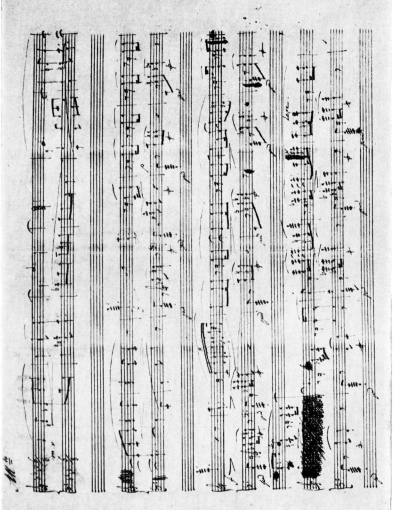

Autograph page of the Ballade in A flat major, Op.47
(Destroyed during the Second World War)

Presto, in which the listener must be carried headlong to the conclusion. It seems inevitable from the beginning that this Ballade must end in violence, and it certainly does. The grinding chromatic scales in octaves start their contrary motion quite wildly from an apparently arbitrary position which will bring them into collision in unison at the right moment; nothing could be more conclusive.

It is strange that this powerful and compelling composition should give rise to a welter of woolly romanticizing, yet such is the case. James Huneker, whose book on Chopin could be described as one long deep purple patch, rightly, if tritely, remarks that the G minor Ballade 'discloses surprising and delicious things'. But he speedily makes up for this understatement. 'There is the tall lily in the fountain that nods to the sun,' he goes on. 'It drips its cadenced monotone and its song is repeated by the lips of the slender-hipped girl with eyes of midnight.' He refers to the introduction as 'That 'cello-like Largo with its noiseless suspension'. Whatever a noiseless suspension may be, the phrase he refers to would sound miserable on the 'cello or any other instrument but the piano. So let us leave Mr Huneker to listen to his drips, while we pay attention to Chopin's music. Schumann thought that Chopin was inspired or stimulated (*angeregt*) by the poems of Mickiewicz when composing this Ballade. Such literary and pictorial associations, or even origins, were, of course, very much in vogue at the time. They were an almost essential feature of the Romantic climate which Schumann himself had done much to bring about. Both Chopin and Mickiewicz were moving in this climate, which pervaded the intellectual life of Paris in those days. (And what days they must have been!) Chopin, the émigré Pole living in France, was the son of an émigré Frenchman living in Poland, and he was fired by all the fervid patriotism common to such a situation. To link the names of poet and musician was obvious, but to pin down the Ballade to a definite story is gratuitous and misleading, for in suggesting extra-musical connotations the attention is distracted from the purely musical scheme which is, as I have tried to show, compelling in itself and completely satisfying. If Chopin had wanted to hang his piece on to a literary framework, there was nothing on earth to stop him doing so and acknowledging the fact in a title. Such things were very fashionable; indeed, Chopin would probably have pleased at least his publishers by giving fanciful names to his

C—C

compositions, instead of the generic nomenclature that he adopted.
His English publishers, in fact, remedied this deficiency by bestowing
titles of their own choosing—*Murmures de la Seine, Les Soupirs*, and so
on. This Ballade fared better than some with *La Favorita*. Mickiewicz is
also invoked as the informing spirit of the next Ballade, in F major—
indeed, he has become a sort of *roux* for the entire Chopin cuisine,
involved in every dish. The only two Polish writers known to the
English, I think, are Mickiewicz and Joseph Conrad; of the first they
know the name but not the works, and of the second the works but
not the name.

The Second Ballade is dedicated to Schumann. No doubt Chopin
owed Schumann a debt of gratitude for the latter's enthusiastic reception of the Variations, op. 2, on 'Là ci darem', in the *Neue Zeitschrift für
Musik*; he does not appear to have had any great liking for Schumann's
music. It was certainly perspicacious to discern genius in this very early
piece, but perhaps not so far-seeing to find the same quality in, say, one
Hermann Hirschbach, who, according to Schumann, possessed an
'overwhelming imagination', and whose string quartets 'are the most
colossal to be met with today'. Perhaps they were, though posterity
does not seem to agree. Then there was Sterndale Bennett . . . However, it is as ungenerous of us to sneer at Schumann's enthusiasm as it
was generous of Schumann to feel it. How much better to shout
'Hurrah!' in a musical journal than to mutter the timid, equivocal
phrases of today!

Schumann seems to have been perplexed by this piece, and with
reason, for apparently Chopin played different versions of it at different
times, sometimes merely an extended version of the first section.
When Chopin first played it to him, writes Schumann, it finished in F
major. When it was published in 1840, however, it finished in A minor.
Chopin must have been turning it over in his mind for several years—
since 1836, in fact, when Schumann first heard it. A long time in terms
of Chopin's woefully short life. And indeed, one can imagine the
composer playing these uniquely seductive strains on the piano, and
wondering which of their enchanting suggestions to follow. We
hardly know when the melody has begun, for although there is no
formal introduction the first two bars are as equivocal in a metrical

sense as was the opening of the First Ballade in a harmonic one. The delicately swaying rhythm rocks through eight bars and then repeats itself with disarming simplicity. The next four bars vary the proceedings slightly by diverging through A minor to C, the dominant, where the second half of the first strain is repeated. Then comes a reprise of the whole first strain, with a codetta to round everything off. Nothing could be less complicated. Yet there is a subtlety here which gives this music its distinctive charm. We are never quite sure precisely where the phrases are going to begin and end. The opening bar suggests a quaver anacrusis, or up-beat, thus:

EX. 5

The first phrase obviously ends at 'x', but the next does not begin on the next note; it shares its beginning with the end of the previous phrase, that is, also at 'x'. This is shown by bar 22, where the preceding phrase has finished a beat earlier. The answering phrase, thus telescoped, manages to shift its rhythmic centre of gravity and its cadence comes to rest on the first beat of the bar, at 'y', instead of the second. This leaves us, so to speak, with two quavers in hand, and we are led back to the beginning by a note, at 'z', which doesn't sound like an anacrusis at all, and consequently gives a delightful freshness to the return. These gentle dislocations are very subtle, obviously not contrived in the pejorative sense of the word, but equally obviously the emanation of an imagination of the most delicate perception.

Some may object that so far we have had little else than a succession of cadences in the key of F major, but to me this is part of the strange hypnosis with which this section casts its spell. In spite of its romantic, dreamy charm, it is, as we have seen, of classic shape. Hidden beneath this easy flow is a finely controlled formal precision. And so there is nothing more to do with this perfectly completed limb but to break it.

So Chopin smashes it well and truly with shattering blows coming from opposite ends of the keyboard, converging in headlong contrary motion. There is nothing hypnotic here; we may be laid out with concussion, but we are no longer mesmerized. It was probably this capricious juxtaposition of two apparently quite disparate units, followed by a repetition of this proceeding with the addition of an irrelevant coda, that caused Busoni to complain that the Second Ballade was 'badly composed'. But there is much more structural organization involved than this. The Presto con Fuoco is a wild, magnificent outburst; glorified passage-work at first, if you like, but later breaking into something which proves, before long, to be very much to the point. In the hammered-out octaves, boldly modulating though simple cadences, which occur in the passage starting at bar 63, I think we must unconsciously feel a relationship to the gently swaying repeated quavers of the opening melody:

EX. 6

At any rate, we are made to recognize it consciously later in the work. This section is a continuous piece of tempestuous declamation; it storms its way on without abatement until it blows itself out and subsides through a long diminuendo to admit the dreamy tones of the first melody once more. But not for long are we back in dreamland. The melody breaks off in its sixth bar, as if unsure of itself, and after a pause starts to develop itself with considerable breadth, making great play with the dotted figure which is an important feature of the theme, and introducing a new, though related, idea.

EX. 7

So powerful a working-out is really astonishing, for it does not seem to be inherent in the mood or the material of the opening. It would indeed have been impossible if the intervening Presto had not changed the temperature of the whole composition. After the violent accents of this Presto, it may display its more grandiose potentialities without being unseemly. This time it fairly crashes into the Presto, and we realize, if we hadn't before, how right this juxtaposition is. And just before the coda the matter is clinched by the powerful octaves of the left hand.

EX. 8

We have started in the key of F major, and then spent some time in A minor; we have returned fleetingly to F major before the rich modulations of the development; we have returned to the Presto in D minor, and now we come resolutely to A minor, with a change of signature, for the coda. In this key we end, with one of Chopin's most magical touches—a whispered reminder of the very opening and a slow full close that 'vibrates in the memory'. And if this piece is 'badly composed', then so is the C sharp minor quartet of Beethoven.

The Third Ballade, in A flat, is perhaps the most light-hearted of the four. More sombre colours are used to introduce the development section, where the material is worked out at some length, but on the whole the mood is cheerful. It was written during 1840–1, when Chopin was living with George Sand in Paris and her country house at Nohant. In the summer of 1840, however, they did not go to the country, as Madame Sand was apparently too hard up; the endless flow of guests at Nohant was expensive to maintain, and the general way of life must have been a drain on her resources. This was a period of Chopin's life when he was reasonably happy and contented. His circumstances were pleasantly organized; he moved in a circle of sympathetic and interesting friends, from whom he could disappear when he wanted without causing affront; in fact, he was living the civilized but not oversophisticated life to which he was most suited. It must have contrasted agreeably with Valldemosa. We might think of this bland composition as a reflection of such felicities, but the Fourth Ballade, written more or less within the same period, proves this to be too naive an assumption. In April 1841, and again in February 1842, Chopin made two of his rare appearances in public. At the second, given with the singer Pauline Viardot, he played the A flat major Ballade.

Presumably this was its 'first performance'. In a contemporary account of the occasion, given in Pleyel's Rooms, we read of 'gilded ribbons, soft blue gauzes, strings of trembling pearls, the freshest roses and mignonettes, in a word, a thousand of the prettiest and gayest hues', and though these observations refer to the audience (which must indeed have looked very pretty) the opening strains of the piece might deceive one into taking a similar view of the music. The first theme has elegance, grace and charm. It is suave and altogether delightful. There is no introduction, for an introduction would only detract from the open-eyed frankness with which the melody introduces itself. The last two notes of this theme's first phrase ('x'), a sort of sub-phrase (and thus marked by Chopin), are of great importance in the structure.

EX. 9

After the theme has been stated, a bold octave starts the next sentence, but this little phrase of two notes, with its gentle fall of a second, continues to sound. Its persistence gives an unconscious sense of logic to the whole paragraph. Presently we arrive, apparently by accident, at the key of C major and this tonality is insisted upon with curious emphasis in a series of repeated cadences and a quite elaborately ornamented version of the triad. But in half a bar we are back in the home key with the opening melody once again, sounding all the fresher for this capricious switch of tonality. It is a characteristic trick—or perhaps feat of *legerdemain* is a more respectful phrase. The section comes to a definite conclusion, after some sequential treatment of the scale-passage contained in the melody, and rests for two bars in the home key. But once again, when the tonality has been firmly and decisively established, we are suddenly whisked into F major for the second section, by an ambiguous C.

EX. 10

The theme of this section must surely refer, once again, to the two-note figure 'x' of the first theme. I do not think it out of proportion to insist on the importance of this, insignificant though the figure may be in itself. It gives life and unity to the whole composition. To some this sort of thing is merely accidental. They are probably right after their fashion, but we must take careful note of accidents. They only show that Chopin accidentally composed in a coherent and logical way. The theme is given a charmingly lurching effect by having the chords on the off-beats and single notes on the strong ones. It is a device which not every composer can bring off successfully. Brahms has tried it in an Intermezzo in E minor,[2] and the result resembles imperfectly cooked porridge. He has marked it 'Grazioso'.

The second strain of this theme, in F minor, builds up the biggest climax we have yet had, and after a fairly systematic passage of relaxation, the first strain returns in the orthodox key, and the section closes in its dominant. So far we have had two units, each complete in themselves, and each of the familiar A B A type. They have been stated and to some extent enlarged upon during the statements; there can be no going back at this moment because of their completeness, and so we go forward to what seems like an episode introduced for the sake of contrast. Possibly it could be extensive and lead to a recapitulation. And certainly it can be called an episode, but it is more, for its graceful arabesques serve to introduce the semiquaver movement so necessary to the development section which presently starts. This development is one of the most powerful Chopin ever composed. It is mainly to do with the second subject, which rises through the turmoil to heights so imposing that one is quite staggered to look back at its winsome origins. But the first subject also makes an appearance after a time, and the two are worked together in a quite wonderful way. This is true creative craftsmanship. The climax is a restatement of the opening theme as a tremendous tutti, with harmonies laid out over the keyboard that fairly make it glow. This serves Chopin (and us) as quite sufficient recapitulation for the purposes of this piece, because Chopin, as I have said before, recognizes form as sensation, not to be calculated in numbers of bars. And surely these triumphant few bars make the point! The composition ends with a reference to the episode, by way of coda, in a blaze of light.

[2] Op. 116, No. 5.

I have found that the beauties of Chopin's Fourth Ballade are sometimes admitted even by those unsympathetic to his work as a whole.
To most of his admirers the work is one of the great peaks of his achievement. It was composed in 1842, and published the following year, as
op. 52.

The introduction is very striking—just as arresting, with its quiet,
persuasive tones, as is that of the First Ballade with its rhetoric. The
phrasing of its melody is intriguing.

EX. II

We may think of the phrase beginning at 'x' as the answer to the first
phrase in the tenor register. But the third phrase, beginning at 'y', shows
us that the second must have already begun before the first has finished.
Perhaps it stretches from the start of the piece. This sort of finesse
pervades the whole work. What exactly are those hesitant three notes
doing, for instance, at the beginning of the main melody when it arrives?
The naive listener will accept them as the start of the tune, and Chopin
includes them in his phrase-mark. But we learn afterwards that the tune
really begins with the last two quavers of this bar, which form an
anacrusis. The three-note figure only occurs once again during the
piece, after the cadenza in bar 134. And though we are reasonably
expecting a four-bar phrase, we find that owing to dallying about in the
fourth bar the phrase has rhythmically occupied four and a half bars;
the position of the melody, in terms of bar-lines, has become dislocated.
Compare Exx. 12(a) and (b).

EX. 12

Far from sounding ungainly the effect is completely convincing and an
added interest is unconsciously felt by the listener, whose business is
not to supply bar-lines, but to respond to the wonderful shape of this

most haunting of melodies. Perhaps a hint of it may be found in the first of the 'Trois Nouvelles Études' of 1839, in the same key, and Liszt has something of the kind in his second Concert Study, also in F minor. Similarity of music in the same key is always a fascinating subject. But nothing quite like this has ever been written. Chopin was a master of such metrical finesse, which seems capricious and ought to sound so, but doesn't. The point of it is that it gives him great freedom in the manipulation of the moments of relaxation or tension in the cadences and modulations with which his phrases open or close. Thus in bar 12 the melody can complete its first sentence on the chord of A flat with leisure to relax. But farther on, at bar 22, there is plenty of time for the modulation which carries it back to the key of F minor. The whole scheme has admirable plasticity, and at the same time is firm and shapely. It was for this purpose, probably, that Beethoven retained the $\frac{3}{4}$ time signature for his scherzos, though there is only one beat in the bar.

So in this metrical freedom the unhurried melody unwinds itself through a richly varied harmonic terrain, until it arrives as a curiously amorphous passage starting in G flat major (bar 38), which rather suggests the introduction of new material. But figures from the tune intervene, and soon we find ourselves, after a characteristic rhythmic hold-up, involved in a counterstatement of the first theme. Fanciful semiquaver decorations accompany this; they build the theme to its first climax, and flow on into a bridge-passage introducing the second idea. Here, having reached his new key of B flat major, Chopin spends four bars in throwing out hints of his next theme in quick modulations —a characteristically wayward proceeding which happily does not take the shine out of the theme proper when it arrives. The beauty of this theme is of a kind no other composer has realized, and although this exquisite tenderness is to be found elsewhere in Chopin's works—in the second theme of the G major Nocturne, op. 37, no. 2, for example—it seems here to have reached its apotheosis. A modulating passage of great eloquence leads to a development which re-introduces the introduction. This is a very fine stroke. Not only is this reappearance very telling in itself, but Chopin shows us at the same time the relation of the introduction to the main melody, namely the four repeated notes in the figure which features so largely in the latter *vis-à-vis* the repeated quavers of the introduction. (Another accident!) The music, as it settles

into the key of A major, has a new significance. The little cadenza
which follows hints that its arpeggios will turn out to be the dominant
of D minor, which indeed they do. A very curious passage now begins
in this key, in which the first phrase of the melody is treated in canonic
imitation—not an aspect of music which one usually associates with
Chopin. These devices are helped, and at the same time made more
fascinating, by the metrical fluidity we have already referred to. In
these circumstances the tune seems to have some difficulty in getting
under way, but eventually it succeeds, and we sail off into a richer
version of the melody than we have had hitherto. It is a statement
embellished with fanciful and luxuriant figuration, but the embroideries
are never extravagant and the shapely melodic contours persist until
the figures dissolve into scale-passages accompanying another version
of the second theme, this time in D flat. Though its characteristic tender
quality never quite deserts it, the theme manages to achieve a strength
and grandeur that one would not have suspected, as it builds a great
climax finishing with a decisive cadence in the dominant, C, and a
fermata. Then follow eight bars of the most breathless suspense in all
music—five chords which prepare the way for the coda. Both time
and emotion seem to cease.

EX. 13

The coda is a perfectly coherent piece of music if it is not reduced to
the amorphous mess favoured by some pianists, apparently anxious
to reach the conclusion without a major disaster. Perhaps there has been
too much loose talk of whirlwinds and the like. Its driving triplets

possess irresistible power, and this extraordinary composition finishes
with a sense of inevitability as conclusive as the crack of doom.

EX. 14

It may seem odd that the most profound of these Ballades, the First
and Fourth, are the ones to have waltz-accompaniments to their main
themes. The melody of the Fourth certainly demands the most delicate
sense of rubato for its execution. In an oration delivered at Lwów in
October 1910, Paderewski speaks of 'an inborn national Arythmia'
which he considers a Polish national characteristic, and which, he says,
would serve to explain the instability and lack of perseverance with
which the Poles are generally credited. 'Not one of those great beings',
he goes on, 'to whom providence entrusted the revelation of the Polish
soul was able to give such strong expression as Chopin to this Arythmia.
Being poets, they were hampered by limiting precision of thought . . .
But Chopin was a musician; and music alone, perhaps alone his music,
could reveal the fluidity of our feelings, their frequent overflowings
towards infinity, their heroic concentrations, their frenzied ecstasies
which lightly face the shattering of rocks, their impotent despairs, in
which thought darkens, and the very desire of action perishes. This
music, tender and tempestuous, tranquil and passionate, heart-reaching,
potent, overwhelming: this music which eludes metrical discipline,
rejects the fetters of rhythmic rule, and refuses submission to the
metronome as if it were the yoke of some hated government: this
music bids us hear, know and realize that our nation, our land, the
whole of Poland lives, feels and moves in Tempo Rubato.'[3]

Rather dangerous stuff, this, and such pianists as are still hampered by
limiting precision of thought, like the poets, should tread warily when
entering the realms of Polish Arythmia. Playing out of time in a cosmopolitan fashion is no substitute.

[3] London 1911, translated by L. Alma Tadema.

It is interesting and even sometimes illuminating to make analogies between Chopin's ballades and sonata-form; sometimes the classical rondo might be invoked. But it is quite unnecessary for their understanding. As I have tried to point out, it is always the principles and sensations that constitute the ultimate form, and not the adherence to a pre-ordained pattern of events. For the events must always govern the pattern in which they occur, or the form will be as dead as Chopin's is vibrating with life. And I would suggest that the student should examine every sonata movement as though it were the first example of its kind he has ever seen.

### *Fantasy in F minor*

To pass from a consideration of the four ballades to the Fantasy in F minor, op. 49, seems a natural thing to do, though the reason is not easy to define. This work is definitely not a ballade; if it is difficult, as I said before, to say what a ballade is, we have at any rate reached the point of being able to say what it is not. Chopin has cleverly outgeneralled his critics by calling this work a 'Fantasy', and fancy certainly seems to be the main force which guides the ideas to their appointed places. It was composed during the period 1840-1, about the same time as the Third Ballade. But that Ballade, though possibly more highly organized, is lighter in calibre. The Fantasy is one of Chopin's very finest compositions, in the richness of its ideas and the breadth with which they are set forth. Yet for all its decisive statements and sometimes even pungent thoughts, it has an elusive quality which makes it difficult, now and then, to follow. It starts in the style of a slow march, with what might be an introduction to something else.

EX. 15

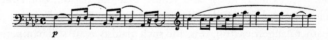

As the music treads solemnly on we begin to feel that the piece has started in earnest, and this is no preliminary material to open the way to more important things. And when a second strain is introduced

this belief is confirmed; when the end of this section is reached we realize that this is a musical unit complete in itself, in simple binary form with a coda. There is no more to be said on that subject, and it never returns. It must have been tempting, one feels, to reintroduce this magical passage, but Chopin was obviously right not to do so. After so compact a statement some little time is needed to get the music under way again, so there now follows quite a considerable passage of questioning triplets, interspersed with pauses, while we feel our way. Eventually the triplets gather speed, and finally rush precipitately into the Allegro. A dark and passionate theme is this, deriving a kind of desparate urgency from its syncopations. At the end of this theme is a figure of some importance:

From this we are suddenly swept into a completely different atmosphere by one of the most triumphantly surging melodies Chopin ever wrote, which lasts for only eight bars before triplets break in again with reckless haste. Much use is made of figure 'x' in Ex. 17, which develops in order to lead to the key of E flat major and what would seem to be a cadence-theme. But unexpectedly we move off again with another march, this time a quick one; when this has run its short span we are jerked into the harmonic no-man's-land of an augmented sixth chord, and once more triplets take over. They bring us back to the syncopated, passionate theme of the first Allegro, and we start again, this time in C minor. We pass through the eight-bar melody, now in G flat major; at last the pressure eases, and we come to rest on a pause. Now begins the middle section, Lento Sostenuto, one of Chopin's most beautiful melodies. On paper this section might appear too short, but its respose and serenity are such that its purpose is perfectly fulfilled in its twenty-four bars. It has succeeded in sounding like what it is—a genuine trio section and not an episode. The rushing triplets once more crash in, and carry us into the recapitulation. As a recapitulation it would not be acceptable to everyone, since it begins in the key of B flat minor, and the material reappears in the keys appropriate to this starting-point. It means that we finally reach the tonality of A flat major, and in this key Chopin has no hesitation in ending his composition. It is indeed a design of fantasy, but it is also a design of inevitability, and served supremely well as a vehicle for some of Chopin's very finest music.

## The Scherzos

With his scherzos Chopin again presented us with a family group of four, but this time the resemblances are much more clearly marked. Possibly this removes an element of fascination which is to be found in the ballades, since one source of resemblance lies in the simplicity of their construction. But the simplicity is always forthright rather than naive, and the method of building, as usual, arises directly out of the nature of the material. And what arrestingly original material it is! Its nature shows immediately that Chopin was not interested here in what the word 'scherzo' might suggest to most people—namely the movements so called by Beethoven in his sonatas and symphonies. About the only characteristic the two types share is the time-signature, and even this has a slightly different connotation. Beethoven's tiny bars are frequently resilient bricks which build themselves into powerful structural patterns. Each gives a small thrust to produce something which becomes, cumulatively, a gigantic momentum. These pieces together form so distinct a species that the wide range they cover individually is quite amazing. But in Chopin's scherzos the music flows over the bar-lines with a quite different sort of impetus. The nearest approach to Beethoven's procedure is possibly to be found in the development passages of the Scherzo in C sharp minor. Again, in Beethoven's scherzos there is sometimes a quality which is usually, for want of a better word, called 'humour'. This will vary from the sardonic to the rumbustious; it can include ländler-like capers or occasionally it can be purposely amusing—as in the F major Violin Sonata (the 'Spring'), for instance. On the whole Chopin's pieces encompass none of these things. A flavour of bitterness may now and again seem to be present which might, I suppose, be thought an equivalent of this quality. But these are rather hazy areas of thought. We can only note that Chopin's idea of a scherzo seemed (for reasons which today we may find hard to grasp) to confuse his contemporaries. Nowadays, when we prefer such nomenclature as 'Aleatoric Agglomeration' or 'Megacycle 23' for our compositions, such a word as 'scherzo' seems quite indecently loose. But then, it still had playful connotations, even if it did not mean a 'Scherz'. 'How is "gravity" to clothe itself', wrote Schumann, 'if "jest" goes about in dark veils?'

The basic form of a scherzo, as everyone knows, is that of the minuet and trio from which it was derived, where the trio is a second minuet introduced by way of contrast before the first is repeated. The more expanded the piece becomes, and the weightier the material it sets forth, the greater, usually, is the contrast which seems to be demanded. Chopin, of course, pays attention to these considerations. Sometimes the trio section of the old minuet would be in the form of a musette, and even this seems to have been in Chopin's mind in his Scherzo in B minor, when he introduces the reiterated F sharps to accompany the tune of the middle section. This work, published as op. 20, was begun in Vienna in 1830, during a rather unhappy period of his life. He was on his second visit to the Austrian capital, and the visit was not proving very successful—a disappointment, in fact, after his decided if moderate triumphs of the previous year. Though he was received socially with some enthusiasm and seems to have wandered about in the grand salons of the day (or, rather, night) he was professionally at a standstill, and no one seemed anxious to help. Then came the Polish rising in November 1830 against the Russians, and Chopin was naturally tormented by fears for his family, his Constantia and his compatriots in general. He was plagued by doubts as to what he ought to do. It has been claimed that this Scherzo is a reflection of his mental state during this period. If this were so, the music would be, amongst other things, indecisive, meandering and rather feeble, and these attributes surely cannot be ascribed to it. But on the other hand, composing music can certainly act as a clarification of individual confusions. The simple act of composition, by generalizing a personal affliction quite unconsciously, can be healthily cathartic. Or perhaps the act is not so simple.

The principal material of the B minor Scherzo consists of two highly contrasted ideas, each of them, however, charged with the same urgency and drive. The first of these is an upward rush of quavers, starting with the familiar pattern of a two-bar phrase repeated, followed by a phrase of four bars. The four-bar phrase is built on a broken version of the following progressions:

EX. 18

and it is worth while taking note of the falling seconds that form the top line. Not only do they contribute a characteristic, one could say thematic, feature of the piece, but they also form a very real link with the second idea. It is one of those links which may only be felt unconsciously, but which is nevertheless a unifying factor. The notes are marked 'x' in both examples.

EX. 19

The rhetoric of this fine passage, with its eloquent dialogue between left and right hands, produces a very grand effect as it crashes in at the climax of the madly rushing quavers.

This section closes with a double-bar and a repeat, giving Ex. 19 the apparent function of a cadence-theme, such as might be found mid-way in an Allemande of Bach. Such an analogy is obviously absurd, however, and it is more realistic to regard this passage in the light of a second subject. At any rate, its frequent dramatic reappearances give it the importance of such, in the general effect of the composition. On the other hand, it *is*, in fact, cadential; in other words, what Chopin does is to follow the classical procedure with such fidelity that, paradoxically, he makes it harder to recognize. Out of these cadence-themes, as we know, emerged the second subject of the classical sonata; Chopin's theme is never developed, thus following an earlier pattern rather than a later. That is to say, he adheres to the plan of a minuet or scherzo.

In passing, I do not think it is too far-fetched to find a relation between this subject and the two massive chords which provide the introduction.

EX. 20

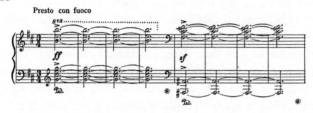

Presto con fuoco

The connexion between the bass notes of these chords and the diminished seventh which plays so prominent a part in Ex. 19 is a real one, and must have been the reason, either conscious or unconscious, why Chopin adopted this particular inversion of the first chord rather than any other.

The music continues after the repeat with an extension, rather than a development of, the quaver patterns; after this the whole thing is recapitulated as from the beginning without the first repeat, followed by a reprise of the opening paragraph to round off the first section. The trio or middle section is based, thematically, on the old Polish Christmas carol 'Lulajze Jezuniu', a title which most of us, I think, could make a shot at translating. I once heard a Polish peasant singing this tune, high up in the Tatra Mountains. The effect was strangely moving in the stillness of the craggy rocks with their patches of snow. His voice came from nowhere in particular, ventriloquially, floating through the mountain air. He sang with abandon, in a quite uninhibited fashion, and with a certain hard, almost ruthless quality that enables the Slavs to get to the heart of their most poignant melodies. It shows how wrong we are

in western Europe to be too tender in such matters. At least, I hope he
was a peasant. He might, I suppose, have been a holiday-making
pianist, but pianists are not very likely, I think, thus to give tongue even
in complete isolation. Polish Arythmia played little part in his performance. Some editions seek to elucidate the melody by notational
devices such as this:

EX. 21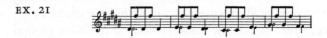

but one hopes that anyone who could not discern the tune from
Chopin's method of writing the passage would not undertake to play
the piece at all. In any case, notation such as this example blurs the
outlines rather than clarifies them. The reiterated dominant pedal, like
the chime of a little bell, is magically hypnotic, and the emergence of
the melody above it at the cadence is deliciously charming. The whole
layout gives a swaying movement to the tune, which sets it off to
perfection. The extensions of the melody are, of course, Chopin's.
The Polish Chopin Institute Edition gives the original tune thus:

EX. 22

The whole paragraph is repeated, after which a reprise of the first
phrases of the melody is interrupted by the violent, almost melo-
dramatic appearance of the fortissimo chords (Ex. 20) which opened the
piece. Gerald Abraham finds this proceeding 'very naive by comparison
with Chopin's later transitions'. He concedes, however, that it is
'effective'. For him the whole piece is 'structurally of little interest'
(amongst other works of this period), and he speaks of ill-concealed
joins in the carpentry.[4] Personally I do not feel that concealment was
much in Chopin's mind here, though there are admittedly cases where
one feels he has attempted such things without being very succesful.
There is a tumultuous coda which leads to a violent conclusion, and the
piece ends with two mighty chords which echo the two with which it
began.

    [4] *Chopin's Musical Style*, p. 53, Gerald Abraham, London, 1960.

The Second Scherzo, op. 31, in B flat minor, was published and probably written in 1837. Schumann called it 'Byronic'. It is a much more highly organized composition than the first, yet at the same time more expansive. The first note is obviously there for rhythmic, or rather metrical, reasons, in order to prevent the second bar sounding like the first. Yet it always seems to me a great pity that it must be so. It never reappears in any of the many reprises of the subject. Not only does it detract from the mystery of these ghostly triplets, but it takes some of the thunder out of the fortissimo B flat when it crashes in four bars later. However, Chopin must have felt that one could not afford any confusion, and here is the subject, in terms of those violent, tearing contrasts which this supposedly elegant and emasculated Pole loved to display:

EX. 23

These fierce antitheses persist and then lead to a broad, lyrical and eminently enthusiastic cantilena, mostly in the relative major. This melody is magnificently sustained through a lengthy paragraph, until a codetta which is little more than a glorified full close brings it to an end. The customary repeat of this whole section follows, this time, happily, without the first B flat, since now we know where we are. The trio section which follows starts with a little duet for the two upper parts, and the subtle difference between the first statement and the second, in the matter of part-writing should be brought out by the pianist more intelligently than is often the case.

EX. 24 (a) and (b)

The accent in Ex. 24(b) must surely apply to the C sharp. This melodic unit consists of three phrases of four bars; Chopin puts a phrase-mark to bind the last two together, in the first instance; the second time, however, he gives the last phrase a wonderful upward lift and extends it to five bars. Polish Arythmia again, possibly. Then follows a passage introducing this tiny figure which makes itself heard in an inner part, and which is to prove of immense importance later:

EX. 25

Clearly it stems from the first subject. It gives way to a passage of waltz-like arabesque, after which the whole section repeats in the customary way. But this arabesque, after its second appearance, proceeds to develop itself into a link leading to a thorough working out of the material associated with Ex. 25. This section is a very fine and compelling piece of work, almost, one might say, the kernel of the whole composition. The little figure with its triplet is irresistible as it drives the music forward, with immense power, through a sustained climax, and subsides again in repetitions emphasizing the dominant of B flat opening the door for the recapitulation. This follows its usual course, until the broad, lyrical melody, blossoming still further, gives way to the coda. Still continuing to develop the material, this coda finishes unusually but very convincingly in the relative major key of D flat. This fine piece is, I suppose, one of the most popular of Chopin's works, and understandably so, but one occasionally feels that in consequence pianists have not devoted quite enough thought to its preparation.

The Third Scherzo, op. 39, is in C sharp minor, and is dedicated to Adolphe Gutmann. Gutmann was a pupil of Chopin at the age of 15, and according to Lenz was 'strong enough to punch a hole through a table'—presumably with the octaves. One doubts whether it was this amiable accomplishment that prompted the dedication. It was composed about 1839, roughly the same period as the first movement, scherzo and finale of the B flat minor Sonata. In a sense the C sharp minor Scherzo is more in the nature of a sonata movement, as understood by Beethoven, than the ones Chopin wrote for his own sonatas.

The nature of its material seems to suggest procedures more akin to those of Beethoven than does that of the other three scherzos. The opening reveals both the elliptical approach and the fierce contrasts so characteristic of Chopin's larger works. Perhaps he felt that such contrasts were inherent in the nature of a 'scherzo'. His introductory bars could indeed be almost called obscure, with four crotchets in the bar instead of three, and a harmonic slant that, to say the least, is equivocal. In order to make things clearer the Chopin Institute Edition has 'corrected' Chopin's notation in a fatherly way, but naturally the sound remains the same. The effect of this introduction is weird in the extreme[5], and when the subject does finally emerge from these curious rumblings it is as though a searchlight had suddenly been switched on.

EX. 26

It is easy to see how these little bars, each a tiny cell with its own explosive power, can serve to force the music forward, much as they do in the 'Eroica' or 'Pastoral' symphonies. Very different from the characteristic bars of the two preceding scherzos, though perhaps the passages concerned with Ex. 25 in op. 31 display something of the same kind. This is the sort of thing:

EX. 27

After some development on the lines of Ex. 26 comes a restatement of the main subject, merging into a modulating bridge-passage to introduce the second main theme, in the key of D flat major (for C sharp, the tonic major). It cannot be said that there is anything particularly

[5]  See p. 247 for more comment on this remarkable passage. ED.

original about this tune as such. Or, at any rate, so I feel. Its opening
phrase has been used by so many composers, in so many contexts, both
before and since, that its appearance at this particular moment comes
almost as a shock. It is as though Henry V were to start his speech before
Harfleur by saying 'Good afternoon'. But its treatment and general
presentation have great originality. Being of the nature of a chorale,
it is capable of pausing at the ends of its phrases, as the Lutheran tunes
used to do, in order, presumably, to allow a sluggish congregation
some chance of starting the next phrase at the same moment. Chopin
fills in those pauses by delightful tinkling cascades of notes, falling from
the topmost reaches of the keyboard towards the tenor register in
which the tune is making its leisurely way. The effect is both new and
enchanting, and quite compensates for any possible banality in the
melody. The melody, by the way, is curiously introduced by a tiny
figure in the left hand which is a retrograde version of the first phrase
in diminution. I am sure that this is enough to cause earnest central
European enthusiasts to conclude that Chopin was unconsciously
yearning for the birth of the twelve-note system. The section is repeated
and developed to lead the way to a recapitulation of the opening
material, somewhat curtailed and leading this time not to the tonic but
to the relative major. In this key the second theme now appears (the
wrong way round, according to the rules!). It rises to a peroration,
however, in the tonic major, over a dominant pedal, and a fairly
extensive coda brings the piece to a strenuous end.

Wierzynski, in his book *The Life and Death of Chopin*, writes of the
E major Scherzo, op. 54, that it 'embodies an emotion so perfectly
sublimated that one can find in it what one pleases, joy or grief, happiness or despair'. This somewhat wild remark is perhaps not so silly as it
seems at first glance, since frequently a piece of music does not, in fact,
convey the same impression to everybody. Indeed, these impressions
may diverge widely, as objects will take on different shapes according
to the point from which one views them. Perhaps this is one of the
glories of music—of all art, come to that. It is a more charming accomplishment, if less morally sound, to be all things to all men than to be
nothing in particular to one. Music is no mere courtesan, but neither
does she necessarily seek to impose her own moods on her audience.

Sad music does not inevitably make one feel sad, though bad music may. Still, one would have to be in a very distressing frame of mind, I would have said, to discern grief or despair in this composition. To me, it is the only one among the scherzos which depends upon the element of caprice, in the wayward and whimsical fashion in which it flits from one thing to another. Yet it is happily quite free from that fatal quality of archness which frequently besets the German romantic composer when he sets about being capricious. It is certainly not a monument of compact form, but it is clearly not in the nature of its material to be so. If its seeming inconsequence and repetitions may occasionally become a little tiresome, it does not demand any great intellectual effort on the part of the listener, and it is easy to relax and succumb to its wiles.

Rather tenuously, a motif of five notes helps to hold it together, by reasserting itself from time to time, sometimes quaintly distorted.

EX. 28

This phrase opens the piece, without any introductory material. It is followed by no less than three other ideas, quite distinct in themselves though very fleeting in effect, and together these make up what might be called the first subject, or main theme, of the composition. Passages of running arabesque which Chopin can rarely deny himself intervene, and the music dances, with many repetitions, through remote keys, in an irresponsible and carefree way. The second subject, or trio section starts off in the darker tonality of C sharp minor, the relative, having arrived in this key by methods which certainly seem a trifle perfunctory. It is not one of Chopin's most distinguished melodies, but it serves its purpose well; it has a slight tinge of melancholy and its sostenuto shows up to good advantage after the fanciful fluttering motions of the preceding music.

EX. 29

PAUL HAMBURGER

# Mazurkas, Waltzes, Polonaises

## Mazurkas

THE transformation of popular dances into forms of serious music is an achievement of genius that provides us with a rather precise yardstick of its greatness. It is easier, and fairer, to compare a Chopin mazurka with the folk-dance that is its primitive model than it is to compare, for instance, his concertos with those of Hummel—though both comparisons are rewarding. In the latter case the divergent aims of fully developed musical personalities have to be precariously assessed before the quality of their products may be compared, whilst in the former a patently pre-artistic utterance may be shown as the source of a highly articulate inspiration.

Most of Chopin's dances, to be sure, cannot be traced to a single, definite folk-model, but arise from a composite recollection of certain types of melodies and rhythms which are then given artistically valid expression in one or more works. In this respect Chopin's Polish-ness is rather like Dvořák's Czech-ness and Bloch's Jewish-ness: all three composers distil national flavours from material that is not strictly folk-loristic—in contradistinction to Bartók, Vaughan Williams, and the Spanish national school who start off from genuine folklore. But in a few cases a definite model is found to exist, such as the folk-tune 'Oj Magdalino'[1]

[1] See Maurice J. E. Brown's *Chopin: an Index of His Works in Chronological Order*, p. 35, London, 1960.

EX. I

which appears in the Poco più vivo of the youthful Mazurka in F
major, op. 68, no. 3 (op. posth.), of 1829:

EX. 2

The distance between model and art-work is small here and, as can
be seen from the return to the main section (last two bars of Ex. 2),
Chopin brought in the folk-song specifically for the sake of its primitive
drone and the typical harshness of its sharpened (Lydian) fourth, so that
he may point a contrast to the more highly developed main section.

This example shows why there are so few direct references to folklore in Chopin's dances: special contexts as the above apart, he felt
hemmed in by the primitive rigidity of these melodies *in their entirety*.
On the other hand, he readily let himself be inspired by their *elements*:
the sharpened fourth, the drone bass, the sudden triplets, the frequent
feminine endings, the repetition of one-bar motifs. If one of these
elements be singled out to show how genius can surmount obstacles
inherent in the material, and indeed profit from them, it should
be the close motif-play of the folk mazurka. Originally an all-
too-convenient unit for the building of square four- and eight-bar
phrases, in the hands of Chopin these motifs are used to counter the
angularity of the predetermined metrical period. He inflects their
intervals, and deflects their harmonic trend far away from the expected

full or half closes. This happens as early as 1830 in the set of Four
Mazurkas, op. 6, completed in Vienna, of which Chopin remarked that
'they are not for dancing'. Here is part of op. 6, no. 1, in F sharp
minor.

EX. 3

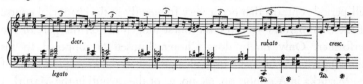

It is to be noted that Chopin, like his admired Mozart, confines
such chromatic flights wherever possible within the bounds of the
regular eight-bar phrase. The chains of side-stepping dominant
sevenths found in the above example are an important feature of
Chopin's writing.[2]

Chains of dominant or diminished sevenths (sometimes, as here,
mixed by way of suspensions) persist right through Chopin's oeuvre
and, in the particular case of the mazurkas, not only provide splashes
of exotic colour, but also counteract the plodding regularity inherent
in the dance's melody-type; moreover, they serve with increasing
frequency as starting-points, not only of transitions within the key, as
in Ex. 3, but of true modulations. Here is an example from Chopin's
last mazurka, written a few months before he died in 1849, and published posthumously as op. 68, no. 4.

EX. 4

The above example starts at bar 9, with a varied repeat of the theme,
which now only lasts six bars. At that point Chopin, instead of turning

---

[2] Their development is most succinctly dealt with in Gerald Abraham, op. cit.,
p. 88.

home to F minor as before, seizes the last seventh on E and, changing it
into the dominant harmony of A major, moves off into that key with a
boldly contrasting new subject. An habitual harmonic pattern thus
provides the late Chopin with a means of abolishing the full stop
between two periods.

Abrupt changes of this very deft sort—as also, of course, the normal
full-period contrasts that occur very frequently in the changeful course
of these miniatures—call for the finest judgement on the part of the
performer. Only rarely does Chopin himself (as opposed to his
editors) give us an actual tempo change such as the Poco più mosso of
the Mazurka in A minor, op. 68, no. 2; or the ritenuti in the Mazurkas
in F sharp minor, op. 59, no. 3, and B major, op. 56, no. 1. But some sort
of change is always implied, for the very life of these pieces depends
on it. Whereas in extended structures such as sonata and rondo forms
changes in character are usually so well prepared that they carry the
performer over the sectional 'dividing-line', in these mazurkas (which
are all built on the A B A form and its variants, i.e. A B A B A, A B C A,
A B A C, etc.) abrupt contrasts appear whose management is very
much left to the performer's discretion. As always, the golden rule
should be first to muster up all our resources of tone-control, dynamic
range and pedalling, and only then to resort to rubato. It all depends
on the width of the gulf to be bridged. A straightforward contrast
such as between A (first sixteen bars) and B of the Mazurka in A flat
major, op. 17, no. 3, can be done by dynamics and pedalling alone.

EX. 5

With a complex contrast, such as Ex. 4, on the other hand, we not only
need the 'animato' supplied there by some kindly editors, but also a perceptible hardening of the legato in the bar before the A major section,
no pedal and slight marcato in the left hand. Above all, we need a sense
of two-bar phrasing in the A major section, as against the one-bar

implications beneath the two-bar melodic arches of the preceding section. This latter contrast is the crucial one: the neater we make it the less 'animato' we shall require. The desire to set strict limits to all prescribed or implied tempo changes in the mazurkas is by no means a puritanical one. In the much more loose-limbed, aggregate forms of the waltzes, for instance, drastic tempo changes are often harmless, and can at times be improvised on particularly frisky days; but the chiselled forms of the mazurkas would be disrupted, and possibly rendered unintelligible and ineffective, by injudicious tempo changes. As in Beethoven's Bagatelles, we have to walk the tightrope between overstating and understating the contrasts that jostle one another in a limited field of action.

Another, less precarious form of tempo change, that of melodic rubato, is invited by Chopin's art of intervallic tension in the first place, and his stupendous gift for immediate melodic variation in the second. Here is the unadorned melody at the start of the Mazurka in F minor, op. 68, no. 4, whose sequel we have quoted above (see Ex. 4).

EX. 6

Now, if the third-beat melody-notes in bars 2 and 4 were 'normal', i.e. an octave lower, they would be dull and unproblematic. The way they are written the rising sixth tempts us to a singer's agogic delay before the note, and a tenuto on it; a very worthy impulse as long as we remember that we are on a weak beat of the bar and the delay must not be so big as to preclude the up-beatish carry-over into the next two-bar phrase, which is indeed urged by the F-F flat (later E flat-D) pull of the alto. I may be labouring a small point here, but it is useful for the pianist to analyse a few examples of this kind in order to realize that with Chopin, more than with any other great composer, the proper rubato results from a nice balance being struck between the contra- dictory claims of melody, harmony and metre. If a guiding principle be wanted one might say that the claims of any two of these elements can usually be satisfied by dynamic and colouristic means, whilst the remaining one calls for a sparing, yet telling rubato. Thus, in the second phrase of op. 68, no. 4, from bar 9 onwards (Ex. 4), when the tune appears as a string of continuous quavers in which the rising sixths become submerged, the top line no longer asks for rubato; the expressive trend is now purely harmonic and metrical, concentrated in the alternating semitone steps of alto, tenor and bass, and for these a purely dynamic realization will suffice.

The innate tendency of the mazurka towards syncopation accents on the third (sometimes the second) beat of the bar, of which we had a refined instance in Ex. 6, presents a constant challenge to composer and performer alike. To be sure, these accents may be no more than a joyous shout at the end of a two-bar phrase, the harmony remaining unchanged; thus at the start of the pretty and nimble Mazurka in A flat major, op. 41, no. 4, every one of the eight two-bar members of the sixteen-bar opening paragraph finishes on this kind of reckless emphasis. Of course, genius compensates for its frivolity by continuing with a B-section where subtle modulating chords are placed just on those third beats, and so turn the texture away from the hopping basses of the beginning into close-harmony four-part writing, with a legato melody for top. But this contrast, appears on second thoughts, as well, too pat to Chopin's fastidious mind, and so he makes fun of the whole piece in a marvellous elliptic ending that lops off the two final bars of the B-phrase, leaving the dancer's leg in mid-air, so to speak, like an automaton run down.

The reverse happens in the Mazurka in B flat minor, op. 24, no. 4. Here it is the B-section (bar 21) that has the purely motoric third-beat accents, falling on every bar, in contrast to the A-section's modulating chords that propel the part-writing over the phrase divisions at the end of every two-bar group. In this Mazurka Chopin is no longer satisfied with the interplay, however adroitly presented, of the clear-cut eight- or sixteen-bar paragraphs of a dance. He opens with a two-part introduction in which an octave on the dominant degree F is gradually narrowed to a plangent diminished fifth which, direct or inverted, remains the characteristic interval in the tortuous chromaticism of the A-section, as well as in the extensive coda (see those C-B flat-G flat phrases). Whereas in the A-section the interval contracts, as a diminished interval should (or, in inversion, expands), and thus is used tonally in a late-romantic, almost Wagnerian sense, in the coda it is the modal implication, that of a Lydian (sharpened) fourth that comes to the fore, giving us a whiff of the orientalism of Balakirev and Rimsky-Korsakov. The form of the mazurka is A B A C D A coda, and it is in the short C-section that this Lydian implication becomes most powerful in a stark unison passage; there follows immediately a purely diatonic F major passage that placates our sense of harmony.

EX. 7

Similar peace-offerings are made by the turns to the tonic major in the coda (a Schubertian touch, reminiscent of those shafts of majorish light that fall upon the first movement development in the latter's posthumous B flat major Sonata). These turns to major are foretold in the modulating D-section, related to the B-section (both are in the relative major, D flat), but tonally much more flexible than the latter, and containing the lush progression D flat major (= C sharp major)→C sharp minor→E major, which is a world apart from the B-section's and the coda's modality.

Arthur Hedley defines a symphonic type of mazurka[3] of which the Mazurka in B flat minor, op. 24, no. 4, is one of the earlier examples. It is preceded, by five years, by the Mazurka in F minor, op. 7, no. 3, which also has an introduction, but no coda. Instead, its main part, consisting of a loose assembly A B C D, is joined to the return of A by the most unexpected modulation, based on the introductory drone, from D flat major, seen as a Neapolitan Sixth, to C major, the latter becoming the dominant of the tonic F minor. As Chopin gradually freed himself from the dance associations of the mazurka the 'tone-poems' amongst them become more frequent. They all contain breathtaking harmonic turns like the one just mentioned, and all are distinguished by a great diversity of material held together in severe structures, just as is the case in op. 24,

---

[3] *Chopin*, Master Musician Series, London, 1964.

no. 4. This is not to disparage the earlier works, some of which, like the deservedly popular op. 7, no. 1, in B flat major, and op. 7, no. 2, in A minor, have an unencumbered freshness of melodic invention and a colourful harmonic charm all their own. But from 1835 the influence of Chopin's large-scale works (both the First Ballade and the First Scherzo had been written then) increasingly leaves its mark on his smaller forms, urging them towards a more symphonic style, often at the expense of simple lyricism.

A case in point is the next 'tone-poem' among the mazurkas, the one in C sharp minor, op. 30, no. 4. The number of constituent sections is here reduced to two, but they both have melodies which, though tuneful, also lend themselves to thematic and motivic use. The resulting ABA coda form is therefore more complex (and longer) than many of the compound ternary forms of earlier works. Attention has often been drawn to the start of the coda with its sliding seventh chords, producing parallel fifths and sevenths that shocked an earlier age, but which *we* feel to be a 'curiously Debussyesque passage'⁴ and moreover one that dissolves the tragic heroism of this Mazurka, at a point when it can no longer maintain itself, into the atonal anonymity of the unconscious.

EX. 8

This is a 'fugue', a flight from reality, in the psychopathic sense of the word, and the Victorians may be forgiven for finding similar passages in Chopin's work 'diseased', 'feverish', 'morbid', for their harmonic instinct balked at such obstacles, being unable to hear across them. Nowadays it is easier to realize how carefully Chopin planned such events. It is not that he himself suddenly and helplessly falls prey to morbidity, but that with great courage he unleashes, and subsequently

⁴ Gerald Abraham, op. cit., p. 88.

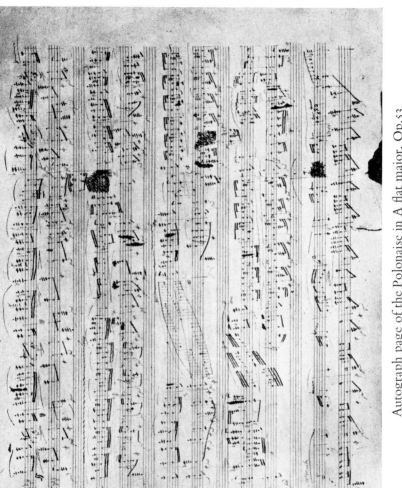

Autograph page of the Polonaise in A flat major, Op.53
(Heinemann Foundation, New York)

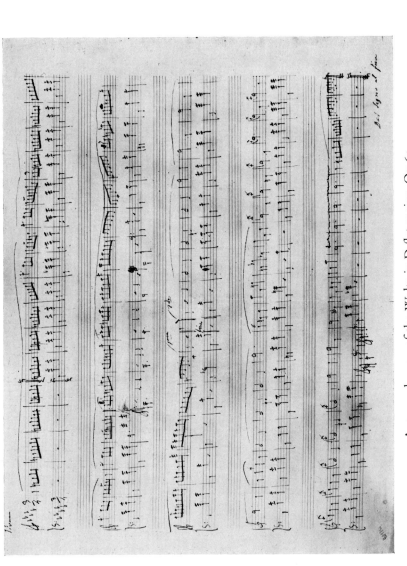

Autograph page of the Waltz in D flat major, Op.64
(Royal College of Music, London)

inhibits, a neurotic streak which runs through his music, and which it is his artistic duty to disclose on occasion. Thus, in this coda of op. 30, no. 4, at bar 6 of Ex. 8, tonality is reapproached with the restatement of a fragment from B in the treble against one from A in the bass. They both fit into the secondary seventh on the home supertonic, to which the 'flight' has ultimately led, but the wonder is that the listener at that point is quite unaware of how near home he is; it is only with the final C sharp minor chord that he realizes how much more tragic than any atonal flight the return to tonal reality may be.

That the great mazurkas of this period are not all sombre, and may even become highly popular, is shown by the lively D major, the second of op. 33 (1837–8). While I hold with Herbert Weinstock[5] that of all Chopin's mazurkas this 'is the closest to being a waltz, particularly a waltz by Chopin', I disagree with his preceding remark: 'It is sprightly and thoughtless dance music engaged in making a cumulative virtue of reiterations.' It is true that in this A B A coda form the A-section consists of one tune only, stated thrice, on tonic, dominant and again tonic. But it is the sort of whirligig affair that has to be hammered in, on the two prime harmonic degrees, to underline its frantic gaiety. And there are 'late style' puns in the other sections: both the second part of the B-section (at the return of the two sharps) and the coda audibly guy the repetitiveness of A by adding, and again retracting, little chromatic alterations to an otherwise self-identical one-bar motif.

A mazurka, on the other hand, which does seem too repetitive to me is op. 33, no. 4, in B minor. Its main phrase *ab* + *ac* forms the C of a C D C form, which in itself is the A of an overall A B A, whose B evolves from the D of the sub-ternary group. Now, if this is a complex statement, so is the form of this piece, and most successfully so, apart from its first section which proffers *a* eight times. Yet even so, *a*, *b* and *c* are in themselves utterly charming. Their beginnings are:

EX. 9

[5] *Chopin: the Man and His Music*, New York, 1949.

Syntactically, *b* and *c* are genuine, and subtly differentiated expansions of the antecedental phrase *a*. The B-section of the total form is in the main taken up by a Maggiore, and the chief point of interest lies in the lead-back from this to the Minore. The 20-year-old Chopin might have plumped for plain juxtaposition; the 28-year-old master, however, supremely confident of the harmonic suggestiveness of his linear writing, invents an unaccompanied recitative of seventeen bars. This is a structural *extension* which, on the one hand, reflects the syntactical *expansion* of *a* by *b* and *c*, and, on the other, makes possible the *compression* of the subsequent, final A-section to a quarter of its former length.

With the Four Mazurkas, op. 41 (1838–9), we arrive at that group of very mature works of which Frederick Niecks, writing in 1885,[6] had this to say:

> 'In the Mazurkas [above op. 41] we look in vain for the *beautés sauvages* which charm us in the earlier ones—they strike us rather by their propriety of manner and scholarly elaboration; in short, they have more of reflective composition and less of spontaneous effusion about them.'

This, unequals being unequal, was also the general opinion on Beethoven's late style for quite some time after his death, and it is the sort of critical pronouncement which is usually prompted by a composer's discovery of new emotional values that have to be communicated in a novel, yet severe idiom. What could be more equivocal to contemporary ears than the Phrygian beginning of op. 41, no. 1, in C sharp minor—an unaccompanied tune that sounds like A major, until the entry of the harmony declares C sharp as the tonic? Or the return of this austere Phrygian tune in fortissimo octave-chords towards the end of a coda that has started by piling up dominant functions right to the eleventh and thirteenth, in a grand, late-romantic climax! The use of the Phrygian mode in this piece is foreshadowed, in a more rudimentary way, by op. 41, no. 2, in E minor, written at Majorca on 28 November 1838.

[6] *Frederick Chopin as Man and Musician*, London, 1888.

EX. 10

The next of the very great mazurkas is another C sharp minor work, op. 50, no. 3, written in 1841–2. Is it fanciful to ascribe to the three great essays in this key (op. 30, no. 4; 41, no. 1; 50, no. 3) a common mood of nostalgia—more than that, of almost regal bitterness over the passing of Poland's glory? Certainly, the Slavic traits of Chopin's style are much in evidence here; modalities and rhythmic asperities that contrast sharply with the highly sophisticated Western chromaticisms in which they are embedded. Op. 50, no. 3, contains five seemingly incompatible strains, which yet by the witchery of Chopin's genius are tied together: *a*, an opening eight-bar antecedent of canonic imitations, improbably linked to *b*, a waltzing consequent; *c*, a chivalric mazurka tune, very plainly harmonized, antecedent to *d*, a Schumannesque phrase of rich suspension chords. After an eight-bar combination of *a* and *d*, there follows (forming the B-section of the total structure) another, much more broadly conceived mazurka, *e*, with the melodic wave motion characteristic of the *oberek*. Nor does Chopin evade the symphonic challenge presented by such diversified material: in a coda of sixty bars he develops all the elements of the A-section by the symphonic devices of motivic work and remote modulation. This is a romantically topical coda in that it extrapolates the development to the end of the piece, and yet Chopin respects the classical proprieties of ternary form—prompted, one should assume, by his deep understanding of Bach, who, after all, fathered the canonic *a* paragraph—in that he finds his way back, twelve bars before the end, to the canonic motif over a tonic pedal, thus satisfying our sense of tonal and structural symmetry.

The developing coda is a feature of Chopin's late mazurkas, and fine specimens are also found in op. 56, nos. 1 and 3, and op. 59, no. 3. Yet the symphonic approach, of which these codas were symptomatic, disappears again in the last set to be published by Chopin himself, the Three

Mazurkas, op. 63, of 1846, which, though full of late-style felicities, cannot compare in breadth of conception with opp. 50, 56 and 59.

One sort of 'felicity' which Chopin seems to shake out of his sleeve in these works is imitative counterpoint, of a strict order. Here is the start of the concluding twelve-bar phrase of op. 63, no. 3.

EX. II

The wonderfully reflective, echoing effect of this is due not only to the closeness of the alto entry (on the second crotchet) which obliterates the rhythmic scansion of the melody, but also to the fact that this passage reverses the order of the opening theme's halves: the more memorable consequent, appearing first, sheds a retrospective light on the (now) ensuing antecedent, whilst the continuing canon elucidates the motivic links between the two.

Canon of a different sort (in the fifth, at an interval of two bars) is used for the very different purpose of structural reprise in op. 59, no. 3, in F sharp minor. This is a fantastic piece of large melodic gestures and sprung rhythms, containing a complex central Maggiore section whose last paragraph (twenty-one bars after the six sharps) consists of a torrent of descending modulations, abruptly brought under control by obsessive insistence on the tonic, F sharp major. Here is the start of the modulations:

EX. I2

and here the 'nailing down' of the tonic:

It is from this point that Chopin has to find his way back to F sharp minor, and he does it by taking away the sharps one by one—modulating, that is, in the shadowy direction of the circle of fifths. Once the cadential six-four of the minor tonic is reached, it takes just this canon

EX. 14

subtly reannouncing the principal theme, to complete the best lead-back ('Rückführung') to be found between Schubert and Brahms.

But the function of this canon reaches into the actual reprise itself: its thematic content makes it possible for Chopin to confine the recapitulated material to the last ten bars of section A, from which point he sails into the coda. This, now, is another miracle: the penultimate bar of the initial A-section (two bars before the six sharps) is built up sequentially to form a rising slope from which the central section's 'modulation torrent' may descend again. This happens twice, with inspired changes of harmony and texture, and then, when tonality has almost gone overboard, the insistent F sharp major rondel comes to the rescue, and, becalmed by its own primly cadential codetta, brings the piece to a major close.

Since this Mazurka is bursting at the seams with invention, some freedom of tempo in its performance will not come amiss. I would certainly speed up the F sharp major Rondel, and take a breather on the coda peaks before plunging down.

Of the other masterpieces among the late mazurkas, it is important that the student of Chopin has a good look at all the numbers of opp. 41, 50, 56, 59, 63, and also at the neglected A minor Mazurka of 1841, dedicated to Emile Gaillard (no opus number). A last glance may be permitted at the big C minor Mazurka, op. 56, no. 3. This has always been considered a dark horse among Chopin's works, for notwithstanding its distinctive bearing and obvious craftsmanship, it contains a number of unintelligible harmonic progressions (see from the five sharps to the two flats; from the two flats to the three flats; bars 11–16 of the coda.) I submit that these are not unintelligible in themselves, but in their context; that is, awkwardly metricized and paragraphed. For once (as also in that notorious passage of the F sharp major Impromptu) compression in the service of experiment has gone too far. But it is certainly true, as has been pointed out, that these progressions herald the style of the mature Wagner—where they become comprehensible.

## Waltzes

In his mazurkas, Chopin did for the three peasant dances *Oberek* (quick), *Mazur* (intermediate) and *Kujawiak* (slow) what Schubert did for the various kinds of *Deutsche* and *Ländler*. In his waltzes and polonaises, on the other hand, Chopin's models were the more civilized, though hardly better organized, ballroom and court dances of his age. Chopin's achievement here is comparable to Bach's in his treatment of the various dance forms, particularly the sarabande. Two stages can be distinguished in Bach: at the first, represented by the French Suites, the binary form A B or AB(*b* + *a*) of the dance is strictly adhered to (though with much finesse of detail); at the second, represented by the partitas for clavier, viola da gamba and violin, the expansion or varied repetition of paragraphs and periods leads to a widening of the structure, which now moves in the direction of the concerto and fantasia. The same evolution is found in Chopin's polonaises and, to a lesser extent, in his waltzes. To be sure, his models were all ternary: ABA, often in the

form of A(*ab*)B(*cd*)A(*ab*) or A(*aba*)B(*cdc*)A(*aba*) in the case of the
polonaises; pseudo-ternary, or potpourri-like in the case of the currently
popular waltzes: ABCDA, or ABACDEA coda. The former design
yields firmer structures, more capable of extension and development. A
clear line may be drawn from Chopin's early polonaises, which are
skilful and brilliant embroideries of the received form (revived much
later in the 'Military' Polonaise, op. 40, no. 1) to the refined 'tone-
poems' of op. 26, nos. 1 and 2, and op. 40, no. 2, and thence to the F
sharp minor Polonaise, op. 44—'a sort of polonaise, but it's more like a
fantasia' (Chopin to Fontana)—and the expressly so designated 'Polonaise-Fantaisie', op. 61, of 1846. In establishing this evolving sequence
it has to be remembered that the freedom or licence implied in the title
'fantasia' is relative to the schematicism of the early models, and not
indicative of any looseness of organization in these works.

No such straightforward progression is discernible in the waltzes.
Apart from some interesting codas—the one section capable of symphonic development, as we know from Johann Strauss—early and late
waltzes alike follow the potpourri pattern, and are thus the most easily
accessible works of Chopin. Of course, this limitation in the nature of
the species was again a challenge to Chopin's genius. He lavishes
melodic and harmonic refinements on almost every single one of the
countless eight- or sixteen-bar phrases of these forms. Moreover, while
the species does not permit structural innovations as do the mazurkas
and polonaises, it does invite motivic and melodic cross-reference, and
even unification, between its various members. Chopin has fully
availed himself of this invitation. In one of his early waltzes, the E
minor of 1830 (perhaps the best of the posthumously published ones),
*all* tunes start on their respective dominants (or function thereof),
creating a unity between the tonic minor, the tonic major and the
latter's relative minor that is distinctly felt in performance as a concen-
tric force. Here are the beginnings of these tunes.

EX. 15

Three consequences arise from this quite naturally, which help Chopin in asserting his personality against the tyranny of the foursquare mould: (1) The eccentric start of the first theme demands a prior confirmation of the tonic; this is given in the ebullient opening flourish. (2) The middle part of the A-section, following upon a full close in E minor, may not only start on the dominant, but may intensify that region by suspension technique within, and sequential technique beyond its two-bar phrases (see (b) of Ex. 15). Having clothed his suspension chords with a rising and falling quaver melody, what is then more natural for Chopin than to continue with a melodic variation in which the quavers become unbroken, and so establish a link with the introduction?

EX. 16

The harmonic identity of these passages is not at all obvious to the listener.

The third consequence of this work's integrated dominants lies in the facility given by a V-I-V-I chord-series to false closes on tonic substitutes. This enables Chopin to restrict his final A-section to one recurrence of the tune (a), and that not even a complete sixteen-bar sentence: three-quarters of the way through he finds a dominant suitable for branching off into the coda.

EX. 17

The expected tonic is replaced by a subdominant diminished seventh; there follows, starting on the Neapolitan sixth, a sequence of chords on rising basses, which is a perfect structural complement to the falling basses of Ex. 15(b)—a little gem of (most likely unconscious) planning that once more proves the punctuality of Chopin's genius (see the similar coda of the Mazurka, op. 59, no. 3, discussed above). When eight bars later the cadential six-four of E minor is reached, the work's harmonic adventures are over; but in the last thirteen bars the 'thematic' V-I progression appears another six times.

The first of the eight waltzes Chopin published in his lifetime, op. 18 in E flat, written in Vienna, 1831, also has a theme starting on the dominant, but while this is a piquant touch, the Waltz on the whole is not closely organized, though it is on a grand, brilliant scale. However, in this Waltz, and in the similar op. 34, no. 1, of 1835, one can admire Chopin's skill in writing salon music of immediate appeal without falling below a certain level. The latter piece, in A flat major, certainly has very characteristic tunes, the first of which provides a charming example of how Chopin, with his gift for on-the-spot variation, can disguise the squareness of an $a + a^1 + a + a^1 =$ sixteen bars phrase.

EX. 18

Harmonically, the phrase just remains I-V-I-V, on the same motif. Melodically, however, it gives the impression of *a* (four bars) *b* (eight bars) *b*¹ (four bars). In passages like the one marked 'x' above, great Chopin players exhibit an enviable flair for ambivalent cross-phrasing. Not successive, but simultaneous ambivalence is wanted in the playing of the coda: this starts with an exhilarating moto perpetuo figure in the right hand, to be played as 'perlé'[7] as possible, against the sumptious subdominant trend of the harmony with its meaningful descending tenor line (bar 246, etc.), which demands fullness of tone and touches of pedal. Here, as also in the second part of the coda, in which thematic fragments float above a reminiscing waltz rhythm, the player has to invoke all his resources of imagination.

This Waltz is the first in which Chopin employs a sort of refrain to tie together the sections of the straggling potpourri form. The same device is used, even more effectively, in op. 42 and op. 64, no. 2. Here are the beginnings of the refrains in those two works:

EX. 19

These refrains work because they are reductions of the surrounding

---

[7] See p. 122 .ED.

waltz material to a simple formula, open to juxtaposition at both ends. Their harmonic and metrical primitiveness is both concealed and emphasized by delightful right-hand arabesques of a pronouncedly motoric character. Thus in op. 34, no. 1, where the refrain harks back to a sub-thematic motif of the introduction, and in op. 42, where it squarely sets itself against the harmonic and rhythmic oscillations (mixture of $\frac{3}{4}$ and $\frac{6}{8}$ time) of the A-section, while aspiring to a fleet two-octave tessitura where the latter, committed, as it is, to its higher organization, had to make do with one.

In the C sharp minor Waltz, op. 64, no. 2, the refrain (see Ex. 19(b)) has an equally exciting top line, particularly impressive here in its contrast to the elegiac A-section; but its one-bar groups are arranged harmonically to form a (repeated) eight-bar sequence that is less primitive than the 2 + 2 appositions of our former example. Yet the difference thus stated is seen to be a purely relative one when each refrain is considered as a function of its A-section. In the case of the C sharp minor Waltz, the preceding material is harmonically and intervallically subtle enough to allow for a relatively 'developed' simplification. There is even greater subtleness in the ensuing B-section, at the other 'open end' of the refrain, where the melodic line appears to become irregular, while the harmonic scheme continues in four-bar groups. An ambiguous melodic overlap of one bar is produced, first by the repetition of the note F, and then by that of the note D flat, implying a 5 + 4 bar structure. In Ex. 20(a) the slurs represent the schematic 4 + 4 + 8 period, the brackets the actual phrase-formation, (x) the overlap, and (y) the apparent extension of the consequent. Ex. 20(b) is an attempt to arrive at the *Urform* that is the primitive background to the composed complex foreground.[8] In Ex. 20(b) the antecedent terminates punctually on the eighth bar, and the consequent is therefore coerced into a feeble motif repetition (x), brilliantly avoided by the extension (y) of the composed phrase. Yet it must be noted that the only extension of the harmonic scheme occurs in the consequent of the phrase, at bar 12, where the apparent extension (y) must be accommodated by a prolongation of the supertonic chord.

[8] For this distinction between background and foreground in a work of music see pp. 228 *et seq.*

EX. 20

It may be due to an unconscious, or even conscious, sense of structural equilibrium on Chopin's part that after such finessing, the C sharp minor Waltz dispenses with a coda. What occurs now is the refrain, the restatement of the finely wrought A-section, and then the refrain once again, completely unaltered, and yet lending the end of the piece an air of modest finality wholly in keeping with its elegiac mood.

The Waltz in A minor, op. 34, no. 2, (1831), suffers from a middle part that is too loose an assembly of B-section and A-section tunes. The tunes themselves, however, are most attractive and, though cast in regular moulds, all have an inherent tendency to progress from initial minims or crotchets to quavers, which gives the piece a springiness in piquant contrast to its minor mode. This piquancy is harmonically underlined at the point of the B-section where the first A major strain, having divided into running quavers, recoups its long-valued beginning, but now in the minor:

EX. 21

In the second strain of the A-section (bars 17 ff.), the split into quavers during the consequent (bars 21–24) is continued into the repeat of the phrase, thus disguising the punctuation of the sentence, and creating an immediate variation of the tune. The actual juncture is not unlike Ex. 18. The ensuing consequent, however (bars 25–36), gains its expansion (from eight to twelve bars, on a modulating arch) through harking back to the ♩. ♪ ♫♩ bar (bar 21) that formed the watershed between long and short values, and so lends itself to summary repetition and cadential dip (Ex. 22(a)). Moreover, the inverted pedal-notes on A and E overlaying the present ♩. ♫♩ motif connect this closing phrase to the opening phrase of the piece; the first, quasi-introductory strain of the A-section, whose tenor line, supported by tonic and dominant pedals, contained in its ♩ ♫ rhythm the germ of all subsequent value divisions (Ex. 22(b)). In fact, the melodic (direct and inverted), motivic, rhythmic, and to some extent, harmonic relation subsisting between bars 1–8 and bars 29–36 can be demonstrated by putting the left hand of the one against the right hand of the other.

EX. 22

This is, of course, intended as a variational, not contrapuntal conspectus.

Before reaching the B-section's A major tune (see Ex. 21), Chopin rounds off the A-section by a very regular sixteen-bar sentence which, starting in C major, twice modulates to A minor. The relative major, C, is introduced here as the function most apt to counterbalance the Waltz's tonic minor-major bias. *Tonally,* the same consideration applies to the C major start of the coda, but *melodically* the left-hand tune here is a (transposed) variation of the initial tune (Ex. 22(b)), which has just preceded the coda (note also the continued right-hand figuration). Thus the onset of the coda signifies, amongst other things, the relinquishment of melodic value-division in favour of continuous variation —a switch that was indeed hinted at in the course of the A-section (see the above reference to bars 21–36). Once the continuous quaver movement of the bass is so well established that it may roll over the eighth-bar caesura, Chopin can place a fresh contrast against it (bars 9 ff. from the start of the coda). This is of a harmonic kind, and consists of the exploitation of the hitherto-neglected home dominant region, complete with its own tune in the treble, and going a long way towards establishing E major as a key (*in* the dominant, not *on* the dominant, as Tovey would have said). Only after twelve bars (bars 20–21 from the coda) does E again turn into the dominant of A, leading back to a last statement of the first tune. These are the crucial bars 7–11 of the coda (bars 175–180 from the start):

EX. 23

It is passages like this C to E major progression that have been felt by generations of music-lovers to embody the quintessential magic of Chopin. (For a general theory about this characteristic see note at the end of the chapter.)

Little need be said about the remaining waltzes published by Chopin himself, except that op. 34, no. 3, in F major (nicknamed 'Cat-Waltz', presumably because of the feline shifts of its principal eight-quaver motif from the first to the second to the third beat of the bar) and op. 64, no. 1, in D flat (nicknamed 'Minute Waltz' due, no doubt, to the childish ambition of some piano gymnasts) both *look* as if they started with a 'refrain', but in fact do not. Actually, the A-section of the former would be schematic and volatile enough to function as such but, as matters stand, it is a real principal section, occurring only at the beginning and end, and leaving the B-section to more developed material. The A-section of the latter turns from its tonic-dominant repetitions into a modulating extension, thus combining the functions of principal section and refrain. In fact, two statements of this *perpetuum mobile*, with a real tune sandwiched between them, suffice for the entire plan of this polished little gem.

Of the posthumously published waltzes, the one in F minor, op. 70, no. 2, of 1841, is uninspired—it is known in six or seven versions, and was apparently kept by Chopin for private gifts to various friends. Much more satisfying are the B minor Waltz, op. 69, no. 2, of 1829, with its charming excursions to the relative major, and, in the middle part, the tonic major; and op. 70, no. 1, in G flat major (1835), whose main part makes great play with widely spaced arpeggios and upward leaps à la Weber (a good test of concert nerves, these!); it also has a meno mosso middle part in which the *Ländler*-like dotted rhythms of the tune lead up to a modulating paragraph that might have come straight out of Schubert's *Deutsche Tänze*.

## Polonaises

Among the polonaises, all posthumous publications (apart from two juvenilia published during Chopin's boyhood) are of works written *before* Chopin himself brought out in 1836 his first mature works in this form, the Two Polonaises, op. 26. It is therefore convenient to start our discussion with the works written prior to that date, and then to proceed to the polonaises provided with opus numbers by Chopin himself (opp. 26, 40, 44, 53, 61).

The polonaise was for the young Chopin what the 'characteristic' suite was for the young Schumann: a form into which he could most easily pour his musical personality and instrumental virtuosity. Up to his twentieth year, virtuosity was the strongest spur, and most of these works (see op. 71, nos. 1 and 3) are too shallow to be viable, as is also the Grande Polonaise in E flat major with orchestra of 1831 (op. 22), which we shall not discuss here (though the 'Andante spianato' for piano solo, added in 1834 as an introduction, is a lovely piece). But the B flat major Polonaise, op. 71, no. 2, of 1828 should be singled out for occasional performance since its passage-work is more melodious than that of other early works, and its trio[9] full of neatly contrived changes of harmony and texture. For the piano student, too, the work is a good choice, as it sounds much more brilliant than it is difficult. Passages such as these

[9] It is usual, in the case of the polonaises, to designate the B section of the overall A B A form as a 'trio', in order to distinguish its own ternary form from that of the main movement. In dealing with all regularly constructed polonaises, of which the one in B flat is an example, I shall refer to the form thus: A B A C D C A¹ B¹ A¹.

EX. 24

are a delight to young hands, and prepare the student for the rigours of

EX. 25

In the eventful trio of the B flat major Polonaise there appears for
the first time a kind of bridge-passage peculiar to Chopin's polonaises,
in which a bass and treble, approaching or receding from each other in
regular contrary motion, form sequences that carry a modulatory
process to its inevitable goal. It is a kind of lead-back particularly
adapted to the stately $\frac{3}{4}$ progress of the polonaise, which, at its most
natural, invites harmonic steps at a frequency of ♩. ♩. or ♩♩|♩♩,
while leaving plenty of room for adumbration by suspensions, changing notes, etc., at a frequency of ♪♪♪ or ♪♪♪. Not that the
*themes* of Chopin's polonaises show this rhythmic-harmonic relation at
its most natural pacing; themes, to be sure, have to react boldly against
an implied, or traditional background, and it is interesting to observe
the tension Chopin manages to accumulate in his most notable polonaise themes. In op. 26, no. 1, in C sharp minor, the progression of the
first theme's antecedent is

$$\frac{3}{4} \left| \quad ♩ \qquad ♩ \, | \, ♩ \, ♩ \, ♩ \, | \quad ♩ \quad ♩ \, | \, ♩. \right.$$
tonic: V, minor subd: V | I  V  I | tonic: V, II | V

—a startlingly original series of chords that gains its point through
asymmetrical, albeit nicely calculated distribution over the weighty

minims and crotchets of a polonaise; in fact, the progression would not make sense either at faster speed, or in any duple-time arrangement one might care to try.

In the great A flat major Polonaise, op. 53, the first theme's antecedent is:

Tonic: I————————→Supertonic IV V I

This reveals an amazing harmonic asymmetry: for seventeen quavers the phrase is stationary on the tonic (in the similarly constructed consequent, it is eleven quavers on the supertonic), whereas the next four quavers spring to rapid life. Naturally, the lengthy tonic is made feasible by repeated melodic suspensions and a bass-line that goes through all the triadic positions in forceful octaves; but again, it is the peculiar embattled stateliness of the polonaise rhythm that makes possible the extension of the tonic as well as the agility of the turn to the supertonic. A pre-form of this is found in the theme of the 'Military' Polonaise in A major; in this very regular eight-bar period (whereas the theme of op. 53 owes its eventual expansion to the rapid harmony changes just mentioned) the antecedent is almost entirely on the tonic, whilst the consequent starts with a scintillating turn to the major mediant, after which A major has 'earned' its full IV-V-I cadence.

It is in the problematic F sharp minor Polonaise, op. 44, that the first theme most closely conforms to the primitive polonaise model, its first four bars each comprising a minim on the tonic plus a crotchet on the dominant. And yet, this is a beautiful theme, since the symmetry of the start not only gives way to, and indeed conditions, the ensuing turn to the natural dominant (bar 15, counting from the introduction) but also serves as a pivot for the modulation to A major and new countermelody during the theme's immediate repeat. Where op. 44 becomes problematic is in its C and D sections (the 'trio', as it were, of this fantasy-polonaise). The former resumes the symmetry of A in yet starker form:

EX. 26

this bar appearing, with minor alterations, five times on end. There is
no harm in this cross-reference to the static start of A, and the entry of
C certainly provides a novel pianistic effect; but when, from bar 6 on,
Chopin tries to develop this motif into a middle-part structure, he
lands himself in a series of forced and repetitive modulations—
apparently the simplification of C has been excessive. Nor is there
a convincing exit: the bridge to the D-section ('Tempo di Mazurka') is
harmonically oblique. And once again, in this central mazurka, we find
a highly symmetrical tonic-dominant theme which—unlike the main
theme!—is at a loss for an unsymmetrical continuation, and begins to
meander instead.[10]

Having seen how important rhythmic-harmonic asymmetry is in
giving profile to a good polonaise theme, and having considered the
borderline case of op. 44, we must return to those properly symmetrical
bridge-passages that, as mentioned above, take their origin from the
B flat major Polonaise of 1828. Here is the passage in question, leading
from D to C (within the trio, that is).

EX. 27

The impression of elegance created by this trio largely rests on the
contrast between the preceding D-section, where the rate of change
between chords is slow in order to accommodate the brilliant figuration,
and this bridge-passage, where the rate of change—first minims to
crotchets, then crotchets to crotchets—is the 'average' rate of the dance,
allowing modulation and harmonic decoration. The subsequent recurrence of C (the trio tune) reintroduces semiquaver movement, first
over a static bass-line (link with D) and then over a crotchet-crotchet
movement (link with the bridge, Ex. 27).

---

[10] I disagree with Paul Hamburger's views about this great Polonaise—the
equal of any Chopin wrote. Its form is never 'problematic' because it nowhere
works *against* the musical content—surely the only valid criterion. That
characteristic, tension-generating build-up which begins at Ex. 26 remains one
of the most original passages in all Chopin. ED.

In op. 44 a similar bridge occurs within the coda, connecting its climactic first part to the resigned conclusion.

EX. 28

Its function is not modulatory, since the tonic chord has re-entered at its beginning, but to confirm the tonic so well that the final seven bars may go through their sullen I–V–I–V– motions without any sense of cadential tension. This purpose is perfectly served by the crotchet rate of harmonic change and the gradually narrowing contrary motion, ineluctably closing in on the cadential $^6_4$ of F sharp minor (Ex. 28, bar 4).

However, most of these bridges in sequential contrary motion are modulatory, and serve as lead-backs. The C minor Polonaise, op. 40, no. 2—a work that has lately fallen into undeserved neglect—not only carries an extraordinary amount of harmonic felicities[11] but also employs a bridge from the A flat major section of C to the return of C minor in section A[1].

EX. 29

[11] Gerald Abraham (op. cit., pp. 91–92) has pointed out the inspired 'tonal parenthesis' in the trio of this work (bars 2–6, *et al.*) which momentarily elevates the Neapolitan Sixth to the status of tonal centre. This is only one instance of Chopin's preoccupation with this harmonic function in this work; for others see bar 15 from the beginning, the start of the B section, and the third-last bar.

This bridge must be made particularly stable, for its one end rests on the narrow ledge of a tonic A flat that has only just been regained from the harmonic vagaries of the trio (see footnote), while its other end should be capable of supporting a fully recapitulatory C minor—a task not made easier by Chopin's intention of compressing his $A^1B^1A^1$ into $A^1 +$ (brief) coda (see Abraham, op. cit., pp. 45–46, on the 'perspective foreshortening' of some of Chopin's structures). To be honest, the near end of the bridge is a little shaky: a full close in A flat major is expected, and the D sharp—E in the bass of Ex. 29, bar 2, comes too late to make Chopin's telescoping of end of cadence and start of bridge quite convincing (though only a genius could have 'fused' like this). The far end, however, is a magnificent engineering feat: the girders that span the 'top' of the bridge (see (a)), and which have gradually come closer to its rising foundations, now go on for a while to overlay the recurring main tune, even though firm C minor land has already been reached. This results not only in a most poetical enrichment of texture—an opening up of a new perpendicular vista, as it were—but also enables Chopin to dispense with his $B^1A^1$; by bar 5 of the recapitulation, when the 'girders' disappear, we feel that the piece is fast drawing to its preordained conclusion.

In the trio of op. 26, no. 1, in C sharp minor, which is in the tonic major, D flat, the bridge-passage has to lead us from the eventual arrival on E flat major of a highly developmental D-section to the return of the tonic D flat.

EX. 30

This is again done by contrary motion (here divergent) of the outer parts, continued until the bass may plunge from the dominant to the tonic, and the treble slide chromatically into the third of the home-triad. The general context is somewhat more contrapuntal here, since the entire trio of this work, apart from its obvious cadential turns, has for its theme the contrapuntal friction of part-writing in contrary motion. Thus, the first bar's treble-tenor opposition

EX. 31(a)

is found partly in direct, partly in inverted form at the start of the consequent between treble and bass, given here schematically

EX. 31(b)

and again in a similar shape, now supporting a 'tonal parenthesis', towards the end of section C.

EX. 31(c)

Between points 'x' and 'y' the treble of Ex. 31(c) inverts and extends the major sixth enveloping the treble motif of Ex. 31(a)—one of many noteworthy features of this 'contrapuntal exercise' of 1834 that will come to life in a good, instinctively felt performance.

Having looked at the themes and bridge-passages of the polonaises, we must now discuss their introductions and developments; by the latter, I mean those B- or D-sections which, wholly or in part, are motivic-harmonic work-outs rather than ternary alternatives. There seems to exist some connexion between introductions and developments, beyond the obvious one that the more sizeable the piece is the more it is likely to contain both features. Sometimes, as in the Polonaise in C sharp minor, op. 26, no. 1, a short development within the B-section is based on a short introduction (compare bars 1–4 with bars 25–32). The clear-cut, almost angular A major Polonaise, op. 40, no. 1, has no introduction, but for a D-section it has a 'tuneless' eight-bar sequence combining a variation of A's semiquaver motif with a sprung rhythm from B. In the main, we find that where a theme was enhanced by being 'introduced', its recurrence as A¹ is being enhanced again, this time by the development of one of the intervening form members. So it is in the A flat major Polonaise, op. 53, whose 'trio' consists, irregularly, of three different, linked sections: C, the famous, rousing 'trumpet tune' over those notorious left-hand octaves; D (at the return of the flats), a developing melody, related to the second half of the B-section; E, a developing paragraph of highly melodious fioriture, drawing at its very end on the material of the introduction and bringing about the entry of A¹. Here are the beginnings of sections C, D and E, and the melody from the B-section:

EX. 32

Apart from the obvious cross-reference between B and D, all these sections have in common the prominent use of the interval of a fourth, marked 'x' in Ex. 32, and are thus heard by the listener as a developing chain, which ultimately fastens on once more to A, the main tune, from which the fourth was derived in the first place. Section E, then, though it is not related to the introduction nor, until its last four bars, is a lead-back, but a central development—this section, then, fulfils in the total structural plan the 'enhancing' function first discharged by the introduction.

The E flat minor Polonaise, op. 26, no. 2—a work in turn mysterious and aggressive, which Niecks found to be 'full of conspiracy and sedition'—presents the singular case of an introduction—here a loose agglomeration of repeated motifs—growing straight into the theme; it is really only with the advent of the very contrasted consequent that we realize the last four bars to have been not only the climax of the introduction but the theme's actual antecedent. These three elements— the semiquaver motif *cum* gloomy, repeated chords of the introduction (Ex. 33(a)), the wide leaps of the antecedent (Ex. 33(b)), and the agitato semiquavers of the consequent (Ex. 33(c))—add up to a statement that is in perfect equilibrium between the poles of absolute unity and absolute contrast (see the relation between $x^1$, $x^2$, $x^3$, and that between $y^1$ and $y^2$, and observe how contrast arises from the progressive alteration of these elements).

EX. 33

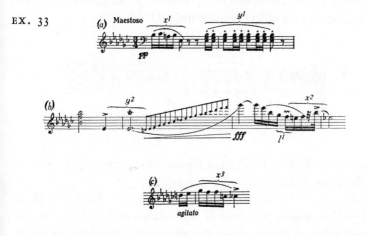

This is one of the most perfectly balanced A-sections in all Chopin's ternary forms, and the rest of the piece cogently utilizes its elements. One of the built-in advantages of (c) is that its close-intervalled shape lends itself to sequential modulation, and thus enables Chopin to write

an astutely disguised double-consequent of eight bars, highly necessary here as a counterweight to the climax-building of Introduction
plus (b). The ensuing B-section, stepping from E flat minor to D flat
major without modulation, is in *tonal* and *syntactical* contrast to A, but
*rhythmically* and *motivically* it relates to all the constituents of A ((a), (b) and
(c)). Within the B-section there is a development that resumes the climax-
building of the introduction (see the above remarks about introduction
—development links in the polonaises), culminating in a paragraph
closely reflecting the former dovetail between introduction and (b).

EX. 34

The downward cascade of Ex. 34 inverts that of Ex. 33(b), and $l^2$ in
Ex. 34 uses $l^1$ of Ex. 33(b) sequentially. Moreover, in the subsequent
lead-back to the resumption of A, 'sedition' is once more reduced to
'conspiracy' by the stifling augmentation of $l^2$ into $l^3$ (Ex. 35).

EX. 35

Ultimately, all forms ($l^1$, $l^2$, $l^3$) of this potent semitone motif derive, of
course, from $x^1$ (Ex. 33(a)) and $x^3$ (Ex. 33(c).

The trio of this work (Meno mosso, B major) dispenses with an
independent middle part, since its close relation to the A B A main part
would make an *alternative* too discursive, and a development on the
lines of B a tautology. The latter possibility is indeed precluded by the
motivic, rhythmic and textural relation between C and B—a relation
that stretches powerfully back across the intervening repeat of A, and
forward to the resumption of $A^1$. Here is the start of C.

EX. 36

|_____ Antecedent _____|_____ Consequent _____|

What saves this theme from undue similarity to B is the contrasting key and the utterly different nature of its consequent, of which the staccato-legato change, in contradistinction to the thoroughgoing staccati of B, is an outward sign. This consequent (bars 3–5 of Ex. 36) is like a remote, faint echo of the A-section's complexities, wherein (m) relates to $y^1$ (Ex. 33(a)) and (n) to $x^2$ (Ex. 33(b)). With such differentiation between antecedent and consequent, and such subtle 'reminiscing' in the motivic material of both, one certainly need not go in for developments. Instead of the missing D-section, Chopin gives us a series of repetitions, varied by simple modulations and refined harmonizations; a static structure that is a perfect foil to the imminent resumption of the dynamic A B A.

Structurally, this E flat minor work stands with the great A flat major as Chopin's best-balanced polonaise. Both works are far removed from the dance origins of the form, but not so far that these are not still felt to exert a schematic influence against which the composer's invention has to assert itself. In the F sharp minor Polonaise, as we have seen, Chopin tried to widen the gap between the primitive dance-model and the finished art-form, with some gain to individuality of utterance, but some loss to formal coherence. He attempted this again, more ambitiously, towards the end of his life in his op. 61 of 1846, to which he openly gave the title 'Polonaise-Fantaisie'. This was the result of an altogether freer approach that was merely hinted at when composing op. 44. Most critics from Liszt on, while admiring the glowing invention and harmonic audacity of op. 61, have found fault with the work's form,[12] contending that op. 44 attained its somewhat less ambitious

---

[12] Liszt himself, however, had oddly prim reservations even about the content of the music: '. . . feverish and restless anxiety . . . deplorable visions, which the artist should admit with extreme circumspection into the graceful circle of his charmed realm.'

aims more securely. Against this I must affirm that, while I have my doubts about the structure as well as some of the invention of op. 44 (see above), op. 61 strikes me as an unqualified masterpiece—in every respect but its end. It is true, however, that its shape is at first difficult to understand and also to realize pianistically, not only in structural sequence, but also in details of 'local colour'. Gerald Abraham's illuminating comparison with the symphonic poems of Strauss (op. cit., p. 110) also applies, as he points out, in the realm of outline, texture and timbre. The pianist is hard put to supply distinctive enough timbres in such orchestrally conceived passages as the thematic polyphony of bars 14–20 and 102–5, and in the final apotheosis of the main themes, where the writing is thicker and somewhat less manageable than in the corresponding passages of the Third Ballade and the Barcarolle. As to formal coherence, any pianist with a soul will succeed in the introduction and the beginning of the Poco più lento, but to continue this latter section, and also to find the right amount of 'pull' and 'give' at the start and end of the various, suddenly arising developments (see bars 76–80, 88–92) requires the specific structural art of a Rubinstein or Perlemuter.

Gerald Abraham—followed by Herbert Weinstock (op. cit., p. 278), who, however, draws a number of wrong conclusions from his scheme—gives the formal skeleton of the work thus:

Introduction: 23 bars, mainly on A: various keys

A: 42 bars; in A flat  
B: 26 bars; A flat but modulating  
A: 24 bars; A flat  
C: 32 bars; B flat but modulating  

Poco  
Più } D: 33 bars; B major, etc.  
lento { E: 34 bars in G sharp minor and B major[13]—2 bars as in the introduction—final 10-bar reference to E  

Transition: 16 bars  
A: 12 bars; A flat  
D: 35 bars; A flat  

---

[13] Here occurs a brief resumption of D, not indicated by Abraham, as he is not concerned, in the context of his book, with analysing this work in depth.

Here are the beginnings of these sections; but the reader is referred to the score, since all the themes of this work are of the gradually unfolding type.

EX. 37

   The first thing that strikes us on looking at these themes (and their
subsidiaries) is that their unfolding, excitingly indeterminate, almost
late-romantic character arises from their preoccupation with the
second and third degrees of the scale at the expense of the tonic; a preoccupation that becomes crystallized in a kind of germinal motif that
goes right through the piece, of falling seconds between the third and
second, and between the second and first degrees of the scale (marked x
in Ex. 37A to E). Taken as a three-note unit, i.e. as two connected
suspensions, the motif is supplemented by its inversion below the
tonic (submediant—leading-note—tonic, marked y) and its retrograde
above (tonic—supertonic—mediant, marked z). In the home-key, A
flat—which, however, is not the only context in which this motif
operates—the 'basic cell' looks like this:

EX. 38

These forms, in their complementary compactness, give an amazing
degree of unity to the piece, a firmness of design which, in the actual
composition, can without detriment be overlaid by hovering themes
and glittering modulations as is a ripe fruit by its bloom. Thus A is
really a suspension on the supertonic, maintained for three bars over a
delicate weave of motif (y). Section B, entering after a development of
A (bars 56–63) in which we have been showered under by the descending form (x), turns to the ascending forms (y) and (z). Here, incidentally,
another form-building motif, the polonaise rhythm on repeated notes,
which was first heard just prior to and as an accompaniment to A, is
renewed with magical effect as an interjection in a wholly lyrical context (p). C is a relation of A, now in B flat major, and so is E (in G sharp
minor), though a more distant one. The relation of E to C, on the other

hand, is that of variation to theme, particularly if one considers—apart from our ubiquitous motivic cell—the rhythmic contraction in both two-bar groups of both antecedents, and the 'through-composed' lines of both consequents. This close affinity between the themes C and E, of which I can find no mention in the scanty literature dealing with Chopin's forms, is instinctively grasped by the listener over the intervening expanse of the D-section (Poco più lento), and is thus an important structural prop. The memory-bridge is all the stronger, since the remainders of the C and E sections follow a similar course: over climax-building modulations to an eventual relaxation into section D and the brief resumption of D respectively.

D itself, the central Poco più lento of the work, in B major, is prefaced by a four-bar group of plain chords which, as it were, present an abstract of the germinal motif. The tune of D itself is a combination of a quasi-ostinato treble in crotchets with a quasi-ostinato bass-line in quavers, both capable of motivic and tonal development (hence the 'quasi'). This sort of combinative melody-writing is a distinctive, though not generally recognized, achievement of Chopin. Basing himself on some remote exemplars in the classics (see the second sentence in the finale of Beethoven's 'Appassionata'), Chopin developed the device as a means of giving constant vertical expression to the pre-established horizontal unity of studies and preludes. The G major Prelude, for instance, shows the device as it is used in the quick studies, the A minor Prelude as it is used in some of the nocturnes, and also, with even greater refinement and purposefulness, in the Polonaise-Fantasie.

While the lower strand of D is mainly built on the x and z forms, the upper one transposes our suspension motive a fifth up (marked $x^1$ and $z^1$ in Ex. 37D). In this variational transposition a static, self-contained formulation is found for a tendency of themes A to E which we have not so far defined, namely their gradual reaching up to the appoggiatura between the sixth and fifth degree of the scale. This is clearest in the *subsequent* theme E, at the places marked $x^1$ in Ex. 37E. But it also occurs at the end of C (marked $x^1$) and in the principal theme A between the note F of bar 2 and the E flat of bar 3. Schematically, then, these are the nascent dominant transpositions of (x)

EX. 39

and this their static formulation in the x¹ of D.

EX. 40

We have said that it is the selection of hovering, suspended degrees that gives the themes their searching, late-romantic air. Is it altogether fanciful to find an intervallic correspondence in the key-scheme of the gradually unfolding, equally searching form? Within each theme the germinal motif tends towards transposition to the dominant—so does the entire first section, up to the Più lento. The palpable vastness of this section is not a matter of bar numbers, but of a progressive shift of key-centres, interspersed with remote modulations. The section would audibly shrink if the resumption of A after B (bar 94) did not start on the dominant, E flat, or if section C were not in the enhanced dominant, B flat. The perspective is made yet grander by the fact that B, on the return from a series of local modulations, once more establishes the tonic A flat, whereas the later key-centre shifts occur more frequently; thus, the B flat major of C soon explodes into its Neapolitan Sixth, B minor (bar 132), which then hands over to the B major of the Più lento. E is in D's relative minor, G sharp, but soon returns to B major, whose dominant is hammered home in the famous triple-trill passage (bar 200 ff.) E on its last appearance (bar 216) is in F minor, and so the circle is closed for the recurrence, after a passage of local modulations, of the (relative major) home-key in which the apotheosis of A and D is to take place.

Here is a graph of the tonal plan, indicating the main centres by white notes for major, black for minor; wavy lines stand for modulatory sections, and the letters refer to our themes A to E and the sections they head.

EX. 41

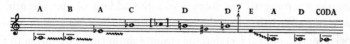

It is a bold, yet logical curve of far-flung, romantic tonal development, in which there is only one unclear point, marked above by a question-mark, and that point is, in aural fact, entirely elucidated by Chopin's use of his introduction.

The introduction, in the extended form it has at the start of the piece, is not only a sublimely beautiful 'improvisation', but has the function of introducing a theme that starts on the supertonic note, and therefore needs a lot of explaining. Chopin's procedure is a stroke of genius: he takes the last interval of his principal theme (A) (marked (a) in Ex. 37 (A) and Ex. 37 Intro.) and twice puts it through three juxtapositions in remote keys. The remoteness of the keys safeguards the improvisatory flair of the introduction (as well as giving rise to the small-note fioriture); the organic intervallic order of the juxtaposition assures the preparation of the main body of the polonaise. That is to say, motif (a) twice describes the arc of the double-suspensions towards the tonic-note which we have called the germinal motif (x) of this work. Thus:

EX. 42

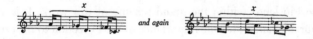

The rest of the introduction is then devoted to an ever-closer approach of A through the gradual entwining of motifs (a) and (x).

When, at our tonal question-mark (see Ex. 41), the A flat major of the recapitulation is to be reached from the B major of D's last return, Chopin once more avails himself, in pregnant abbreviation, of the introduction's ability to progress from harmonic tangents to a tonal centre. Two steps of motifs (a) suffice to bring him from B major to C major, which, as the dominant of the home-key's relative minor, readily opens up the A flat major sphere (bars 214–16). This progression, although dangerously brief, is emphatically not one of Chopin's over-compressions, such as we found in the Mazurka in C minor (op.

56, no. 3). In a good performance the return of E in F minor may give momentary pause to the listener (it's the adding of the seventh, B flat!), but after half a bar, the ear feels secure. Nor do I, with Weinstock (op. cit., p. 282) feel that the ensuing modulation transition to the return of A is 'fragmentary'. Certainly, bars 222–6 need careful dynamics and rubato, if the resumption of harmonic movement away from F minor is to be made palatable—but this can be done, and redeemable demands on the performer must not be held up as the composer's weaknesses. In fact, I feel that the whole climactic movement towards A and the latter's apotheosis, with its fantastic harmonic and coloristic enrichment, are as good as the comparable apotheotic passages in the A flat major Ballade.

What, to my mind, does not come off is the subsequent apotheosis of D. To be sure, the variational devices are as good, or even more startling than those operating in the apotheosis of A: the two strands of the theme now roll along in thunderous triplet-chains, and soon a wildly exciting, coda-forming sequential modulation, tending to the subdominant, is introduced (bars 260–8) as a link to the plain A flat major unison statement of the lower strand that forms the beginning of the actual coda. But the mere fact that this coda has to renounce the upper strand of D, and to content itself with skippy V–I movements to arrive breathlessly, at the subjoined codetta, is enough to make one doubt, in retrospect, Chopin's wisdom in admitting the transfiguration of the Più lento within the grand scheme of this work. It is a most honourable failure, for the importance of the D-section to the centre of the work cried out for some sort of confirmation at the conclusion. And yet, this is an infringement of the fundamental symmetry of the ABA form (an infringement that was to bedevil many symphonic finales of the later nineteenth century), and Chopin had no precedents for it in his own works. The apotheosis of the A flat major Ballade turns straight into its own coda; that of the Barcarolle into an extended 'coda-development', held firmly together by a tonic pedal-point. Perhaps this final aggrandisement of D might have worked but for the fact, so fortunate in the Più lento, but so unfortunate here, that the upper strand of D uses $x^1$ and $z^1$ instead of x and z (see Ex. 37 D). That is, the germinal motif tends to the dominant here, instead of the tonic, as it should for the sake of finality, and this is really why Chopin has to discard the upper strand and coerce the lower strand into a string of compulsively repeated V–I harmonizations.

But this is a small defect at the very end of one of Chopin's most original conceptions. Chopin was 36 years of age when he published this 'late' masterpiece, and if tuberculosis had not killed him off after another three years of misery, we should now look upon the Polonaise-Fantaisie as the first work of a new 'middle period' development. My private guess is that this middle period would have brought us some more polonaises of the stature of op. 61, followed perhaps by a further exploration of the structural principles of the F minor Fantasy, and eventually, leading into a 'late style', a renewed confrontation with the principles of sonata form on the lines of the Cello Sonata, op. 65.[14]

*This note refers to Ex. 23 on p. 94.*

[14] Passages of this kind all have in common the introduction of a contrast against a constant; in the case of the Waltz in A minor (Op. 34 no. 2) harmonic contrast against constant melody at the beginning (bar 9), melodic contrast (resumption of the first tune) against constant cadence (V–I in A minor) at the end (bars 20–21). Indeed, it seems that the small forms of Chopin—as distinct from his or anyone else's sonata movements, where relations are much less stratified—frequently reveal a special application of the structural principle of 'contrast in unity'. That is to say, unity is maintained in one dimension (for example, the melodic) while contrast is introduced in another (for example, the harmonic); subsequently, unity may be maintained in the latter dimension, while contrast is introduced in the former. Graphically, this might be expressed thus:

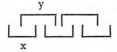

where 'x' equals unity and 'y' equals contrast. The magic wrought on us by these concatenations affects the sensual, emotional and intellectual planes of our personality: on all these planes, that is, we rejoice in penetrating from the known to the unknown, in reducing the unknown into the known.

ROBERT COLLET

# Studies, Preludes and Impromptus

## Studies

JUDGEMENTS of the value of works of art are always highly subjective, but it can be cogently argued that in many ways Chopin's studies and preludes are the most permanently significant of all his works. From the point of view of sheer harmonic and melodic originality, the mazurkas may be more remarkable; the large-scale (mostly later) works like the ballades, the two great sonatas, the Fantasy, the Polonaise-Fantaisie, and the Barcarolle may in their best moments move and astonish us to a greater degree. (Indeed, there is hardly any section of his work that does not contain passages of piano-writing that still dazzle us today by their ingenuity and by the profound understanding shown of the possibilities of the instrument.) Yet, what I think can be said is that in the studies and preludes, virtually without exception, there is a consistently high degree of integration and fusion of musical content, form, style, and technical exploitation of the instrument. In a work like the F minor Ballade, a work of unique richness of musical and pianistic invention, one feels at times that the underlying structure of the work is lacking in solidity[1], something that one never feels in the longest of the studies. Here Chopin's more obvious limitations, his lack of sense of the monumental, either seem to be unimportant or to be positive virtues; in these works he never attempts

[1] But see Rawsthorne, pp. 56–60. ED.

anything basically unsuited to his natural genius. They are in some ways the most universal of his works, which does not imply that they are on that account the most popular; to an unusual degree (and perhaps more than any other piano music of his period) they transcend barriers of time and nationality. The romantic nostalgia of the nocturnes (beautiful as many of these are) is unmistakably the expression of a particular epoch; not everybody can appreciate (still less do justice to in performance) the extremely national character of the mazurkas. But it is difficult to think of *any* music of the decade in which the studies and preludes were nearly all written (1830–40) that has dated less.

In an interesting essay written in 1900, Tovey said:

> 'Chopin's Études stand alone. With the single exception of Brahms in his *Variations on a theme of Paganini*, no other composer has so nobly overcome the immense difficulty of writing works that shall systematize and exhibit one by one the extreme resources of the modern pianoforte while at the time remaining spontaneous music of a high order.'

Tovey, as so often, particularly in his earlier writings, overstates his case. What is true is that in this field no composer succeeded as consistently as Chopin. The essential character of a study (and in many ways a prelude is much the same thing) is that it is a short, or at most a medium-length piece, embodying *one* principal technical problem (perhaps with some other secondary difficulty) and homogeneous in texture and musical character. None of the classical composers wrote true studies, although individual numbers of some of Beethoven's extended variations are in a sense studies on a very small scale, and the last movements of the Sonata in A flat major (op. 26) and the Sonata in F major (op. 54) are somewhat étude-like in character. The great Viennese composers were developing sonata forms, which depend above all on successive contrasts of texture, rhythm and mood; all of which conflict with the whole idea of the study. But there were plenty of studies written in the seventeenth and the first half of the eighteenth centuries, the majority unfortunately very dull; even the more obviously pedagogic pieces of so gifted a keyboard writer as Thomas Tomkins are uninspired.

### Origins

In 1717 there appeared a didactic work by François Couperin *L'art de toucher le Clavecin*. This little treatise, together with an illuminating and at times witty discussion of the problems of harpsichord playing, contains a number of finger-exercises, and a set of eight preludes that are really studies in Chopin's sense, albeit on a smaller scale. Several of these preludes are little masterpieces, yet are hardly ever performed. Most of the shorter preludes of Bach, and quite a number in the 'Forty-eight' are also in the same class; for example, the Preludes in C minor, C sharp major, D major and F major in Book I, in D sharp minor, G sharp minor and B flat major in Book II; one could name a good many other examples. In Bach's keyboard music one hardly ever feels that a piece is written purely to exploit the resources of the instrument; equally there are few pieces that do not show in some way a subtle awareness of the strength and limitations of the medium. The balance of emphasis may shift from one work to another, but only in a very few works is Bach anything like as abstract as he is generally thought to be. Virtuosity and musical thought are intimately blended. The same is nearly always true of Chopin, the few examples of technical writing for its own sake occurring in very early works; and the same is true of the best work of Liszt, however often this may have been denied.

Chopin was introduced to Bach at an early age by his first teacher, a Czech musician named Wojciech Zywny, and I think it is true that this early study of Bach had an important though somewhat masked influence on the development of Chopin's style. Chopin's music, of course, is hardly ever truly *contrapuntal*; that is to say, his basses could seldom be upper parts or the other way round; there is little invertible part-writing or canonic imitation. There is often *polyphony* of a subtle and unobtrusive kind, with frequently a very special role for the left hand. The daring and variety of Bach's harmony, especially its chromaticism, must surely have affected Chopin profoundly, and in spite of the basic differences between the harpsichord and the pianoforte his feeling for the keyboard reminds one of Bach more often than of Beethoven. Perhaps more than anything else the two composers share the gift of writing figuration that suggests a potential harmony. None of Chopin's contemporaries equalled him in this. EX. I

Six Little Preludes (No. 2) - Bach

EX. 2

Prelude in B flat minor - Chopin

There is no evidence that Chopin had any extensive knowledge of Couperin, but the two composers had a significant affinity in their extreme preoccupation with the legato possibilities of their instruments. In one very important respect Chopin was nearer to the outlook of the baroque period than to the Viennese; a high proportion of his most successful works are built round the development of one musical idea, not of successive contrasted ideas. This is above all true of the studies and the preludes.

In the early decades of the nineteenth century a number of collections of pianoforte studies were written, some of which are to this day of great value (it was, incidentally, during the same period that the studies of Kreutzer and Rode were written, which still play so large a part in violin teaching). The most important works are the four books of studies by J. B. Cramer (which Beethoven regarded as an excellent preliminary to the study of his own work) and Clementi's monumental *Gradus ad Parnassum*. Chopin knew these collections intimately and used them as the basis of his own teaching. They contain in embryo much of the expanded technique of Chopin and Liszt, however different the final artistic results may appear. Cramer had an excellent understanding of the instrument, and a genuine if minor talent for composition. His studies often have musical charm as well as exceptional technical value. The following two extracts from studies by Cramer have a definite anticipation of Chopin.

EX. 3

EX. 4

Clementi as a composer is in a different class; for stretches of twenty to thirty bars he will compose music that sounds unquestionably like the work of a great composer; but he suffered from a curious lack of creative staying power—the strength and the weakness of his temperament appear in his *Gradus* much as they do in his sonatas. These few bars from a study from the *Gradus* might have come from a Chopin nocturne.

EX. 5

The Clementi studies have many poetic moments. They are seldom merely extended *exercises*, which is what the longer pieces of Czerny almost invariably are.[1a] It would be perverse to apply the word genius to Czerny, but as a writer of exercises he combined extreme ingenuity with an astounding fertility. His work in this field (for example, the 'Forty Daily Studies'—really groups of exercises) and the 'School of the Virtuoso' are still extremely important. The works he wrote in the form of extended studies are often of lesser technical value, and as music they are much inferior to the best work of Cramer and Clementi.[2]

[1a] An *exercise*, let me add, is a short fragment (usually to be practised in different keys) designed to present a particular instrumental problem in a highly compressed form. In a certain sense it is bound to be mechanical, and except by pure accident to be without musical value; its importance lies in its concentration of technical difficulty which is the compensation, even the justification, of its aridity. All instrumentalists to some extent need to practise exercises. A *study*, on the other hand, sets out to be a piece of music, not merely something to be repeated over and over to develop manual skill.

[2] I stress the importance of these two men for more than one reason. Their studies, even at their best, lack the imaginative power of Chopin's; but it would be true to say, not so much that they made Chopin's achievement possible, but

Chopin learnt much from these composers; and it should be said that the Viennese influence in his style was important, perhaps as important as the influence of Polish folk-music and Italian *bel canto*. I am not thinking of the greatest Viennese composers, Haydn, Mozart, Beethoven and Schubert, but rather of about half a dozen writers for the piano who, even when not themselves Austrians, worked in Vienna during an important stage of their careers. Vienna, up to about 1830, was really the true home of piano playing. Chopin loved Mozart, but he was temperamentally unresponsive to Beethoven and little influenced by him in his instrumental style; he absorbed far more from Hummel. To say this is in no way to indulge in the anti-Beethovenism that was fashionable forty years ago. Not only was Beethoven the greatest of the composers who wrote for the piano (which some people would concede on the strength of his orchestral and chamber music), but it could well be argued that no one did more to develop the resources of the instrument. Hummel in stature cannot for a moment be compared with Beethoven; but it is often easier for other men to learn from a lesser composer, particularly in technical things. Most of Chopin's early work shows his debt to Hummel, more especially the rondos and the two concertos, though in their best moments they have a lightness and a poetry that were outside Hummel's range. John Field, who was a pupil of Clementi, belonged to the same school; the fact that he wrote nocturnes has caused his influence on Chopin to be rather overrated, and

---

that they made it easier. Without their work Chopin would scarcely have reached so soon the degree of understanding of the piano shown even in his very earliest studies, written before he was 20. Moreover, the studies of Cramer and Clementi form an admirable preliminary to a thorough study of Chopin. Many young pianists are too ready to attempt a frontal assault on Chopin's studies, imagining that this is the shortest way to acquire a virtuoso piano technique; an understandable point of view, but in reality an error that can lead to much unnecessary disappointment and frustration. Before a student embarks on a systematic study of these works, it is essential that his technical equipment should already be so well developed that most of their purely physical difficulties will be comfortably within his resources. If this is not the case the technical mastery of the works eludes him and he becomes bogged down in a morass of mechanical problems; the spontaneity and musicality of his approach to these incomparable masterpieces is sometimes permanently damaged. A careful study of twenty to thirty studies of Cramer, Clementi and Moscheles, backed up with appropriate doses of Czerny, is the best way of avoiding this disaster; though it is, of course, true that even to the most technically accomplished pianist in the world the major works of Chopin will still present their own unique problems.

has possibly led to his own merits as a composer being misunderstood.

It is not true to say that in the studies and preludes Chopin covered the entire field of piano technique. Whether the nature of his own gifts as an executant led him to explore some aspects of technique more than others or whether his choice was decided by purely musical considerations is a question that cannot really be answered. In the case of a composer writing for an instrument which he himself plays, the two approaches normally converge; though one can imagine the case of a pianist-composer gifted, say, with an unusually easy and rapid trill who from a musical point of view was not much interested in exploiting it. I doubt if this happens very often, and the reverse must happen hardly at all. A pianist-composer would be most unlikely to write in a way that would fail to show his special gifts to the best advantage. Chopin's technical grounding in boyhood must have been sound, but it does not seem to have been particularly severe or systematic; his natural gift for the instrument must have been very unusual, and it seems to have developed both rapidly and steadily without ever having been through a forcing-house. At the age of 20 he met Kalkbrenner (who seems to have been a sort of early nineteenth-century Godowsky), who pointed out various shortcomings in his technique, and suggested a course of three years' intensive training under his (Kalkbrenner's) supervision. Chopin declined the proposal, probably very wisely. He had no ambition to be a super-virtuoso, and neither in his playing nor his composition did he set out to cover systematically the *whole* field of the possibilities of the instrument as Liszt undoubtedly did. There was nothing Faustian in Chopin's personality; Liszt, on the other hand, especially as a young man, was passionately interested in experiment (even if always with the aim of developing the means of expression) and experiment over an enormously wide field. This, together with his almost excessive receptivity to the ideas of others, is the true reason for the many unevennesses in his work. Chopin, on the other hand, is one of the most perfect examples of the type of artist who instinctively knows and accepts his strength and his limitations, and who knows exactly what he can truly assimilate in the work of other artists and thus achieves a rare degree of perfection and completeness.

In Chopin's work we find few really difficult trill passages; no interest in tremolos or broken octaves; no passages to be played with alternating hands (the chopsticks formula); comparatively few octave passages, particularly of the kind frequent in Liszt, demanding a rather heavy arm-technique. Above all we find a consistent bias towards treating the piano as being primarily a legato instrument. In this, though in little else, he resembles Beethoven, and stands in rather sharp contrast to Liszt. Busoni's remark that the piano is essentially a non-legato instrument lends itself to misinterpretation. It would be truer to say that as a non-legato and staccato instrument it has great natural advantages through the percussive attack of the hammer which starts the vibration of the string; this gives a possibility of exceptional incisiveness and clarity. The dying away of the tone after the attack obviously means that the piano is at a certain disadvantage as a legato and cantabile instrument compared with the violin or the clarinet, particularly in the higher registers. This limitation needs to be recognized, but there is no need to overemphasize it; a skilful player can achieve a very high degree of relative legato. Of course, all true piano composers have had a deep understanding of the possibilities of the instrument in both fields, and the same is true of all really good players. But throughout the history of keyboard music, with the harpsichord as well as with the piano, composers have tended to have a certain natural bias in one or the other direction. The preoccupation of Couperin with legato playing has been mentioned; Domenico Scarlatti is naturally staccato-minded and significantly he makes frequent use of the very un-Chopinesque device of alternating the hands. Of course, there are numerous staccato pieces of Couperin, and legato pieces by Scarlatti, but I think most people who have studied the works of the two men will agree with my point.

In the nineteenth century from many points of view Liszt, Mendelssohn and Alkan are in the Scarlatti tradition; Beethoven (insofar as he can ever be classified), Chopin and Henselt in the Couperin tradition. There is an interesting passage in the preface by Edward Dannreuther to his edition of Liszt's 'Transcendental' Studies; Dannreuther heard Liszt play many times. He says of Liszt's technique: 'Chopin's or Henselt's legato, legatissimo, cantabile, bass and all was possible to him, but not congenial. Thus, his rattling octaves, his rapid chromatic scales of thirds and sixths . . . owe their startling effect to "quasi-staccato"—they are ineffective if played, no matter how quick, with an

apologetic sort of legato as is usually done.' This applies to most of
Liszt's figuration, but this touch is seldom really appropriate to Chopin
whose brilliance is much less glittering, less metallic—neither of these
objectives being used with an implied derogatory sense. Cortot in his
commentary on the 'Black Keys' study, says that the piece demands
'legato brillant—nommé "jeu perlé" '. Some schools of piano playing
no doubt were obsessed by the *jeu perlé*, but no pianist can afford to be
without it. Many people seem to imagine that because the two men were
almost exact contemporaries one can talk of a Chopin-Liszt style of
piano writing; in reality they were in some respects antithetical, in
others complementary. The similarities are mostly superficial; musically and technically their music needs a very different approach. There
are Chopinesque moments in Liszt, though Chopin was not attracted
to Liszt's compositions; but his admiration for his playing is shown by
his having dedicated his First book of Studies, op. 10, to Liszt himself,
and the Second book, op. 25, to his mistress the Countess d'Agoult.
For some of the studies demanding great physical endurance Liszt may
well have been a more completely satisfying interpreter than Chopin
himself.

Between them Beethoven, Chopin and Liszt contributed most to
the great enrichment of the literature of the piano that took place in the
first half of the nineteenth century. There has been further development
since then, but it has been less significant; in the art of composition as a
whole the role of keyboard music has become less important.

### Later developments

Liszt's studies, particularly the *Douze Etudes d'exécution transcendante*,
are very important works. It is true that Liszt was less consistently
happy than Chopin in achieving a perfect fusion of pianistic brilliance
and musical content, and if I were asked to name the twenty-five most
musically satisfying works of Liszt, I would only put three of these
studies in this category: *Paysage*, *Harmonies du Soir* and *Chasse-Neige*.
But all the studies are fascinating pianistically and the last-named,
together with *Mazeppa*, *Eroica*, *Wilde Jagd*, and the titleless A minor
(EX. 6), are particularly interesting in their exploitation of many very
un-Chopinesque devices.

EX. 6

In the essay from which I have earlier quoted, Tovey implies that Liszt's studies must have been impressive when performed by the composer as a vehicle for communicating his magnetic personality and colossal technique, but that they are almost devoid of musical content. One wonders whether he really knew them at all intimately.

An interesting contemporary of Chopin was the German pianist Adolf Henselt, a pupil of Hummel, who settled in Russia and by his teaching did much to lay the foundations of the later excellence of Russian piano playing. Among other compositions he wrote two books of twelve studies each, often with quaint titles like *Pensez un peu à moi, qui pense toujours à vous*. All pianists should know them. Both musically and pianistically he owed much to Chopin, though without a trace of Polish vivacity; in his preoccupation with legato playing he is even *plus royaliste que le roi*. The technique of widely spaced broken chords, which appears occasionally in Beethoven, and is used by Chopin in several of his studies and preludes, as well as in the sonatas, is here pushed to its extreme limit. Musically these pieces are a bit monotonous and undeniably sentimental; at their best they have a delicate flavour, and a sincerity that is rather touching. Henselt's studies are hardly ever heard in the concert hall, perhaps because when well played they sound a great deal easier than they really are. Concert pianists do not as a rule care for that.

Charles Alkan wrote two books of twelve studies (one would like to know if Chopin started the practice of writing studies in sets of twelve), one book in all the major, the other in all the minor keys. Several of them show better than anything else the originality, the sombre lyricism, and the unevenness of his strange and fitful genius. In the second half of the nineteenth century a good many studies were written, usually influenced by Chopin and Liszt and usually of minor musical interest. Those of Anton Rubinstein and Saint-Saëns are well worth practising. In our own century the Twelve Studies of Debussy are of major importance musically, and are fine examples of his later development, which until recently was misunderstood and underrated. Significantly they are dedicated to the memory of Chopin, with whom of all composers Debussy had the deepest affinity. From a pianistic point of view, for all their skill and subtlety, they are hardly landmarks in the sense that the studies of Chopin and Liszt are; after the expansion of piano technique in the nineteenth century (thinking of technique as 'means of expression', not mere mechanism) there remained no new continents to be discovered, but there were a number of mysterious and fascinating islands. One wonders how many even of these remain.

The studies of Rachmaninoff, Stravinsky, Bartók and Szymanowski all deserve attention, but they hardly count amongst the major works of their composers. One should add in the case of Rachmaninoff that many of his preludes could be called studies; as with Chopin there is no clearly defined borderline between the two genres. Those who are attracted to Scriabin's music may find his studies rewarding; they are admirably written for the piano, and they show just about how much can be learnt from Chopin by a composer with only a small fraction of Chopin's genius.

There exist four books of exercises and *Études de travail* by Busoni, including some interesting technical variants of passages from the Chopin studies; these four books explore many unusual by-ways of piano technique, and used selectively they can be of great benefit to an advanced pianist. They are not really *Études de Concert*. The musically significant work of Busoni is to be found elsewhere.[3]

Mention must be made of a curious collection of pieces called *Studien über die Etuden von Chopin*, by Leopold Godowsky (1870–1938). There are fifty-three of them; nearly twice the number that Chopin wrote. Of these, twenty-two are studies for the left hand alone, including a C sharp minor version of the 'Revolutionary' Study. There are seven different versions of the study on the black keys; and a further one in which it is ingeniously combined with the 'Butterfly' Study— one study in each hand. In another piece, no. 11 of op. 10 is combined

---

[3] It is worth mentioning that some musicians who disliked Busoni's general approach to Chopin were greatly impressed, if not always convinced, by his interpretations of the studies and preludes.

with no. 3 of op. 25 in the same fashion. All these pieces show a phenomenal ingenuity in exploiting to the outside limit the technical possibilities of the piano and of the human hand; in detail almost any pianist could find them useful as practising material, particularly if he is aware of weaknesses in his left hand. But there is something monstrous and slightly repellent in this total obsession with technique, something from which Chopin himself was quite free. Godowsky's pieces are not really acceptable in the concert hall, although he himself thought they were. It appears that Godowsky, perhaps because of this obsession, was a somewhat inhibited and disappointing player on the platform, though all those who heard him in private were deeply impressed.

It is hoped that this introduction will help to place Chopin's work in its historical setting, though it cannot be too strongly emphasized that the true value of a work of art lies in its uniqueness, not in any relation to other works that preceded or followed it. This uniqueness can seldom be usefully described or explained; the work must be its own commentary.

Before passing to an examination of individual works a few general points need to be made.

I consider Chopin's pedalling marks to be very revealing. Beethoven was the first great composer to sense the technical and expressive possibilities of the use of the sustaining pedal, and, in fact, to write music that could not be played on an instrument without one. Some of Beethoven's effects are so daring (for example, the opening of the last movement of the 'Waldstein') that most pianists and even some editors fight shy of them. Looking at Chopin's markings, one realizes that as a player he must have given great attention to the pedal, showing equal skill and courage in using and in not using it; the two things are complementary. He must have left nothing to chance. It is true that some of his pedal effects sound unclear on the more resonant instruments of today, but not as often as one might think. A great deal can be done by delicate adjustments of touch and a correct balance between the different registers of the instrument; some notes slightly emphasized, others much in the background. The effect should be like a mist through which the outlines are still clearly discernible. It is not realized

enough that good pedalling is not mainly a matter of skilful footwork,
but of carefully co-ordinating the work of the pedal with the work of
the hands, from the point of view of dynamics, tonal balance and articu-
lation. Slight differences in these matters can make the difference between an identical use of the pedal sounding ravishingly beautiful or
confused and ugly. The only rule that works ultimately is 'listen and
adjust, the whole time'. Listening to good pianists, one can often admire
pedalling that is quite different from what one would do oneself, provided one never feels one is hearing something haphazard or insensitive.
Probably in most cases Chopin would not have regarded his markings
as the only possible pedalling; the pedalling often has to be modified
according to the degree of resonance of the instrument or of the room
or hall in which one is playing. I quote three examples of unusual pedal
effects of Chopin's; the first two seem to me altogether admirable, the
third very risky.

In one respect Chopin's notation is ambiguous. Like other composers, he uses the German sign *Ped* to indicate the moment where the
pedal is depressed; he invariably follows it sooner or later by the
asterisk ✳. Liszt, on the other hand, generally uses the asterisk to indicate

that the pedal is to be raised and not depressed again immediately; there is to be a gap of 'no-pedal' whether of half a beat or of several bars. On the other hand, if the pedal is to be put down again immediately after being released (which is what is called 'legato' pedalling, 'legato' being used in its literal sense of 'joined'), then Liszt simply writes a succession of *Ped* signs. One is not always sure whether Chopin intends a break or not. It is almost inconceivable that he never used legato pedalling, though he may well have used it much less than most later pianists. A further point: one should not conclude that when no use of the pedal is indicated the passage should necessarily be played without pedal, though this is often the case. Chopin was well aware that 'no pedal at all' is sometimes the best 'pedal effect'. But to take two interesting cases from the first set of Studies, no. 6, in E flat minor, and no. 12, the 'Revolutionary' Study. In neither piece is there a single pedal mark; this cannot mean that no pedal is to be used, but simply that here at least Chopin thought it best to rely on the discretion of his interpreter. It is a curious point that, as far as I have been able to discover, Chopin never marked the use of the soft pedal, though its use is sometimes indicated by Beethoven and frequently by Schumann and Liszt. I do not know how far this is to be regarded as significant; it would be pedantic and probably incorrect to conclude that one must never use it in playing Chopin!

Chopin's metronome marks certainly present a problem. He wrote metronome marks in the op. 10 and op. 25 Studies, none in the 'Trois Nouvelles Études', and none in the preludes. In his work as a whole they are rare. In some of the more obviously bravura pieces the speeds indicated seem to me definitely too fast: for example, in nos. 1, 4 and 8 from op. 10 and in nos. 10 and 11 from op. 25. Chopin may, in fact, have thought that from the point of view of sheer virtuosity it would be useful sometimes to *practise* these studies in these tempos, rather than that they were the musically right ones. In op. 25, no. 1, a piece one often hears played too fast, Chopin's marking $\downarrow = 104$ seems to me perfect; equally so in nos. 3 and 6. It is interesting to observe that for the last-named study (G sharp minor, in thirds) Friedman marks $\downarrow = 138–168$. As it happens, the lower figures coincides with Chopin's own $\downarrow = 69$, but the fact is not mentioned. No doubt we are always pleased when a composer's markings agree with what we ourselves want to do, and ready enough to find good reasons for disregarding them when they do not. Chopin's metronome marks should be treated with much caution, but they should always be printed along with the text. In the majority of cases they are helpful.[4]

The studies and preludes, with the exception of the Prelude in C sharp minor, op. 45, were all written between 1829 and 1839. Chopin lived for another ten years, but he wrote no further works designed to illustrate particular aspects of piano technique; he may well have felt that he had said, not everything that could be said, but everything he needed to say in the field of specialized virtuosity. The earliest studies were written in 1829; namely op. 10, nos. 8, 9, 10 and 11. The rest of the set were written over the next three years; in several cases in pairs—a study in a major key followed by another in the relative minor. They are amongst the most original and mature works ever written by a very young man; one can think of few parallels apart from the 'Midsummer Night's Dream' Overture and some of the earliest Schubert songs.

The music written in the last ten years of Chopin's life is not inferior to his earlier work, indeed it has its own special subtlety; but in his case there is nothing comparable to the steady evolution of style that we find in Beethoven or Wagner. The op. 25 Studies were written between 1832 and 1836; they really form a continuous series with the earlier set. The preludes were mostly written between 1836 and 1838, the earliest, no. 17 in A flat major, dating back to 1834. In many ways they can be regarded as a continuation of the same series. It is true that a number of the preludes can be played by a performer without advanced technique, though they still set real problems. The Preludes in G major, F sharp minor, G sharp minor, B flat minor, D minor and several others could well have been called studies; if they are easier than some of op. 10 and op. 25, it is mainly because they are rather shorter, and demand less staying power. In detail they are as difficult as the studies.

Many pianists have played the two sets of studies, and the twenty-four preludes, as cycles; the practice has been severely criticized. Naturally if these pieces are treated only with the idea of exhibiting the more obvious kinds of virtuosity the effect is devastating; but I have heard performances of each of the three cycles that I have found completely

4 See p. 19 for another view of Chopin's metronome markings. ED.

satisfying. On the whole it is easier to play the preludes convincingly than either set of studies, though their very brevity does create its own problems. One is definitely helped by the simple key-sequence (C major, A minor, G major, E minor, etc.), and the contrasts and transitions between successive preludes are without exception admirable; almost certainly this was deliberate. The player must make up his mind in each case whether to proceed without a break from one prelude to the next, or to make a brief pause. In the op. 10 Studies there is a sort of key-sequence in the first six: C major, A minor, E major, C sharp minor, G flat major, E flat minor. No. 7 reverts to C major, a bizarre change of key that does not give the impression of being quite intentional. Nos. 8, 9 and 10 follow on well enough, but I feel the juxtaposition of nos. 11 and 12 is not very happy. The studies op. 25 give much more the impression of having been arranged as a series though this is possibly accidental. The main difficulty comes with the last three. Nos. 10, 11 and 12 could all have been entitled *Études de haute tragedie*. Apart from the exhausting physical demands on the player (which must have taxed Chopin's strength to the utmost), the effect on the listener is almost too overpowering—three dramatic finales in succession. In spite of this, it is not, I think, justifiable, if the studies are played as cycles, to rearrange their order, or to make one's own set of twelve selected from the two books. To play all twenty-four studies in the same programme seems to me an error of judgement. There is, of course, no reason why the studies should not be played singly or in smaller groups devised by the player; this is, in fact, how they usually sound best.

## Twelve Studies op. 10

The first of the op. 10 Studies, in C major, is obviously a bravura piece, but much else besides. It has great harmonic originality. It is rather dangerous to follow Chopin's metronome mark $\quad = 176$. The piece will usually sound rushed, and the performance full of split notes, apart from the danger of sounding exhausted before one is half-way through. It should sound allegro but also *con grandezza*. The study is based on the typical Chopin-Henselt-Liszt technique of the widely spaced broken chord, yet it should be regarded as a study in contraction as much as in extension. Klindworth in his suggestive but unreliable edition adds staccato dots to the first note of each group.

EX. 10

This, I think, is quite contrary to Chopin's intentions. The liaisons I have added in Ex. 11 show what I think Chopin wanted. The accents are the composer's. Klindworth may have slipped into the fallacy that accents mean staccato, or that staccato means accents; he sidetracks what is perhaps the main technical problem here. In playing this study it helps to remember the first prelude of the 'Forty-eight'.

EX. 11

In the next Study, in A minor, we have an obvious virtuoso piece, but the technical side, after being completely mastered, should be subordinated to the musical. It need not sound like Czerny. It is most effective if the crescendos, when marked, are on a rather small scale; when they are not marked none should be made. The effect can be quite eerie. The main technical problem is the crossing of the fingers over each other, a method much employed by the harpsichordists (see the didactic works of Couperin and C. P. E. Bach), but in piano music usually reserved for scales in double notes or in passages where the thumb being otherwise engaged is not free to turn under. It is a tech-nique that should be practised systematically, not regarded merely as a dodge one resorts to when there is nothing else one can do. The pianist who can play this study without fear of fatigue can think himself unusually fortunate. Practice the chromatic scale with the three fingerings given in Ex. 12.

EX. 12

The following Study, in E major, is one of the most hackneyed pieces in the whole piano literature. In spite of all the occasions when one has heard this piece maltreated, instrumentally and vocally, it can still sound moving if played with simplicity and without exaggerated rubato. We have often been presented with a distorted view of Chopin as the ultra-romantic Schwärmer, with a highly morbid streak in his character. That this streak existed is true enough, but it was one element among many. The passion in Chopin is always most moving if expressed with reserve, a certain elegance and even the slightest hint of irony.

The Study in C sharp minor (no. 4) has more than a hint of something elemental, demoniacal and even sinister. I have *once* heard it played convincingly at the tempo indicated by Chopin, ♩ = 88; it can sound equally convincing at considerably slower speeds. In this Study the two hands have virtually identical but alternating roles; except in the middle section where both hands are playing together in semi-quavers the figuration is transferred from one hand to another, usually at intervals of four bars. This procedure is common in Bach, but rare in Chopin, who makes great demands on the left hand, but seldom treats it as if it were a second right hand. The left hand is often given a very specialized role. A typical Chopin virtuoso passage is usually conceived definitely in terms of the right or the left hand, and is often really awkward to play with the hand for which it was not written. These two bars from the first movement of the E minor Concerto show what I mean.

EX. 13

The so-called 'Black-Keys' Study, in G flat major, is one of the most popular. It needs to be played with real gaiety and wit, though not without tenderness; after all, Chopin is known to have been a brilliant amateur comic actor. The two hands have different roles, but both are vital. One sometimes hears the left hand played as if it were an accompaniment to a Donizetti aria; other players make the left hand all-important and reduce the right hand to a role of mere decoration. A true equilibrium is essential.

The Study in E flat minor (No. 6) is a good example of Chopin's uncontrapuntal polyphony—not all Bach's polyphony is contrapuntal either. There is also more than a hint of Wagner. There is a very characteristic use of chromatic auxiliary notes played on the beat and approached by disjunct motion. It is this device rather than his use of particular chords that gives so much of its unique flavour to Chopin's harmony; though in his use of major ninths he sometimes anticipates Debussy[4a], and his fondness for the French form of the augmented sixth is almost a mannerism. In the last seven bars a most beautiful effect is produced by the repeated use of the chord of the Neapolitan sixth to delay the final cadence. There is even a brief modulation into the remote key of A major—or is it really B double flat?

EX. 14

There are no original pedal marks in this piece, but a discreet use of the pedal is essential. At the same time it is useful to practise a piece like this one, or the E major Study, without pedal, aiming at the greatest possible degree of legato and cantabile playing.

In spite of its being based entirely on a single technical formula, the Study in C major (no. 7) is a charming piece. The technical problem is to combine a high degree of legato in the upper part of the right hand

[4a] See Badura-Skoda, pp. 269–72.

with the repeated notes in the lower. The device of rapidly repeated notes with changing fingers is rather infrequent in Chopin; it was much exploited by Liszt.

The Study in F major (no. 8) is another of the pieces that are sometimes made to sound like mere bravura pieces; there are perhaps weaknesses in the middle section, which are more than compensated by the poetry of the last two pages. Here again it is most important to play throughout with expressiveness and virtuosity in both hands.

The same remark applies to the Study in F minor (no. 9), an essentially lyrical piece. Chopin wrote an interesting fingering for the first bar.

EX. 15

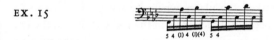

This is a bit awkward for many hands; most pianists would use 531413 or 531313. But there is a reason for Chopin's fingering; the constant employment of the very strong third finger on C is apt to give that note undue prominence. The strength of the third finger, as of the thumb, is sometimes an embarrassment, and although one works hard to equalize one's fingers, no one ever succeeds completely. One should not lament this unduly; the differences of strength can be treated as a positive asset. Numerous fingerings by Chopin show that he understood this well enough.

In the A flat major Study one again has to say, 'Don't let the great brilliance of this piece destroy its lyrical feeling.' It is a study in contrasted accentuation; Chopin's markings should be scrupulously observed.

The E flat major Study (no. 11) is one of the most perfect examples of the extended broken-chord technique. It is a mistake to suppose that a piece of this kind needs to be played, or is even necessarily played better, by unusually large hands. What counts is finger control, and the lateral flexibility of the wrist and forearm.

The Study in C minor (no. 12) is the famous 'Revolutionary' Study, written in September 1831 at the time of the final collapse of the Polish insurrection against the Russians. It is one of the few pieces of Chopin that remind one of Beethoven—the Beethoven of the last movement

of the 'Appassionata' and the first movement of op. III.[5] The left-hand
part in the first bar is marked *legatissimo* and this applies throughout
the Study; the touch should be brilliant, but not too metallic, not too
Lisztian. The right-hand part needs very careful practice; it is often
neglected!

*Twelve Studies op. 25*

Now we come to the Second set of Studies.

The first, in A flat major, was the last to be composed. Superficially
it is just like dozens of nineteenth-century pieces; a melody in the right
hand supported by an accompaniment in broken chords. In fact, both
its perfection and its originality are beyond analysis. Note that Chopin
has very carefully marked the places where he wishes the bass to be
brought out, and on occasion inner parts in the right as well as the left
hand. This should be done very discreetly; not too much in the manner
of the incomparable but sometimes naughty Josef Hofmann.

EX. 16

The F minor Study (no. 2) is perhaps the most perfect example
of Chopin's fioritura, ornamentation that never ceases to be expressive.
It is worth while making a comparative study of Liszt's *Étude de
Concert* in the same key, obviously inspired by Chopin, and to analyse
the subtle but important differences needed in the style of performance.
In Chopin's figuration one should seldom aim at a completely even
tone over long stretches, something that suggests the harpsichord or
the organ rather than the piano. Small dynamic inflexions are constantly

---

[5] A comparison of the 'Revolutionary' Study with the coda of the first movement of Beethoven's op. III is highly fruitful. The likeness is enhanced by both
works being in C minor.

demanded. There exist manuscript fragments of a pedagogic work
that Chopin never completed. In one place he says: 'Nobody will
notice unevenness of tone in a very rapid scale when it is played evenly
from the standpoint of rhythm; one's aim is not to play everything
with an even tone. The property of a developed technique is to combine
variety of shading with good tone quality.' Words that give much food
for thought. The metronome mark $\downarrow = 112$ seems to me just right, but
if a pianist feels he can play it better in a slower tempo he is fully justi-
fied in doing so.

In the Study in F major (no. 3), as in no. 10 of op. 10, the differences
in accentuation marked by Chopin must be observed. The study
should sound really gay; Chopin's metronome mark $\downarrow = 120$ is quite
fast enough.

No. 4 in A minor is a staccato study, something rare in Chopin.
There is no real example in op. 10. The combination of held notes with
staccato in the same hand was first used by Weber, a composer to whom
Chopin was much attracted.

In the case of no. 5 in E minor the question is sometimes asked: A
study in what? In the main it is a study in lightness of touch, perhaps
also in the avoidance of wrong accents on the thumb. It is the least
obviously pedagogic, and one of the least showy of all the studies.

The Study in thirds, no. 6 in G sharp minor, has the same will-o'-
the-wisp character as no. 2 of op. 10. Here again the crescendos should
not be exaggerated. I think it is impossible to improve on Chopin's
pedalling marks; the following bars are characteristic, and contain the
essence of Chopin's method.

EX. 17

The Study in C sharp minor (no. 7) is one of those elegiac pieces about which little can be said. Many regard it as the most musically perfect of all the studies. Great care should be taken to make the accompanying chords in the right hand as sustained as possible, independently of support from the pedal. All the same, it is, I think, quite impossible only to use the pedal when Chopin marked it.

EX. 18

The Study in sixths, no. 8, in D flat major has perhaps less poetry than most of the others. It needs much brilliance, but also lightness. Before Chopin, the composer who had done most to develop the technique of double notes was Hummel.

Once again, there is not much one can say about the charming 'Butterfly' Study (no. 9). It is important to realize that the problem in the right hand is the *alternation* of legato and staccato. The staccato needs to be played from the wrist, almost throughout.

The B minor Study (no. 10), by contrast, asks for a 'heavy' technique; I feel convinced that Chopin wrote this Study with the idea of its being played by Liszt. A passage in the manuscript fragment which I have mentioned makes it quite clear that Chopin realized that the forearm and upper arm have an important role in piano playing, whereas among many nineteenth-century pianists the use of the arm (except on the rarest occasions) was regarded as the first step on the road to ruin. Chopin says: 'One should not set out to try to play everything from the wrist, as Kalkbrenner makes out.' At the same time he would not have agreed with those who think that arm-weight, together with rotation, provides the answer to all problems.

This Study and the E minor (no. 5) are the only two in the entire series that have contrasted, though thematically related, middle sections.

It is interesting to know that in no. 11 in A minor ('the Winter Wind') the four opening bars were added later at the suggestion of a friend.[6] This Study must be treated throughout as a polyphonic duet

⁶ Charles A. Hoffmann. ED.

between the two hands with attention to the melodic writing implicit
in most of the semiquaver figuration.

EX. 19

I would point out that the additional quaver tails seem to me to con-
form to the composer's intentions; but in a printed edition one should
not make an addition of this sort without making clear in some way
what one has done.

The last of the set, no. 12, in C minor, is extremely convincing, and
has a perfect structural solidity—again rather Beethovenian. It is advis-
able not to play forte throughout; the climax at the end will be more
impressive if one has played rather softer in the middle section.

The 'Trois Nouvelles Études' were written in 1839 without an opus
number as a contribution to a pedagogic work by Moscheles called *La
methode des methodes*. They are all three beautiful and original pieces,
especially the first, which is the least played. They are perhaps insufficiently contrasted to be suitable for performance as a group. The
opening of the first, in F minor (Ex. 20(a)) has a family resemblance to
the opening of the Study in F minor, op. 25, no. 2 (Ex. 20(b)), and to
the principal theme of the Fourth Ballade also in F minor (Ex. 20(c)).

EX. 20 (a)

EX. 20 (b)

EX. 20 (c)

The second piece, in A flat major (which might well have been called a prelude), is often taken a shade too slowly, which takes away from its freshness and overstresses a certain underlying melancholy. In Chopin this can usually be left to look after itself.

The last of the set, in D flat major, is a graceful study in legato and staccato played in the same hand. Ignaz Friedman mentions that Rosenthal used to play the lower part entirely with the thumb, which is difficult, but gives a wider choice of fingers for the upper part.

EX. 21

## Twenty-four Preludes

Many judges would put the Twenty-four Preludes on an even higher level than either of the sets of Twelve Studies. There is the same concentration and consistently high quality of musical thought, the same perfect harmony between form and content, and an equally perfect sense of the instrument. Although I would not care to say that they are on that account superior to the studies, there is obviously a less consistent preoccupation in the preludes with questions of virtuosity and technique, although as has been pointed out, at least half a dozen of the preludes could equally well have been named 'studies', and there are another seven or eight that could be classed as 'quasi-studies'. At the other extreme are pieces like the Preludes in A major and C minor which are in no way *etüdenhaft*. Pieces like the E minor, B minor and A flat major Preludes present no obvious technical problems—except in the sense that real cantabile and legato playing on the piano is always in itself a problem. These pieces are, in fact, pure lyrics; it is really these balanced contrasts between the lyrical and dramatic elements and the imaginative exploitation of the technique of the instrument that give the preludes as a set their special character as a summing-up of nearly every aspect of Chopin's many-sided genius.

The real forerunners of Chopin's preludes are Bach's two sets of Short Preludes, the preludes of the 'Forty-eight', and some many numbers in the suites and partitas, particularly among the allemandes and

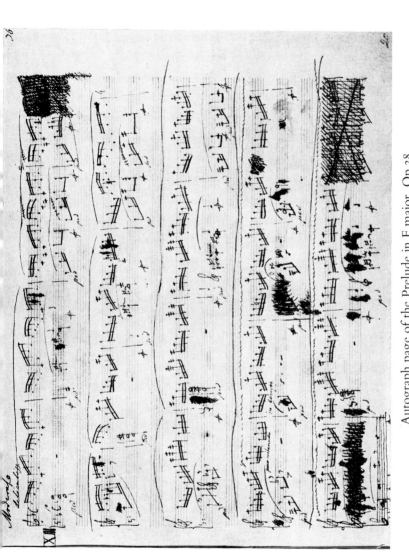

Autograph page of the Prelude in F major, Op. 28
(Chopin Institute, Warsaw)

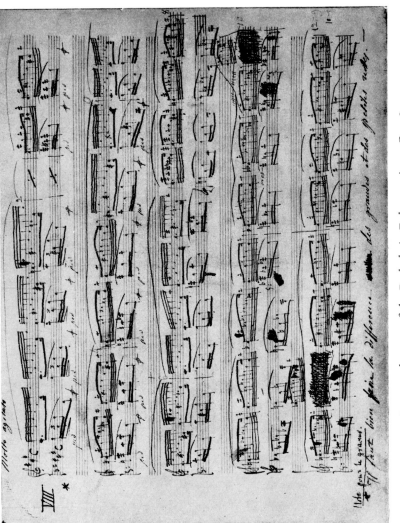

Autograph page of the Prelude in F sharp minor, Op.28

(Chopin Institute, Warsaw)

sarabandes, and there is evidence that during the period when most of the preludes were composed Chopin was more than usually occupied with Bach.[7] In the instrumental music of the Viennese period the lyrical miniature hardly exists, although curiously enough there are a few striking examples in Beethoven's Bagatelles particularly in several of the op. 126 set; Beethoven was perhaps the least miniature-minded of all the great composers.

The classical sonata form, with its complex interplay of contrasts and its emphasis on development, has striking affinities with drama. Chopin's preludes, which are the most perfect examples of the romantic lyrical miniature, have affinities with the type of poem known in German literature as the *Gelegenheitsgedicht*, the poem 'occasioned' by a single deeply felt event or spiritual experience. Much of the best poetry of the nineteenth century in all European literature tends to approach this type, and in all nineteenth-century music Chopin's preludes are the purest expression of the trend. A number of the best of Mendelssohn's *Lieder ohne Worte* are comparable, but in spite of the great elegance of the instrumental writing, Mendelssohn only occasionally gave of his best in his piano music. Debussy's preludes seldom have the concentration of Chopin's, whatever their other qualities may be. The indebtedness of Rachmaninoff and Scriabin is obvious[7a].

One hears the Prelude in C major played in different ways. Everything depends on how the first bars are conceived. As so often the guiding principle is that everything should be regarded as important. The part played by thumb in the right hand is sometimes played with such emphasis that the first note in the left hand is made to sound like an up-beat. The bass should be given due weight; only then will one have the impression of a syncopation in the right hand, which I am convinced is what Chopin intended.

 EX. 22

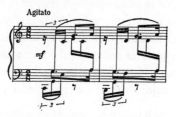

[7] See p. 10. ED.     [7a] See Badura-Skoda, p. 263f. ED.

The originality of the Prelude in A minor is so striking that many listeners have been disconcerted and even repelled at a first hearing. The false relations, in bars 10–11 (including an example of the diminished octave), are very unusual, but are, in fact, an example of Chopin's characteristic chromatic auxiliary notes.

EX. 23

The basic harmonic progression of these bars (10–16) is simple enough.

EX. 24

The Prelude in G major I regard as one of the most dangerous little pieces ever written. It should be played with great lightness and evenness, with only the most occasional touches of pedal, and as fast as is compatible with control.

In the D major Prelude one is above all struck by the richness and variety of the harmony and the economy of the means by which it is achieved. The rhythm in this piece should not be so wayward that the cross-accents which frequently occur are no longer felt as such.

The F sharp minor Prelude is a marvellous piece that is not as well known as it should be. Baudelaire paraphrasing Delacroix referred to 'cette musique légère et passionnée qui ressemble a un brillant oiseau voltigeant sur les horreurs d'un gouffre'.[8] These words seem to me to be a most apt description of this Prelude. Nos. 9, 10 and 11 are all miniatures; I think the evanescent and magical no. 10 sounds best if played in nearly strict time, but with no feeling of breathlessness.

In the F sharp major Prelude Chopin's pedal markings are rather

---

[8] 'This music, swift and passionate, resembles a brilliant bird flying over the horrors of an abyss.'

sparse, and most pianists use here a good deal more pedal. This is quite admissible, but an effect of unusual delicacy can be obtained by keeping close to the original. One must have a piano with an unusually good singing tone.

The resemblance between the E flat minor Prelude and the last movement of the 'Funeral March' Sonata is obvious, but I think Cortot is right in saying that that Prelude requires a more harmonic treatment with less finger-articulation, and a slower tempo.

EX. 25

The demoniacal B flat minor Prelude is in the same class as the C sharp minor Study in op. 10 and the last pages of the B minor and C sharp minor Scherzos. It is incomprehensible that anyone who has heard music like this can still think of Chopin as primarily a composer of drawing-room music.

The tender A flat major Prelude forms an admirable contrast. The F minor Prelude should be interpreted as an excerpt from a grand opera, and played in a frankly declamatory style. Chopin, particularly as a very young man, was a great devotee of opera, especially Italian. This piece shows that it is not only Italian lyricism that attracted him. His composition teacher, Joseph Elsner, always hoped that Chopin would eventually write operas.

EX. 26

The Prelude in E flat major is both an extremely exacting study and a perfect lyric. Throughout the piece the melody in the right hand and the bass notes should be slightly emphasized, producing this effect.

EX. 27

It is dangerously easy to overemphasize the second notes of each group played by the thumbs in each hand. This produces a wrong balance of tone and an impression of overpedalling, even though one's pedalling may, in fact, be perfectly correct.

It should be pointed out how perfect the contrasts are between the nocturne-like B flat major and the tempestuous G minor, and between the wistful F major and the heroic D minor, which is such an admirable concluding piece to the whole series. It is an interesting fact that the number of pieces by Chopin in this last key is extremely small.

The beautiful Prelude in C sharp minor, op. 45, should, of course, always be played as an independent piece in no way linked with the op. 28 series.[9]

## *Impromptus*

The Impromptus, of which there are four, are not among Chopin's most important works, but they should not be underrated. There are definite thematic links between them, as is clearly shown by the following extracts.

EX. 28

[9] There is also a solitary Prelude in A flat major composed in 1834, two years before op. 28. It is a piece of some charm, but no particular significance.

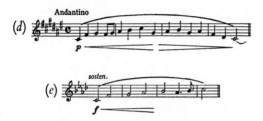

It would be interesting to know how far Chopin was aware of these resemblances, which have often been pointed out. All four impromptus are basically in ternary form.

The Fantaisie-Impromptu is the earliest of the series and the least interesting, in spite of the elegance and charm of the semiquaver figuration; the middle section in D flat is rather too much in the sentimental salon style that is regarded as typical Chopin.

The Impromptu in A flat major has been played by hundreds of thousands of players of all standards; this is in no way to be held against it. It is a little masterpiece. The original pedalling marks are extremely helpful, to my mind the best possible.

The Impromptu in F sharp major contains some interesting hints of variation form; a type of structure to which Chopin as a mature composer was seldom drawn—the one outstanding example being the Berceuse. The arabesques in the final section are among the most perfect examples of this florid writing. The left hand should be played expressively, but not at the expense of the right.

The Impromptu in G flat major is little played; it is one of those treacherous pieces that sound much easier than they really are. The resemblance between this and the A flat major Impromptu should not lead one into the error of playing this one too fast; it is different in character from the other, reflective though not morbid.

PETER GOULD

---

## Sonatas and Concertos

EVER since Schumann's famous remark about Chopin's Sonata
in B flat minor to the effect that it was an arbitrary family consisting of four of his most unruly children, it has been assumed that
Chopin was incapable of writing in larger forms. His perfect miniatures
have been held as proof that, since he excelled in them, he must therefore be incapable of succeeding on a larger canvas. It is true that some
of the early, more extended works show a lack of direction and cohesion
that could only have been rectified by a degree of compression of
which at that time Chopin was wholly incapable. But his composing
career is remarkable for an almost unbroken process of development,
and on reaching maturity the substance had become so intense that the
musical activity contained in a relatively short work far exceeded that
of large-scale works by other composers. An abundance of ideas is not
necessarily ideal for extended forms; moreover, the stop-watch is no
measure of the *size* of a piece of music, only its length.

The seven works I shall consider in this chapter are among the largest
in Chopin's output, and they range from the very early C minor Sonata
to the late Cello Sonata, one of his most mature, if not wholly successful, compositions.

The Sonata in C minor, op. 4, is the immature work of a young man out to impress his teachers and his family.[1] It has all the gestures and rhetoric needed for an impressive piece, but as yet Chopin's technique was quite incapable of accomplishing the ambitious task too soon imposed on it. In spite of this, there are intermittently many features, quite apart from the obviously talented keyboard writing, which show that the composer was to become one of the most original in the history of musical composition. The sombre opening subject already has character,

EX. I

but the atmosphere it creates is unfortunately soon dispersed by the repetitive sequences and the almost total lack of growth. But the recapitulation immediately draws attention to a tonality awareness far beyond his years which became such a striking feature of his later work and which was to have a substantial and cumulative effect on the history of tonality. Later on he was to discard or dilute the first subject in the recapitulation; but here in a C minor movement he recapitulates the first subject *a tone lower*, in B flat minor. (Something rather similar happens in the subtle tonal arrangement of the F sharp major Impromptu, where the main subject returns with veiled drama in *F major*.)

EX. 2

[1] The work is dedicated to Josef Elsner, Chopin's principal teacher.

More dramatic, though less subtle, is the return of the first subject in
*E flat*, in the rondo of the E minor Concerto.

EX. 3

The late Mazurka in A minor, op. 59, no. 1, a constantly modulating
piece, has the return of its main theme also a semitone lower, in G sharp
minor. But in this context the listener is hardly aware of the actual
shift in tonality, since it has taken the whole of the second section to
arrive there.

EX. 4

To return to the C minor Sonata: the Minuet is unremarkable
(Ex. 5), but is followed by the often-quoted slow movement in five-
four (Ex. 6). Again this shows originality, but although the movement
is perhaps the most successful of the four and has a genuine lyrical poise,
there are few significant pointers to the future.

EX. 5

EX. 6

The opening figures in the finale are bold, as might be expected from a beginner writing while Beethoven was still alive and who had heard perhaps Schubert's 'Wanderer' Fantasy.

EX. 7

But the movement is tedious and square and suffers from Schumann's fatal fixation on four-bar phrases. Having said all this, one might conclude that this is a bad beginning and so in a sense it is. The perceptive musician will merely note the signposts which were to lead to such overwhelming mastery and originality and will leave this sonata where it is and accept it for what it is. The composer was perfectly aware of its inadequacies and was furious when in 1839 Tobias Haslinger proposed to publish it.[2]

Let us turn now to the two concertos, written successively just before his twentieth birthday. Chopin had composed various pieces for piano with orchestral accompaniment, but they were very much virtuoso works intended to show off the brilliance of his technique; he still thought of his future in the conventional terms of a pianist who also composed. Chopin had taken what he found in his senior contemporaries and had seemingly been content, not to imitate (for he was compulsively original) but to use their method and their idiom to

---

[2] Years earlier Chopin had submitted the manuscript to the Viennese publisher Haslinger, who was not prepared to publish it at that time, but who shrewdly kept the manuscript. Chopin was then virtually unknown in Vienna.

express his youthful precociousness. However, with these two concertos there was a definite and unmistakable distillation of style. Here
there was a new confidence, an emerging individuality, and with it a
formation of style, in which content and technique were matched.
Here the harmonic outline hardened and struck home meaningfully at
every modulation; here melody was emboldened and enriched with
the perfect fusion of line and embellishment which only Mozart before
him could equal. Consider this example from the first movement of
the E minor Concerto.

EX. 8

Gone is the vapid, formal decoration so beloved of his formula-ridden
age, the polite, graceful trivialities which found a natural home in the
aristocratic drawing-rooms of the period. It is only incomprehension
that can link Chopin with one of these embroiderers, and it was only
through incomprehension that his music was accepted as falling within
this category. Even at this early age his spirit was totally alien in this
milieu, had his listeners but known it. While alive, a man's character
and personality can overshadow, in concourse with his fellow mortals,
his inner being, his innermost thoughts, so that one who lives in a society
is accepted as one of that society. It seems wholly likely, then, that the
mask which is almost always to the fore in his letters concerning his
music was equally so in his social contact with his friends and colleagues. The candid jesting remarks of Mozart in his letters, the voluminous manuscript evidence of Beethoven, is by comparison totally
lacking in Chopin. Nowhere in all the correspondence that has come
down to us is there more than a chance reference to his own music,
apart from instructions to copyists like Fontana as to details of publica-

tion and the price he was demanding for his music. Not even by reading between the lines can much be gathered except a few admittedly important facts as to the music and the artists he enjoyed hearing. No real evaluation of his contemporaries, no substantial evaluation of their merit as composers. Thus we may only deduce that the flamboyant Liszt was anathema to him when Chopin reckons he would become King of Abyssinia or Ethiopia. Thus we may only infer that he held the problematical Allegro de Concert in greater esteem than the great Fantasy in F minor, since from the publishers he was demanding 600 francs for the former, and only 500 francs for the latter. Such reticence became second nature to the artist vividly described by George Sand as 'meticulous and irresolute'.

Meticulous he was in all things; a glance at the manuscripts confirms this. Irresolute he was in many of the ordinary decisions of life and often so in style in his earliest compositions. But with the two concertos his composing character resolves and is now truly set on the path of development that was to continue for the rest of his life.

The F minor Concerto, op. 21, described as 'number two', was actually written first. There is no comparison with the first movement of the Sonata in C minor; the style is confident and the whole line is now extended and continuous. People have been so concerned with the comparative inadequacy of the orchestration and the minor role given to the orchestra that the fact that these two concertos are masterpieces so often seems to escape notice. It is undoubtedly true that Chopin was to all intents and purposes a composer solely for piano, and the fact that these two works represent his total output in concerto form confirms that he himself was aware of his shortcomings. Other composers, Balakirev and Granados, for example, have thought it worth while to improve and alter the orchestration, but their action springs from the fundamental misconception, not of orchestral technique, but of the pianistic style which this orchestral writing was intended to accompany. The work, as indeed are all Chopin's other works, was conceived in terms of the keyboard, and the keyboard writing throughout is exceptionally full to the point of self-sufficiency. The curtailment, modification or elaboration of the orchestral part cannot be accomplished without modifying the piano writing also. No improvement is, in fact, possible.

The first movement of the F minor Concerto is a maestoso movement which begins with that characteristic dotted rhythm x, seen
first in the C minor Sonata, then here in the E minor Concerto, again
in the Allegro de Concert, and finally in the late Cello Sonata.

EX. 9

Whatever the association, and it may have been Hummel or Kalkbrenner, or merely some association of ideas unknown to us, the
dotted-rhythm is common to all these works. Taken purely from the
point of view of form and design, this first movement does not show
any particular mastery or, in fact, originality. The inspiration is there,
but, characteristically, the material tends to be too eventful for such
large formal designs. Nevertheless, once the very beautiful piano entry
is reached with its atmospheric preparation, the piano carries the music
forward unchecked through a spontaneous and never-failing elaboration of the exposition. Perhaps one of the most important features,
particularly important with regard to future developments, is the use
made of decoration which becomes more and more thematic and
truly meaningful and less and less ornamental for its own sake.

EX. 10

This fusion of the decorative with the substantial is reminiscent of Mozart's later writing,[3] and it is a fascinating study to observe how Chopin's development throughout his life, apart from his superbly original new ventures in form, was centred on this particular facet of his writing. The appoggiatura and the suspension, so naive and superficial in the music of his lesser contemporaries and in his own early works, becomes the basis of all his later harmonic originality, and he evolved a harmonic and contrapuntal technique that was superb in its sureness of touch and in the unfailing, uncanny skill with which he was able to manoeuvre. There are sure and unmistakable signs in these concertos of the road he was to follow later.

The development section in the F minor Concerto is not a true development as understood by Beethoven. Chopin seldom argued. He was not naturally an intellectual, his greatest attribute being that of sensitivity, and in his development he wrote what could be better described as a commentary on what had gone before. The tonal scheme of this movement is unremarkable and the recapitulation is little more than a restatement of the exposition, somewhat compressed admittedly, with conventional lip service to classical form.

The slow movement is masterly, a continual outpouring of intensity and lyricism which differs only from the greatest of his later works in the comparative simplicity of its harmonic style.

EX. II

[SOLO PIANO]

*molto con delicatezza*

Once again we see the increasing meaningfulness of the ornamentation, increasing to the point of identity with the material it is intended to decorate. The dramatic middle section with its unusually apt orchestral accompaniment is memorable by any standards, and its harmonic scheme is miraculous when placed in historical perspective, for it appeared not long after Beethoven's death. The form of this piece is, of

[3] For example, his A minor Rondo (K.511).

course, the simple ternary form which was the basis of so much of Chopin's most powerful and spontaneous writing. It could be used to argue that it was content, not form, that interested him, but a glance at the Polonaise-Fantaisie will be sufficient to disprove this contention.

The finale of this Concerto is related to the mazurka;

EX. 12

it is a rondo with a third subject in mazurka rhythm.

EX. 13

The coda is, perhaps, not particularly significant, but it is an ideal dramatic close to a work that has its fair share of drama.

The E minor Concerto, called 'number one' because of the delay in publishing the F minor, has much in common with its companion piece, though it does not really break very much fresh ground beyond showing a further development along the lines indicated in the F minor. The tonal scheme of the first movement is unusual, but it is not clear what purpose Chopin had when keeping to the tonic for both the first and second subjects. By the time the exposition is over, apart from some very interesting and subtle tonal digressions, there is certainly some

feeling of tonal monotony. Tovey could see no redeeming feature in it,[4]
but the beginning of the development may well provide a clue. For
the appearance of first-subject material in C major is one of the most
beautiful events in the whole of the work.

EX. 14

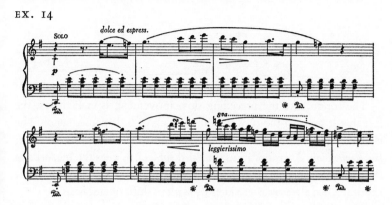

In the recapitulation the second subject appears in the relative major
key, again a choice whose purpose it is not easy to understand. But
such near-eccentricities do not detract from the essential majesty of this
maestoso.

EX. 15

The slow movement is entitled Romance. This is as good a word as any
to describe a movement which is clearly the elder brother of the
larghetto of the F minor Concerto. Here the contrasts are less dramatic,
but perhaps there is greater unity. Certainly the continuous outpouring
of melody is as spontaneous and convincing.

[4] He described the tonal scheme of this movement as 'suicidal' (*Essays in
Musical Analysis*, Vol. III, p. 103).

EX. 16

The rondo, like the preceding slow movement, is in E major, the fact that it starts in the relative minor being of little consequence. The character of the movement is derived from the Polish national dance, the *Krakowiak*. This appears as the third subject, as does the mazurka in the previous concerto. The theme has subtle, ambiguous accents whose rhythm is not always easy to identify with its shifts of emphasis.

EX. 17

The return to the first subject once more illustrates Chopin's adventurous attitude to tonality, for the re-statement appears a semitone lower in E flat, a feature touched on earlier in this chapter. The coda is a wonderful piece of piano writing, wholly consistent with the simultaneous creative work on the Studies, opp. 10 and 25.

EX. 18 (a)

(b)

Having completed these two concertos, there is evidence that Chopin intended to write a third. Indeed, there is reference to this in one of his father's letters to him (1834); he apparently knew that his son found this a particularly taxing task, for he charmingly advises him not to bother too much, as his health might sustain an injury through the worry entailed in its completion.

However, it would seem more than concern for his health which prevented Chopin from completing this in the manner one would expect from its two predecessors. To judge from the evidence, there is no further mention of this work until approximately seven years later (1841), when he writes to his copyist Fontana that he has ready amongst other things a maestoso or Allegro de Concert in A major. The projected Third Concerto would appear to be the origin of this Allegro. Indeed, from the characteristic dotted-rhythm to the transparently obvious first movement's concerto form, the signs are quite clear. What is not clear, however, is the date at which the various sections of the movement were actually written, for here alone among Chopin's work we find some transparent inconsistencies of style. The opening tutti sounds very much like a piano reduction of an orchestral score. There is certainly an advance in some respects on the two concertos, but the thematic material was clearly conceived at the earlier date, if indeed not before.

EX. 19

Once this rather unwieldy-sounding tutti is complete, there is the characteristic preparation of the solo entry with a complete change of keyboard style. It is almost as if the composer was freed from his self-imposed shackles and the piece immediately blossoms into a spontaneous outpouring. Unlike the first movements of the concertos, the exposition is not repeated and the solo part begins with new material, material that is not unrelated, for the transition is both apt and gives a real feeling of continuity. The second subject which in the exposition proper is in the tonic, here appears greatly elaborated in the dominant. At one point there is an interesting decoration (Exx. 20(a) and (b)) very similar to that in the late Nocturne in B major (Ex. 20(c)) and also to that in the Study in C sharp minor, op. 25 (Ex. 20(d)).

EX. 20(a)

EX. 20(b)

EX 20(c)

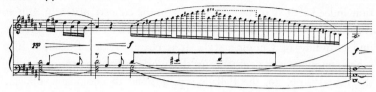

EX. 20(d)

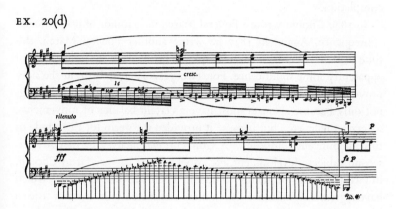

Also, a recurring pedal point is introduced in this second subject, not admittedly very interestingly, but it was to become one of Chopin's characteristic harmonic devices, particularly in his later years.[5]

The second subject leads by way of some extremely complex and elaborate pianistic and harmonic passages to the development, which restates the second subject in modified form. From here, sonata form as preached in all the respectable textbooks becomes somewhat obscure. Much new material is introduced, originating, I think, at the later of the two dates of this composition. The movement ends with a quasi orchestral climax devoted to a small and relatively unimportant late section of the tutti. This is an absorbing and indeed fascinating work, uneven maybe, but with many examples of superb inspiration and blazing originality. I suppose it is not ideally a piece for performance in public, for it does sound like a piano reduction of a concerto with all

[5] See, for example, the F minor Study, op. 10, the B flat major Prelude and the Barcarolle.

the inevitable awkwardness. It needs very careful thought and preparation indeed if it is to be convincing on the concert platform. But it is certainly a work which repays study and which leads to a greater understanding of Chopin's style. It is characteristic of Chopin that when announcing the existence of this work to Fontana together with the Fantasy, op. 49, the Ballade, op. 47, and the Polonaise, op. 44, he makes absolutely no mention of the circumstances attending its completion.

In 1829 Chopin wrote a Funeral March in C minor of no particular consequence. Again, in 1837 he wrote another Funeral March, this time in B flat minor, a piece simple in form, stark in outline, but of apparently some significance. For, two years later, it became the slow movement of the Sonata in B flat minor, op. 35, to which it belongs not only because a sonata must have a certain balance of movements, scherzo, finale, etc., but because it provided the germ for the whole of this magnificent composition.[6] Conventional analysis of first subject, second subject, development, etc., does not get us very far in Chopin. In fact, the points of interest to be noted here are precisely those which have a greater significance than a mere conducted tour. It is not true to say that this work is an uneasy amalgam of disparate and unrelated movements. There is a unity of purpose which goes much deeper than the easily demonstrable thematic and motivic relationships which recur throughout the work, though even these are often ignored by detractors. Of course, the best demonstration of a work's unity is a performance through which its essential unity of purpose is more truly felt than by a demonstration of superficially related motifs. It is of interest, however, to note that at least in the first three movements there is a recurrence of repeated notes in their first subjects and that the semitone features prominently in its thematic make-up.

The opening movement has an interesting problem in theory if perhaps not in practice, for there is no actual indication of tempo. The performer is faced with four bars marked 'Grave', meaning solemn or portentous, followed by the very clear but inexact command to proceed at double the speed—'doppio movimento'.

[6] See p. 246. ED.

EX. 21

However, this is not a problem which would have exercised the composer's contemporaries. The conventions of notation were still a comparatively implicit science, and beyond a minimum of direction, little more was usually necessary than careful observation of the time-signature and the notation involved. Thus to Beethoven, Mozart and Haydn 'two-four' time indicated a very special kind of motion, for which careful observance of printed verbal instructions is no substitute. Handel was not merely being vague when he instructed his interpreters to proceed 'a tempo ordinario'. Quite the contrary. The briefest glance at the text was sufficient to show that this ordinary tempo was a precise description of the proceedings.

It is possible to draw an analogy between the opening four bars of this work and the first bar of the slow movement of Beethoven's 'Hammerklavier' Sonata. We know for certain that the latter was added as an afterthought, and very meaningful it has proved to be. In the case of the B flat minor Sonata, the opening four bars are not part of the exposition, but are used meaningfully in combination with the first subject in the development section. It would be fascinating to know when this introduction came into being; I suspect after the movement itself had been completed.[6a] The repeat of the exposition begins, of course, without repetition of these four bars. Incidentally, as in all music where repeats are indicated, it is especially important to observe them here, otherwise their omission completely destroys the balance of an exceptionally finely shaped movement.

The scherzo, a difficult piece to project successfully, is related more

[6a] In which event, it would not be the first time Chopin had composed an introduction last. Compare the 'Winter Wind' Study (see Collet p. 136) and the Andante Spianato and Grande Polonaise (see Searle, p. 215). ED.

to the Beethoven scherzo than to Chopin's own separate and highly individual examples of this form.

EX. 22

The end of the movement shows a keen dramatic sense and an awareness of continuity in its subtle preparation for the succeeding funeral march. We have already noted the absence of a precise tempo indication in the first movement; the scherzo likewise has no further instruction than its description, and the funeral march is both an instruction and a description.

EX. 23

The finale, on the other hand, is inscribed with the word 'presto', and the very clear and unequivocal 'sotto voce e legato'.

EX. 24

From this point to the end (where there are two chords marked fortissimo) there is only one crescendo and diminuendo. However, this lack of detailed advice is, in fact, the clearest indication of the approach intended by the composer. Of course, it should be played fast, but there is such a wealth of harmonic subtlety that superimposition of effects detracts from the fascination of this strange other-worldly fantasy. In this piece Chopin has indeed moved away from the pre-

Autograph page of the "Krakowiak," for piano and orchestra, Op.14

(Czartoryski Library, Cracow)

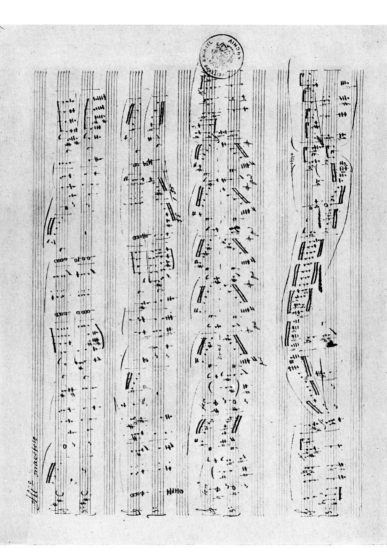

Autograph page of the Sonata in B minor, Op. 58
(Chopin Institute, Warsaw)

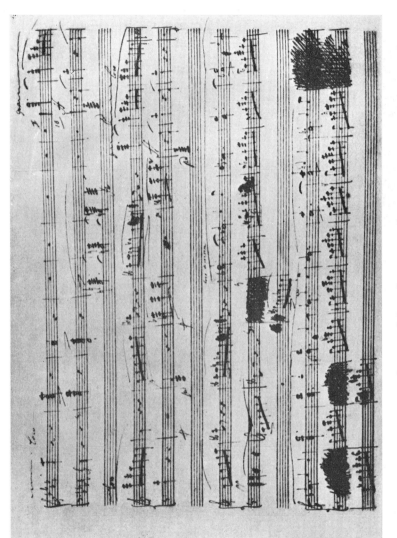

Autograph page of the Scherzo in B flat minor, Op. 31

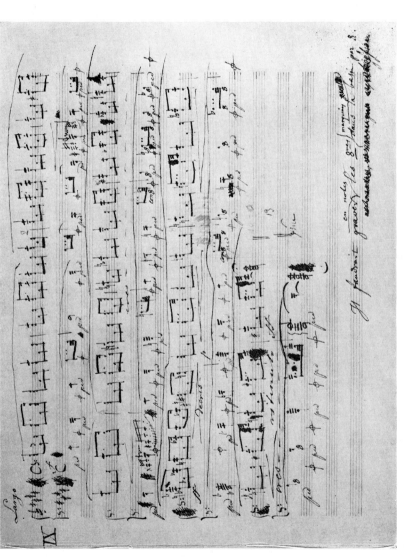

Autograph page of the Prelude in E major, Op.28
(Chopin Institute, Warsaw)

viously accepted canons of tonality and has set the scene for revolutionary developments. There is such a wealth of detail and technical skill that it is eminently satisfying even played at half speed. The movement brings this masterpiece to its close in a manner both fantastic and inevitable.[7]

The Sonata in B flat minor was followed five years later by the Sonata in B minor, op. 58, and the development in Chopin's style is immediately striking. There is at once a greater complexity of harmonic device, and the total integration of the decorative element into the substance of the material. Judged from the structural point of view, this Sonata is perhaps less satisfactory than its predecessor, due to the lessening of the clarity of the main outline. By the time Chopin's technique had achieved the necessary manipulative mastery his style had become too complex, detailed and eventful to span the vast arches which the greatest masters of sonata form bestrode. Nevertheless, the inspiration is of such uniform superlativity that the attention of the listener and the performer is held by the sheer miracle of continuous creation. Here there is little that is beyond Chopin's accomplishment, and he handles his material in all its widely varying aspects with superb mastery. The first movement, another maestoso incidentally, is packed with material sufficient for twenty-five sonatas by a composer twenty-five years previously. The interesting, and now characteristic, point to be noted in the first movement is that, as in the B flat minor Sonata, the first subject is developed or commented on to such an extent that the recapitulation virtually begins with the second subject. In the earlier sonata the first subject is not recapitulated, since it forms the basis of the development. Here, likewise, its complete reiteration would be redundant and its exclusion once again demonstrates Chopin's awareness, if not mastery, of sonata form.

EX. 25

Allegro maestoso

[7] For a further detailed discussion of the B flat minor Sonata, see pp. 239–49. ED.

The scherzo, as in the previous sonata, is again a smaller version of the form and is not to be confused with Chopin's separate scherzos. It is in E flat major, a miniature of simple design but striking originality.

EX. 26

Its tonic is enharmonically transformed by suggestion into D sharp at the opening of the succeeding Largo, a movement in ternary form. Here the opening four bars show, if it were needed by now, Chopin's unerring sense of modulation and his prodigious resources of invention.[7a]

EX. 27

These four bars can serve a useful purpose in demonstrating one of the more important aspects of Chopin's composing character. In considering his stature as a composer, so much critical stress has been laid on his attitude to form as understood by the Viennese classics that the importance of the *episode* in Chopin's music is often lost sight of. For it is in these structural devices, these parentheses, that a significant outpouring of his imagination is to be found. Without them, his music would be unrecognizable, and indeed without his uncanny gift for integrating apparently irreconcilable ideas such material would have had to be rejected. Sometimes, of course, passages of this nature fulfil a very definite and important structural purpose, as a glance at the four bars preceding the return to the slow movement's main theme will show.

[7a] And related passages later in the movement such as Ex. 28.

EX. 28

But it is not in works such as the sonatas that this particular example of Chopin's creative character most frequently occurs; rather is it to be found in the highly organized and personal forms which he himself created as in the Barcarolle (Ex. 29 (a)) and the Polonaise-Fantaisie (Ex. 29 (b)).

EX. 29 (a)

EX. 29 (b)

The finale is a very clearly organized movement of great brilliance and uninterrupted vigour which maintains an unflagging eventfulness despite its virtual restriction to two main ideas.

EX. 30.

The coda contains an example, if one were still needed, of the extent to which Chopin's harmony had developed, in particular how the innocent and expressive appoggiatura of his earlier Bellinic associations had become the instrument of a taut and highly organized workshop or armoury which he used with unerring skill. It is a far cry from the technically related passage in the earlier but none the less highly individual Bolero.

This movement would be more successful in performance with a more faithful application of Chopin's instruction 'presto non tanto'. Too frequently does a performer's enthusiasm exceed his judgement, with the result that the semiquaver sections (especially Exx. 31 (a) and (b)) are either hopelessly unrhythmic and lacking in clarity or, as is more often the case, these sections have to be played at a slower tempo. The remorseless surge which should span the whole movement is thus inhibited.[8]

EX. 31 (a)

[8] For a further detailed discussion of the Sonata in B minor see pp. 250–6. ED.

EX. 31 (b)

Two years later there appeared the last and final sonata that Chopin was to write: the Cello Sonata in G minor, op. 65. Written for his great friend, the cellist Franchomme, they performed the final three movements in Paris at Chopin's last concert there in 1848. Chopin's last major composition, it is a work of great beauty, though uneven in some respects. This is possibly due to the inclusion of an instrument other than the piano. The opening, though more complex, is curiously reminiscent of the style of the two early concertos.

EX. 32

One can almost hear the orchestra in the opening four bars. The following keyboard flourish, however, immediately dispels this illusion. The cello writing in this piece may not be instrumentally ideal, and the infrequency of its performance suggests that cellists share this view, but there is no doubt that the instrument is handled with a very natural understanding of its *melodic* possibilities. The piano part is, as one would expect, rather too complex and detailed for an equal partnership. The first movement in particular often makes less than its potential impression through the difficulty some string players have in fully understanding the nature of Chopin's writing. While *rubato* is

frequently misunderstood by pianists, the peculiar needs in this respect
in Chopin's music are often incomprehensible to instrumentalists whose
relatively small repertoire is based on major works by Bach, Beethoven
and Brahms. And there are many passages in this movement which
suffer from the inability of string players to gauge the relaxations and
tensions implicit in the constantly shifting emphases of Chopin's
harmonic and melodic writing. In this respect it is possible to observe
Chopin's unerring harmonic instinct through subtle juxtaposition of
contrasted chords and textures. A musical novice studying, say, the
mazurkas or the polonaises can, with the aid of imagination and
intelligence, find out exactly the nature and character of these stylized
national dances. Nothing has to be superimposed, an accent on the
second or third beats never needing deliberate imposition. It is there
in the music, in the texture. So, in this Sonata, lack of experience of
Chopin's style leads cellists to impose a wholly foreign, Brahmsian
eloquence which obliterates the finely calculated *minutiae*. This movement is not adventurous in form, and does not break much fresh
ground stylistically. Chopin was reaching the end of his life, and it is
not surprising that although his inspiration and technique were still
fully in evidence he had perhaps ceased to develop as strikingly as in his
earlier years. Nevertheless, who else could have written a passage of
such beauty as this?

EX. 33

The brilliant scherzo (Ex. 34) is a successful venture with a distinct

Polish flavour and some surprising tonal adventures. The Largo (Ex.
35) is a uniquely striking piece of autumnal beauty, a perfect miniature.

EX. 34

EX. 35

The finale (Ex. 36) is in the nature of a tarantella, a convincing
movement full of taut, meaningful harmonic progressions, and certainly well judged in the balance between cello and piano. The second
subject (Ex. 37), with its brooding melancholy, is a perfect foil to the
cutting vivacity of the first subject.

EX. 36

EX. 37

There is a problem of notation in this movement which illustrates that Chopin was, neither in time nor in convention, so very far from Bach. The simultaneous triplet-and-dotted-quaver (which, when it occurs in the Polonaise-Fantaisie, for instance, is clearly soluble) here present is some ambiguity. It is curious that Chopin, usually so meticulous, should have left room for doubt, but it is not always possible to say with certainty whether the semiquaver should be *exact* or treated as the third triplet. In the Polonaise-Fantaisie the following examples show clearly Chopin's view of conventional notation. For, quite apart from musical sense, the arrangement of the notes vertically is exactly as they appear in the manuscript.

EX. 38 (a)

EX. 38 (b)

Moreover, the photograph of the manuscript of the E major Prelude (facing page 169) should lead, at least, to a reappraisal of the conventional interpretation. Comparison with performing editions gives an idea of the dangers of neglecting the historical evolution of notation. Familiarity with one particular solution to the problem should not absolve each player from approaching each problem afresh whenever it occurs. Valuable as tradition can be, its unquestioning adoption in this respect, as over the whole field of interpretation, reduces the conviction and the authority of a performance to a mere imitation. In the music of no other composer is this more true than in that of Chopin. Meticulous he was, as George Sand affirmed. He should not therefore be denied the courtesy of the most searching scrutiny of his each and every wish. Only then can interpretation begin. Only then will the implicit emerge from the explicit.

LENNOX BERKELEY

## Nocturnes, Berceuse, Barcarolle

THOUGH the nocturnes cannot be said to occupy as important a place among Chopin's works as do the preludes and the studies, they are in no sense minor compositions. As with the mazurkas, one feels that in them he was less concerned with pianistic considerations, and more with his most intimate thoughts and feelings. Nevertheless, it is clear that they derive in great measure from his very personal style of playing, contemporary accounts of which invariably stress the extreme delicacy and the beauty of sound he could achieve in cantabile passages. Though by all accounts he was capable of astonishing virtuosity, it was always the poetic quality of his playing that made the deepest impression. Indeed, it was thought too intimate for large concert halls, and better suited to a more restricted audience. The nocturnes therefore correspond to a very individual feeling for the piano, and one that had been little exploited before, the first reactions to the instrument having been more to take full advantage of its powerful tone and percussive potentialities.

The word 'nocturne', as used by Chopin, bears no relation to the *notturno* that we find in eighteenth-century music, which does not conjure up any picture that one could call specifically nocturnal. Only John Field had previously used the word in this sense, and it is generally admitted that it was from him that Chopin derived the style and atmosphere of his nocturnes. Since Chopin, the word has been widely used for the more descriptive type of piece, most successfully perhaps by Fauré, while later composers have made a still freer use of it. Debussy, for example, employs it as the title of one of his most important orchestral works.

There are nineteen nocturnes in the standard editions of Chopin's works. Apart from these, there are two, in C minor and C sharp minor, which are not always included. The C minor Nocturne was not discovered until recent times and was published in 1938. The other one, the C sharp minor Nocturne, is best known by its title *Lento con gran espressione*, and it has an interesting history. Found among the composer's manuscripts after his death, it was first published in 1875. A later edition bears the dedication 'To my sister Louise to practise before she starts playing my Second Concerto'. In the piece there appears a tune from the F minor Piano Concerto in this form.

EX. I

But in the original autograph copy in the possession of Mr Arthur Hedley the passage is written so that the tune remains in $\frac{3}{4}$, as in the Concerto, while the accompaniment is in $\frac{4}{4}$—the time-signature of the piece.[1]

EX. 2

This astonishing passage is particularly interesting in view of the important part that cross-rhythms play in the later nocturnes. Chopin

[1] See p. 21f. for further discussion of this piece. ED.

must have decided that it was beyond what the average pianist could manage with accuracy, and therefore simplified it by sacrificing the original rhythm of the tune.

The nocturnes comprised in the 'official' volume spread over the period from 1827, when Chopin was 17, until 1846, three years before his death. The Nocturne in E minor op. 72, published after the composer's death, is actually a very early work, written when he was only seventeen.[2] It could well be thought a product of his maturity, for it has an austere simplicity, a directness and clarity, that give the impression of a piece on a bigger scale. The regular left-hand triplets are, it is true, typical of the earlier nocturnes, but they are given a greater intensity than usual by the fact that the middle note of the second and fourth triplets continually forms an appogiatura to the harmony. This is most effectively seen in the crescendo that starts at bar 16.

EX. 3

The section in the major key immediately following this passage is of great beauty. It is repeated in the tonic key at the end of the piece. Calm, and yet intense in feeling, the romantic idiom here achieves a classical poise and dignity. It was Chopin's wish that his unpublished manuscripts should be destroyed after his death; had it been carried out, this beautiful piece, among others, would have been lost to posterity.

As might be expected, the debt to Field is more evident in the first set

[2] See Maurice Brown, op. cit., p. 18. All Chopin's posthumously published compositions were dated by Fontana.

of Nocturnes op. 9, but even here his influence amounts to little more than the idea of a quiet reflective piece having a melody in the right hand and an accompanying figure in the left; the melodic character already bears the imprint of Chopin's personality. In the first, in B flat minor, the form is a straightforward ABA, the middle section being simply a prolongation of the melody involving a change of key but preserving the same accompaniment. Already the decoration of the theme is characteristically elaborate and subtle. The rhythmical independence of the hands that is such a feature of Chopin's piano writing is found in the very first bars.

EX. 4

The form, too, is somewhat freer than in Field, the recapitulation being 'telescoped' so that the tune jumps from bar 4 to bar 13 of the exposition, and leads straight to the coda.

The second Nocturne, in E flat major, is the best known of this group, its graceful melody and the simplicity of its form making it easy to assimilate and remember. It is in $\frac{12}{8}$ time. The four-bar theme is immediately repeated in a decorated form which is followed by a continuation of the melody of equal length. The original four bars then reappear in a new variation, the second part of the theme is repeated, then once again come the original bars leading to a coda. The form can be summarized as A1 A2 B1 A3 B2 A4 coda.

The last of the group foreshadows the development Chopin was to bring both to the shape and the content of the nocturne. It is laid out on a much bigger scale, and includes a middle section using quite

different material. The opening, with its bare accompaniment and
restless chromatic theme, is strikingly original.

EX. 5

As in the preceding Nocturne, the decorations of the theme are of
extraordinary grace and freedom. For the first time the central portion
presents a deliberate contrast to the initial idea. This was to be a form
that Chopin often used, sometimes in quite different contexts—in the
studies, for example. Here, between a quiet first and last section, is an
agitated and fast-moving episode. It is in contrast to, and yet essentially
a part of, the overall conception of the piece.

Although composed hardly more than a year later, the next group
of Nocturnes, op. 15, shows material of deeper significance and a subtler
control of form. The first, in F major, is memorable for the beauty of its
opening melody, more classical in shape than is usual with Chopin, and
floating in rapt calm over an accompaniment of triplets. The tune
itself has the spontaneity and distinction that are characteristic of
Chopin's genius, its shape wonderfully controlled by the bass line that,
after remaining on the tonic for the first phrase, descends in a scale
from F to E, a ninth below, thereby leading the music back to the
key-note and restatement of the theme.

EX. 6

The middle section provides a violent contrast of mood, its stormy character being accentuated by the tranquility that surrounds it.

The Nocturne in F sharp major is of roughly the same shape, though of totally different character. It is among the best-known and most frequently played of all Chopin's works. Compared with the first group of Nocturnes (op. 9), there is here a great advance in the handling of the material. An example of Chopin's skill can be seen in the delayed cadence that occurs at the end of the recapitulation. In its original form it goes to the dominant.

EX. 7

Finally, where the cadence must be in the tonic, the resolution is delayed with great effect.

EX. 8

There is much more here than the solution of a technical problem, for though the device of prolonging a final cadence is a common one, it rarely adds such intensity, and one feels that what started in the composer's mind as a mere technical expedient became a matter of great emotional significance. The final piece in this group, the Nocturne in

G minor, begins innocently enough; there is even a studied simplicity in the harmonization of the theme, but in its development we are soon in much deeper waters; unexpected, and what must then have been surprisingly novel chromatic modulations, similar to those found in the mazurkas, are followed by a powerful crescendo.

EX. 9

A highly unusual feature of this Nocturne is the complete absence of any recapitulation. A new theme marked 'religioso', which comes immediately after the passage just quoted, leads to the end of the piece without any reference to the thematic material of the opening. This epilogue grows out of the second theme and forms an unexpected commentary upon it. Its strongly marked rhythm is in complete contrast to the rest of the piece, and brings it to a somewhat enigmatic conclusion.

The next nocturnes in chronological order are op. 27, nos. 1 and 2. They are as different in character as they possibly could be. The first, in C sharp minor, is one of the most evocative in the whole series. The beginning is indeed a picture of the night. A deep and mysterious stillness pervades the opening bars; a glimmer of light appears as the music moves to the major key, only to sink back into the dark.

EX. 10

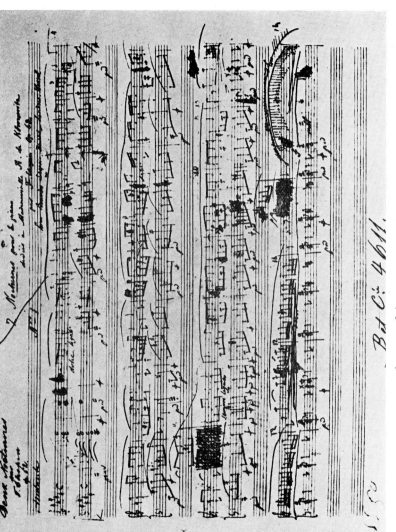

Autograph page of the Nocturne in B major, Op. 62
(Chopin Institute, Warsaw)

Autograph page of the Barcarolle, Op.60

At the tenth bar the melody, as though momentarily lost in the impenetrable darkness, disappears altogether. The piece is in conventional form, having a central episode, marked più mosso, which, after a restless and agitated beginning, moves to a vehement climax before returning to the initial theme; but the gloom of the opening is soon dispelled, the music slides imperceptibly into C sharp major, and the piece ends in an atmosphere of serenity and calm. This ending foreshadows the mood (and the key, for it is in D flat major) of the second piece, whose opening is as gentle and limpid as that of the first is uneasy and brooding. There is no contrasting section here, only a long continuous melody, over slow $\frac{6}{8}$ semiquavers, elaborately decorated with great rhythmical freedom. A close study of this piece reveals the individuality of Chopin's piano writing; the proliferation of the arabesques that embellish the theme are of a kind that is his own invention, bearing little resemblance to the work of any other composer. Chopin here reaches his full maturity. The somewhat languid theme is transformed into variants that are surprisingly strong and virile. A passage in the middle, leading to the recapitulation, is a striking example of the harmonic subtlety and boldness of conception that he could now command.

**EX. II**

The coda is of exceptional beauty; over a tonic pedal, lasting for sixteen bars, a series of chromatic fourths slides gently downwards; they are repeated in a variation, and the piece is concluded with an elegance and charm that Chopin rarely surpassed.

    The Two Nocturnes op. 32 date from not more than two years later.

The first, in B major, is chiefly remarkable for the freedom and originality of its form. The first part of the melody is spread over twelve bars, made up of two sections of seven and five bars respectively; a repeat of the first seven bars leads to a new theme, similar in mood, but rather unpredictable in its course, containing allusions to the initial idea, but no further statement of it. The coda is astonishing by reason of its complete change of atmosphere—the quiet, reflective character that has prevailed hitherto is suddenly interrupted by a forceful and menacing recitative, as though the composer's thoughts had been put to flight by some sinister apparition. It is an ending that defies analysis, but compels acceptance.

Op. 32, no. 2, is more familiar to many people in another form, for the orchestral version plays an important part in the ballet *Les Sylphides*; indeed, to those who know the ballet well it has become difficult to think of it as a piano piece. The middle section in particular might well have been written for the theatre, and has something of the atmosphere of the great Tchaikovsky ballets. Nevertheless it is one of the best examples of the kind of piano writing that Chopin evolved in the nocturnes—the cantabile line in the right hand continually varied by subtle changes of rhythmical emphasis, and the regular triplets that accompany it in the left hand, are the basic elements of many pieces in the series. It must be admitted that it is more conventional than some of them, and to that extent less interesting.

The next pair, op. 37, are among the more well known. In the first the form is so clear that it calls for no comment. The tune is varied by small touches that look of little account on paper, but are highly effective in performance. The central portion is a passage of the 'religioso' type that was popular in mid-nineteenth-century music, which, in the hands of lesser composers, so easily turned into the worst kind of sentimentality, but with Chopin, natural taste and sheer musicality prevent any suspicion of this. The second of this pair, a considerably longer piece, has the basic form A B A B A, but this does not mean exact repetition. At the first repeat of A, for example, the six bars, identical, in the right hand, with the opening six, now appear over a dominant pedal, giving them a different shade of feeling. The second appearance of B is transposed, but goes through a parallel sequence of keys; it joins up with the third statement of A, but cutting out the first bars altogether, and the piece ends with a reference to B. Thus a traditional form is used, but with great freedom and important modifications. The principal theme with its thirds and sixths is a particularly felicitous piece of piano-writing.

EX. 12

This at the seventh bar becomes

EX. 13

The Nocturne in C minor, op. 48, no. 1, stands out as a work of major significance, surpassing in breadth and grandeur all its predecessors. The opening phrase

EX. 14

is immediately repeated, differently harmonized (this time in the relative major) and leading to the key of the dominant. At this point a bold modulation takes the music into D flat before the return of the first phrase, once more with a different harmony. The middle section is a slow march-like theme in C major to which is later added an under-current of triplets; these gradually increase in volume, and finally take possession of the whole situation, bursting out in vehement double octaves. The first theme now returns, but the triplet figure remains as its accompaniment. This has the effect of altering its character—its former majestic calm being replaced by a feeling of passionate urgency, enhanced by the cross-rhythms that the coming together of four notes to a beat in the right hand, and three in the left, cause. An interrupted cadence skilfully resolved brings to an end one of Chopin's most eloquent and moving pages.

In none of Chopin's works is his capacity for maintaining long-sustained melody more happily exploited than in the nocturnes. The second of the pieces that constitute op. 48 is a particularly good example of this. After an introduction of two bars, a slow melody that might have been written for the voice unwinds itself in a passage lasting for twenty-five bars, and is at once repeated with slight modifications. It is a line of great purity and simplicity that in spite of its length is never tedious, but seems propelled by an organic growth. The più lento episode that follows is less compelling; made up of short phrases, it serves rather as a kind of diversion or breathing space before the cantabile is resumed.

Op. 55 consists of two pieces in F minor and in E flat major respectively. The former is a lesser work than the latter, and for this reason has sometimes been dismissed by critics in a rather summary fashion. It is true that it lacks the wide-ranging melodic line that is found in so much of Chopin's music of this period, and the più mosso section is more obviously contrived than usual, but the form is satisfying, and the way in which the tune at the reprise slides imperceptibly into the coda is skilfully managed. The E flat major Nocturne, however, that follows it is one of the most beautiful and flawless in the whole series—a small masterpiece in which technical skill and inspiration go hand in hand. Here no analysis can explain the natural growth of the melodic line. It has many striking features; the falling sixth of the first bar, for example (almost immediately echoed by a similar interval) seems like the middle or end of a phrase rather than the beginning, and indeed in a sense it is, for the theme's real first notes are only revealed later. It would be difficult to find in the whole of music a parallel example of this.

EX. 15

After a passage in which a third voice is introduced between the other two comes a cadence in G major, but the music modulates at once back to E flat, and now we are given the first notes of the theme which even here sound more like an ornamented version of something already heard.

EX. 16

Not the least remarkable feature of the piece is the perfect blending of the tune itself with the accompanying figure, which shows an infallible ear, not only for the harmony, but for the choice of the actual 'note against note' between the two parts. This contrapuntal approach to harmony is still more striking in the three-voice passage that occurs towards the middle of the piece.

EX. 17

The Nocturne ends in rapt and serene calm with a coda of outstanding beauty.

With the Two Nocturnes, op. 62, nos. 1 and 2, the tendencies that we have noticed in these later pieces are still more marked: freedom of melodic line, richer and more unpredictable harmony, and a looser and less stereotyped form. Op. 62, no. 1, is a quiet reflective piece in the familiar A B A pattern, but the individual sections are less symmetrical in themselves than in the earlier pieces. Thus the first section of the theme is only three and a half bars long instead of the usual four, the cadence being merged into the repetition. At the eleventh bar, the original melody continues underneath a new figure that gives fresh impetus to the music. Towards the end of the first section there is a strangely haunting passage.

EX. 18

A modified form of this appears at the end of the Nocturne. The middle part of the piece is typical of Chopin's later manner in the range of the melodic line and individuality of harmony which now becomes much more chromatic than in his earlier music, as, for instance, in this passage leading to the coda.

EX. 19

It is true that op. 62, no. 2, reverts to an earlier type of theme, the first part being in eight-bar phrases, but the middle section belongs very definitely in style to the later period, as can be seen by the freedom with which the theme moves first over a bass of running semiquavers, and later over a syncopated accompaniment. This is, in fact, new material, distinct from what has gone before, and in a slightly faster tempo, yet one feels that it has not been introduced for the sake of contrast, for it is but another facet of the prevailing mood, which here takes on a more urgent note and only gradually returns to the calmer feeling of the opening. The first theme reappears for a brief moment and the piece ends with part of the central portion slightly modified.

### Berceuse

It is not surprising that this piece, in which technical adroitness is matched by seemingly effortless and inexhaustible invention, should have become one of Chopin's most popular compositions. No analysis can give any idea of its compelling grace and charm, but it is put together with such skill that a brief examination of its construction is rewarding. A tonic pedal (D flat) is sustained throughout all seventy bars of the piece, and the ostinato figure with which it begins remains virtually unchanged from beginning to end.

EX. 20

The tune itself is no longer than the four bars above, but each repetition is, in fact, a variation of them. Thus the next phrase adds another part and is prolonged for another two bars; there follow a series of differently decorated variations of the tune, each one enhancing the basic idea with amazing skill and delicacy. The resourcefulness of the ever-changing presentation of the theme is such that the listener is hardly aware that the underlying harmony remains practically the same. At the fifteenth bar the tune appears in grace-notes over an interior pedal (A flat).

EX. 21

This is followed by a variation in gently rippling demi-semiquavers. Sometimes only the accompaniment and a purely decorative figure remain. Even when, at the thirty-fifth bar, a new melodic phrase appears, it is so near in feeling to the original theme that one is hardly aware of any difference. When the penultimate variation is reached, the seventh degree of the scale is flattened for the first time, suggesting that a modulation to the subdominant is coming, but this does not, in fact, occur; the harmony returns to the tonic key for a final variation of the tune, which now drops down the scale over the common chord of D flat.

This elaborate treatment of a very simple melodic idea might so easily have become something overloaded and fussy; in fact, the variants grow so naturally out of each other that its essential simplicity is retained, and one has the impression of listening not so much to an ingenious musical construction as to an inspired improvisation.

### Barcarolle

Beyond the fact that it comes from Venice, little seems to be known about the barcarolle in its original form. The word means 'boat-song', but there is no evidence that it derives from any form of folk-music; it is more likely that it was simply a type of popular song with which the gondoliers of former times were wont to regale their customers. Its chief characteristic, in the form in which it has survived, is its atmosphere of languorous ease and opulence. This may be because we know it only through the ears of the contemporary sightseer, who heard its strains, as he reclined in his gondola, wafted across the waters of the Venetian lagoon. No such sound beguiles the traveller's ear today; the *gondolieri* are silent as far as music is concerned, and the barcarolle, even as a piano piece, which is the only form, apart from a few operatic excerpts, in which we are likely to encounter it now, is a thing of the past. Indeed, were it not for the fact that composers of the stature of Chopin, Mendelssohn and Fauré transcribed it into piano music, it would hardly be remembered.

Chopin wrote only one Barcarolle, but it has long been a favourite, and remains one of his most popular and effective works. The opening is striking and typical of Chopin's innate sense of what is effective in performance. Feeling, no doubt, that to start straight into the accompanying figure would be insufficiently arresting, he writes a brief introduction, already taut and intense in harmony.

EX. 22

The theme follows immediately. The style of a song with guitar accompaniment is at once recognizable, but as the piece develops, the full resources of the piano are brought into play. Thirds and sixths give glitter and brilliance to the melody, replacing the colour and expressive quality of the voice, much in the same way in which Liszt transferred vocal effects to the piano in his operatic adaptations. One feels throughout the piece that vocal music is its basis, but a pianistic equivalent is always found, as, for example, where the tune comes to an end, a series of rising chords produce an effect similar to the excitement and tension of a vocal cadenza.

EX. 23

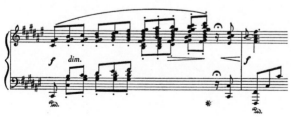

Now come two bars, heard earlier in the piece, which close the first part, and a short bridge-passage leads to the middle section. Here one is still more conscious of the rocking motion that is the traditional accompaniment of the barcarolle.

EX. 24

This theme modulates to several keys, and finally breaks into what might indeed almost be a popular song of the period. The passage that follows, linking it to a repeat of the first part, is interesting, for some bars it lingers over a pedal E, as though unable to decide where it is leading, settling down in the end in C sharp major before returning to the real key of the piece (F sharp). The recapitulation is much condensed; at the fifth bar a mutation occurs causing the music to jump to bar 28 of the exposition, and this passage is followed by a restatement of the 'popular song' theme, now fortissimo and grandioso. The coda is particularly memorable; it consists of fourteen bars over a tonic pedal, the first seven of which form a kind of pendant or epilogue to the main theme. They are extraordinarily rich and original in harmony. The remaining bars round off the piece with rapid and graceful figuration in the right hand. The perfect proportion of these elements in relation to the whole brings a rare sense of fulfilment and completeness to this sumptuous and exciting work.

BERNARD JACOBSON

---

# The Songs

THAT Chopin wrote songs, though an unfamiliar fact, is not a surprising one. The song was a natural field for a composer whose gifts were suited, not to the more expansive and formal kinds of music, but to smaller, essentially poetic compositions.

Two distinctions need to be drawn here: between two senses of the word 'small' and between 'poetic' and 'literary'. The forms of music can be small in physical extent without being small in emotional depth or musical significance, and Chopin's genius lay precisely in his ability to make a mere handful of notes say a great deal: it is the concentration, rather than the sheer brute quantity, of feeling that gives any composer's work its value.

In a way the distinction between 'poetic' and 'literary' is an analogous one, in that it is a distinction between the spiritual and the physical elements. If we call a composer literary, we generally mean that literary forms, concepts, characters, and trappings enter into the way he goes about his work. Schumann, Berlioz, and Liszt are all, in their different ways, good examples of literary composers. Almost alone among the romantics, Chopin had no interest in using literary procedures as starting-points or methods for shaping his music. But he is a pre-eminently poetic composer in that the essence of his work is the communication of feelings and moods which, though thoroughly transmuted by a purely musical way of thinking, are nevertheless entirely parallel in kind to the feelings and moods portrayed by poets.

Applying these considerations to Chopin's nineteen surviving songs, we find first of all that most of them are small in length and not extreme in dynamic range, but that in intensity they vary considerably. The majority are settings of agreeably romantic but unprofound lyrics, and they catch the mood of the poems without far transcending them. A handful are more ambitious in the depth of emotion they set out to explore: these are *Precz z moich oczu*, *Melodia*, *Nie ma czego trzeba*, and *Leci Liście z drzewa*. (The last-named is of disputed authenticity, but the arguments against it are far from conclusive, and its intrinsic qualities weigh heavily in favour of its acceptance.[1]) These four songs are larger than the others in dramatic gesture, and are closer in spirit to Chopin's bigger and more ambitious piano works. The others are akin to the dances, and indeed several of them are mazurkas; only one of these, *Moja pieszczotka*, resembles the more mature mazurkas in scale—its melodic line expands grandly in an exciting coda. The rest are simple strophic mazurkas, with the exception of *Gdzie lubi*, which is in a ternary form much less expansive than that of *Moja pieszczotka*.

The Lieder of Schubert, Schumann, and Brahms show how wrong one would be to suppose that strophic songs tend to be less profound than through-composed ones, but in Chopin's case it is notable that, while thirteen of the nineteen songs are strophic, only one of these thirteen (*Nie ma czego trzeba*) falls among the more ambitious group listed above. This leads us to the second distinction already discussed. Chopin's songs are good songs because they catch the moods of their poems with great perception and sensitivity, but he does not show the same intensely imaginative feeling for words as his German counterparts.

Thus an inflexion like the G sharp in the melody of *Poseł*, see Ex. I. is an essential part of the musical and expressive scheme, but it is not linked with the words in such a way as to make the strophic repetitions doubly significant, in the almost unbearably moving manner of the refrain in such a song as *Gute Morgen* in Schubert's *Schöne Müllerin*

---

[1] This song is, in fact, now reliably considered to be authentic. ED.

EX. I

cycle. In the same cycle the sudden little embellishment in *Trockne Blumen* (X)

EX. 2

is a moment of poignancy directly derived from the composer's perception of the words. In Chopin's *Smutna rzeka*, the modifications by which the last two lines of the melody

EX. 3

become

EX. 4

are not connected with the words; this beautiful embellishment is musically, not verbally poetic. It need hardly be added that none of this constitutes a value-judgement either way: there is more than one way of composing songs. But it perhaps helps to explain why Liszt's transcriptions of six of the songs are so unusually effective.

Chopin's songs range in date from 1829 (*Życzenie* and *Gdzie lubi*) to 1847 (*Melodia*), and they were not collected and published till after his death. His choice of poems was probably dictated more by personal than by literary considerations: far the greatest number of poems, ten, was contributed by Stefan Witwicki (1800–47), a minor figure in Polish literature but Chopin's closest associate among the six poets whose work he set.

In the following chronological survey of the songs, alongside the original texts, I have included translations which are as literal as I can make them without departing entirely from the bounds of the English language. All the existing translations are so approximate as to afford no help whatsoever to the singer who wants to deliver the words with more than the vaguest of nuances. I have kept his needs primarily in mind, and so the few departures from literal rendering are such as make no difference to the expression—for example, such grammatical transpositions as 'Flowers bloom on my banks' for 'My banks bloom with flowers' in *Smutna rzeka*, where the change has been made so as to preserve the original word-order. The order has been kept wherever possible within lines, and transpositions between lines have been made in only a few places where they were unavoidable, and where they are indicated by brackets.

In the preparation of these translations, I have had the invaluable help and advice of Mrs Doris Kaye.

## 1. *Życzenie* (*The Wish*) op. 74, no. 1. 1829 (Stefan Witwicki)

This, like all the Witwicki poems set by Chopin, was published in his *Piośnki Sielski* (*Pastoral Songs*) in Warsaw in 1830; but Chopin knew them in manuscript, as his inclusion in *Czary* of a stanza omitted from the published edition indicates. The first phrase of this Song's accompaniment presents a textual problem. In Chopin's manuscript[1a] the right-hand part is as follows:

EX. 5

Fontana, the editor of the original edition of opus 74, published by Schlesinger in Berlin in 1857 (Polish edition) and 1859–60 (German edition), changed this to:

EX. 6

It is hard to see any musical reason for the change, one of many made

[1a] The complex situation with regard to Chopin's manuscripts of the songs is, briefly, as follows. Chopin appears to have retained them all his life, with no thought of publishing them. After his death they were acquired by Fontana who made a complete manuscript transcript of them, edited them and published sixteen of them as op. 74 in 1857. (In 1872 Schlesinger added one more song 'A Hymn from the Tomb'; the remaining two songs 'Spells' and 'Elegy' were not discovered until 1910.) Unfortunately, most of Chopin's manuscripts have since been lost, although Fontana's transcript still survives. The *Maria Wodzińska* album, however, contains manuscript copies of songs which, according to Arthur Hedley, are in the hand of Chopin's sister Louise. This makes them the most authentic texts we have, for they were undoubtedly copied from Chopin's originals during his lifetime and with his full approval. ED.

by Fontana, and the manuscript reading seems preferable, though it has not been kept in the Polish Complete Edition.

*Życzenie*, a gay mazurka, is typical of Chopin's smaller strophic songs.

| | |
|---|---|
| Gdybym ja była słoneczkiem na niebie, | If I were the sun in the sky, |
| Nie świeciłabym jak tylko dla ciebie. | I would not shine except for you. |
| Ani na wody, ani na lasy, | Neither on water nor on forest— |
| Ale po wszystkie czasy | only for all time |
| Pod twym okienkiem i tylko dla ciebie | under your window and for you alone |
| Gdybym w słoneczko mogła zmienić siebie. | if I could change myself into a sun. |
| Gdybym ja była ptaszkiem z tego gaju, | If I were a bird of this grove, |
| Nie śpiewałabym w żadnym obcym kraju. | I would not sing in any foreign country. |
| Ani na wody, ani na lasy, | Neither on water nor on forest— |
| Ale po wszystkie czasy | only for all time |
| Pod twym okienkiem i tylko dla ciebie. | under your window and for you alone. |
| Czemuż nie mogę w ptaszka zmienię siebie! | Why can I not change myself into a bird! |

2. *Gdzie lubi* (*What she likes*) op. 74, no. 5. 1829 (Stefan Witwicki)

This is one of the only two Songs Chopin composed in A BA form (the other is *Moja pieszczotka*). It is a simple piece, again in mazurka style, but there is subtlety in the harmony that leads into the middle section. The third section is not a slavish repetition of the first. The first note of the melody is changed, and the phrase:

EX. 7

becomes:

EX. 8

Again, this alteration is a purely musical one not dictated by the words.

The editions leave out the direction *naïvement*, which appears at bar 25 in the manuscript.

| | |
|---|---|
| Strumyk lubi w dolinie, | The stream likes to be in the valley, |
| Sarna lubi w gęstwinie, | the deer likes to be in the thicket, |
| Ptaszek lubi pod strzechą, | The little bird likes to be under a thatched roof, |
| Lecz dziewczyna z uciechą | but a girl finds pleasure |
| Lubi gdzie niebieskie oko, | and likes to be where there is a blue eye, |
| Lubi gdzie i czarne oko, | and likes to be where there is a black eye, |
| Lubi gdzie wesołe pieśni, | and likes to be where there are gay songs, |
| Lubi gdzie i smutne pieśni. | and likes to be where there are sad songs. |
| Sama nie wie gdzie lubi, | She does not know where she'd like to be, |
| Wszędzie serce zgubi. | everywhere she'll lose her heart. |

3. *Hulanka* (*Drinking song*) op. 74, no. 4. 1830 (Stefan Witwicki)

This Song presents problems of arrangement. It is not certain which order the stanzas, the introduction, and the interlude should take. However, this is an editorial matter, and the Polish Complete Edition solves it well enough. The Liszt transcription offers some clues—for instance, it does not repeat the introduction as the Fontana edition does —and the Complete Edition largely agrees with what the Liszt version seems to suggest.

The actual music is completely unproblematical, and Chopin captures an uncharacteristically boisterous mood with conviction.

| | |
|---|---|
| Szynkareczko, szafareczko, | Mischievous barmaid, |
| Co ty robisz? Stój! | what are you doing? Stop! |
| Tam się śmiejesz, a tu lejesz | There you're laughing, here you're pouring |
| Miód na kaftan mój! | mead over my jacket! |
| | |
| Nie daruję, wycałuję! | I'll not let it go by, I'll kiss you all over! |
| | |
| Jakie oczko, brew! | What a little eye, what eyebrows! |
| Nóżki małe, ząbki białe, | Little feet, little white teeth, |
| hej! spali mnie krew! | hey! it will burn my blood! |
| | |
| Cóż tak bracie wciąż dumacie? | Why, brothers, do you go on dreaming? |
| | |
| Bierz tam smutki czart! | The devil take sorrow! |
| Pełno nędzy, ot pij prędzej, | There's plenty of misery, drink up quickly, |
| Świat ten diabła wart! | the world can go to the devil! |
| | |
| Piane nogi zbłądzą z drogi, | Drunken feet stray from the road, |
| Cóż za wielki srom? | what great shame is that? |
| Krzykiem żony rozbudzony | With the shout of your wife when she wakes up |
| Trafisz gdzie twój dom. | You guess where your home is. |
| | |
| Pij, lub kijem się pobijem! | Drink, or with a stick we'll have a fight! |
| | |
| Biegnij dziewczę w czas, | Run, girl, in time |
| By pogodzić, nie zaszkodzić, | to bring peace, not harm; |
| Oblej miodem nas! | pour the mead over us! |

4. *Precz z moich oczu!* . . . (*Out of my sight!*) op. 74, no. 6. 1830
(Adam Mickiewicz)

This fine Song is unusual in form. It consists of a free introduction
followed by two strophes. The opening gesture immediately establishes
the song's expressive power:

EX. 9

and the shift from imperiousness to pathos in the words is beautifully enshrined in the strophic melody:

EX. 10

Altogether this is a worthy setting of one of Poland's greatest poets. Mickiewicz lived from 1798 to 1855, and was the author of the poem *Świteż* on which, according to Schumann, the F major Ballade was based. Chopin became acquainted with him in Paris, and played the piano at his home about 1835.

Precz z moich oczu! Posłucham od razu!
Precz z mego serca! I serce posłucha.

Out of my sight! I shall obey at once!
Out of my heart! And my heart will obey.

Precz z mej pamięci! Nie! tego rozkazu
Moja i twoja pamięć nie posłucha.

Out of my memory! No! This order my memory and yours will not obey.

Jak cień tym dłuższy gdy padnie z daleka,
Tym szerzej koło żałobne roztoczy,

As the shadow is so much longer when it falls from a distance,
as the sad circle spreads so much wider,

Tak moja postać, im dalej ucieka,
Tym grubszym kirem twą pamięć pomroczy.

so my being runs farther away,
with so much thicker a shroud your memory darkens.

Na każdym miejscu i o każdej dobie,

In every place and during every day and night,

Gdziem z tobą płakał, gdziemsię z tobą bawił,

where with you I wept, where with you I played,

Wszędzie i zawsze będę ja przy tobie,

everywhere and for ever I shall be by you,

Bom wszędzie cząstkę mej duszy zostawił.

for everywhere I left a piece of my soul.

5. *Poseł* (*The Messenger*) op. 74, no. 7. 1830 (Stefan Witwicki)

The haunting melody of this strophic Song has already been quoted (Ex. 1). In addition to *Andantino*, the manuscript has the instruction *z chłopska, ale nie wesoło* (in a rustic fashion, but not gaily) which does not appear in the editions.

| | |
|---|---|
| Rośnie trawka ziółko, | The blade of grass is growing, |
| Zimne dni się mienią, | cold days are changing; |
| Ty, wierna jaskółko, | you, loyal swallow, |
| Znów przed naszą sienią. | are again in front of our passage. |
| Z tobą słońce dłużej, | With you here the sun stays longer, |
| Z tobą miłą wiosna; | With you comes pleasant spring; |
| Witaj nam z podróżyy, | greet us from your journey, |
| Śpiewaczko radosna. | gay songster. |
| | |
| Nie leć, czekaj, słowo! | Don't fly, wait, a word! |
| Może ziarnka prosisz? | Perhaps you are begging a crumb? |
| Może piosnkę nową | ⌠Perhaps you bring a new song from |
| Z cudzych stron przynosisz? | ⌡foreign parts? |
| Latasz, patrzysz wkoło | You fly, you look all around |
| Czarnymi oczyma . . . | with black eyes . . . |
| Nie patrz tak wesoło, | Don't look so gay, |
| Nie ma jej tu, nie ma! | she's not here! |
| | |
| Poszła za żołnierza, | She went after a soldier, |
| Tę rzuciła chatkę, | abandoned this cottage, |
| Koło tego krzyża | by this cross |
| Pożegnała matkę. | she said good-bye to her mother. |
| Może lecisz od niej? | Perhaps you come from her? |
| Po wiedz że mi przecie, | Then tell me, please, |
| Czy nie są tam głodni, | if they are not hungry, |
| Czy im dobrze w świecie? | if it is well with them in the world. |

6. *Wojak* (*The Warrior*) op. 74, no. 10. 1830 (Stefan Witwicki)

EX. 11

This is a vigorous Song in strophic form, but the last stanza is treated individually as part of a long and exciting coda. The fourteen-bar phrasing of the tune is noteworthy, and at the end the piano part develops enormous momentum (Ex. 11).

| | |
|---|---|
| Rży mój gniady, ziemie grzebie, | My horse neighs, paws the earth; |
| Puśćcie, czas już, czas! | let me go, it's time already, time! |
| Ciebie, ojcze, matko, ciebie, | You, father, mother, you, |
| Siostry, żegnam was! | sisters, I say good-bye to you! |
| | |
| Z wiatrem, z wiatrem! niech drżą wrogi, | With the wind, with the wind! let enemies tremble, |
| Krwawy stoczym bój! | we shall wage bloody battle! |
| Raźni, zdrowi wrócim z drogi, | Brisk, healthy, we shall come back from the journey, |
| Z wiatrem, koniu mój! | with the wind, my horse! |
| | |
| Tak, tak, dobrze! na zawody! | So, so, well! on with the contest! |
| Jeśli polec mam! | If I have to perish! |
| Koniu, sam, do tej zagrody, | Horse, alone to that cottage, |
| Wolny wróć tu sam! | come back free and alone! |
| | |
| Słyszę jeszcze sióstr wołanie, | I still hear my sisters calling; |
| Zwróć się koniu, stój! | turn yourself, horse, stop! |
| Nie chcesz? Leć że, niech się stanie! | You don't want to? Run then, let it happen! |
| Leć na krwawy bój! | Run on to bloody battle! |

7. *Czary (Spells)* Complete Edition, No. 18. 1830 (Stefan Witwicki)

EX. 12

This Song was rejected by Fontana as unworthy of Chopin, and not included in opus 74. To me, however, it appears to possess considerable charm, and the ten-bar phrasing of the strophic melody is skilfully handled:

To są czary, pewno czary!
Coś dziwnego w tym się święci;
Dobrze mówi ojciec stary,
Robię, gadam bez pamięci.

These are spells, certainly spells!
In this something strange glitters;
old father is right,
I act, I chatter without memory.

W każdym miejscu, każdą dobą
Idę w lasy czyli w jary;
Zawsze widzę ją przed sobą!
To są czary, pewno czary!

In every place, every day,
I go into the forest or into the ravine;
always I see her before me!
These are spells, certainly spells!

Czy pogoda sprawia ciszę,
Czy wiatr łamie drzew konary;

Zawsze, wszędzie głos jej słyszę!
O! to pewno, pewno czary!

Whether the weather creates a calm,
whether the wind breaks the trees'
    branches,
always, everywhere I hear her voice!
O! these are certainly, certainly
    spells!

W dzień się myślą, przy niej stawić,

W nocy kształt jej biorą mary;
Ona przy mnie w snach, na jawie:
Jestem pewny, że to czary!

During the day in thought I stand
    by her,
in the night dreams take her form;
she is by me in dreams, in daydreams:
I am certain that these are spells!

Gdy z nią śpiewam, czuję trwogę;
Gdy odejdzie, zal bez miary;

Chcę być wesół, i nie mogę!
Ani wątpić, że to czary!

When I sing with her, I feel awe;
when she goes away, sorrow without
    measure;
I want to be merry, and I can't!
Without doubt, these are spells!

Na to miłe słówko rzekła,
Przywabiła mnie do domu,
By zdradziła, by urzekła!
Ufajże tu teraz komu!

When she said a pleasant little word,
she enticed me to her home,
to betray me, to bewitch me!
Trust anybody here now!

Lecz czekajcie, mam ja rade,
Po miesiacu znajde ziele;
A gdy zdrada splace zdrade,

Bedzie, musi byc wesele!

But you wait, I have a remedy:
after a month I'll find a herb;
and when with betrayal I pay back
    betrayal,
there will, there must be a wedding!

8. *Smutna rzeka (Sad river)* op. 74, no. 3. 1831 (Stefan Witwicki)

Though not one of the best songs, this has a spacious and poignant strophic melody. One of its phrases has already been quoted (Exx. 3 and 4). The D sharp in this passage is also a piece of musical rhetoric worth pointing out:

| Rzeko z cudzoziemców strony, | River from foreign regions, |
|---|---|
| Czemu nurt twój tak zmącony? | why is your current so murky? |
| Czy się gdzie zapadły brzegi, | Has the bank fallen in somewhere, |
| Czy stopniały stare śniegi? | have old snows melted? |
| | |
| Leżą w górach stare śniegi, | The old snows lie on the mountains, |
| Kwiatem kwitną moje brzegi, | flowers bloom on my banks, |
| Ale tam, przy żródle moim, | but there, by my spring, |
| Płacze matka nad mym zdrojem. | a mother weeps at my spring. |
| | |
| Siedem córek piastowała, | Seven daughters she has brought up, |
| Siedem córek zakopała, | seven daughters she has buried, |
| Siedem córek śród ogrodu, | seven daughters in the middle of the garden, |
| | |
| Głowami przeciwko wschodu. | with their heads facing the east. |
| | |
| Teraz się zduchami wita, | Now she greets their ghosts, |
| O wygody dziatki pyta | she asks the children about their comfort, |
| | |
| I mogiły ich polewa, | and she waters their graves |
| I żałośne pieśni śpiewa. | and sings pitiful songs. |

9. *Narzeczony (The Bridegroom)* op. 74, no. 15. 1831 (Stefan Witwicki)

In spite of its swiftness, the tune of this fine Song has a skilfully achieved poise, as is shown by the last ten of its fourteen bars:

EX. 14

In the last stanza the cadence is modified.

Wiatr zaszumiał między krzewy,          A wind rustled among the shrubs,
Nie w czas, nie w czas, koniu!          too late, too late, my horse!
Nie w czas, chłopcze czarnobrewy,       Too late, black-browed lad,
Lecisz tu, po błoniu.                   do you run here across the meadow.

Czy nie widzisz tam nad lasem           Do you not see there over the forest
Tego kruków stada?                      that flock of ravens,
Jak podleci, krąży czasem               how they fly up, circle sometimes
I w las znów zapada?                    and into the forest again sink down?

Gdzieżeś, gdzieżeś, dziewczę hoże?      Where are you, where are you,
                                            high-spirited girl?
Czemuż nie wybieży?                     Why don't they pair off?
Jakże, jakże wybiec może,              How, how can she pair off,
Kiedy w grobie leży?                   when in the grave she lies?

O, puszczajcie! żal mnie tłoczy,        O, leave me alone! grief hems me in,
Niech zobaczę onę!                     let me see her!
Czy konając piękne oczy                ⎧When she died did she turn her
Zwróciła w mą stronę?                  ⎩beautiful eyes in my direction?

Gdy usłyszy me wołanie,                 When she hears my call,
Płacz mój nad swą głową,                my lament over her head,
Może z trumny jeszcze wstanie,         perhaps from the coffin she will yet
                                            rise,
Zacznie żyć na nowo!                    will start to live again!

10. *Piośnka litewska* (*Lithuanian song*) op. 74, no. 16. 1831 (Ludwik Osiński)

The text of this charming through-composed ballad is by Ludwik Osiński. In his section on Chopin's poets, Maurice Brown,[2] through some momentary aberration, attributes it to Witwicki, who merely quoted it in the notes to the first edition of his *Pastoral Songs*. In Brown's actual index (no. 63) the attribution is correct, though here the name is given in its genitive form.

| | |
|---|---|
| Bardzo raniuchno wschodziło słoneczko, | The little sun rises very early, |
| Mama przy szklannym okienku siedziała, | the mother was sitting by the little glass window, |
| 'Skądże to,' pyta, 'powracasz córeczko? | 'From where,' she asks, 'are you coming back, little daughter? |
| Gdzieś twój wianeczek na głowie zmaczała?' | Where did you get your garland on your head wet?' |
| 'Kto tak raniuchno musi wodę nosić, Nie dziw, że może swój wianeczek zrosić.' | 'If one must carry water so early, no wonder that it can bedew one's garland.' |
| | |
| 'Ej, zymślasz, dziecię! Tyś zapewne w pole Z twoim młodzianem gawędzić pobiegła.' | 'Eh, you invent, child! You certainly ran to the field for a chat with your young man.' |
| 'Prawda, matusiu, prawdę wyznać wolę, | 'True, little mother, in truth I want to confess, |
| Mojegom w polu młodziana spostrzegła, | I spotted my young man in the field. |
| Kilka chwil tylko zeszło na rozmowie, | A few moments only I spent in conversation; |
| Tymczasem wianek zrosił się na głowie.' | meanwhile the garland became dewy on my head.' |

11. *Pierścień* (*The Ring*) op. 74, no. 14. 1836 (Stefan Witwicki)

Musical symbolism is always a subjective matter, but it is hard not to detect it in the morbid involution of this Song's melody, which inevitably suggests the circularity of a ring:

[2] Maurice Brown op. cit.

EX. 15

Every one of these first eight bars is centred on the mediant, which fulfils a similar function to the dominant in Schubert's *Die liebe Farbe* in underlining the obsessive, persistent sadness of the words.

The manuscript, reproduced by Binental,[3] does not give the opening four bars which serve as prelude in the editions: it has them only as postlude, and with B flat, not C flat or B, in the second bar.

| | |
|---|---|
| Smutno niańki ci śpiewały, | Sadly nannies sang to you, |
| A ja już kochałem, | and I already loved you, |
| A na lewy palec mały | and for your left little finger |
| Srebrny pierścień dałem. | a silver ring I gave you. |
| | |
| Pobrali dziewczęta drudzy, | Others have married girls, |
| Ja wiernie kochałem, | I faithfully loved; |
| Przyszedł młody chłopiec cudzy, | there came a young lad, a stranger, |
| Choć ja pierścień dalem. | though I gave a ring. |
| | |
| Muzykantów zaproszono, | Musicians were invited, |
| Na godach śpiewałem! | at the wedding I sang! |
| Innego zostałaś żoną, | To another you became a wife, |
| Ja zawsze kochałem. | I still loved. |
| | |
| Dziś dziewczęta mnie wyśmiały, | Today the girls jeered at me, |
| Gorzko zapłakałem: | bitterly I wept: |
| Próżnom wierny był i stały, | in vain have I been faithful and constant, |
| Próżno pierścień dałem. | in vain did I give a ring. |

12. *Śpiew grobowy* (*Hymn from the tomb*) op. 74, no. 17. 1836 (Wincenty Pol)

This Song was not included in the original edition by Fontana, but was

---

[3] Chopin: on the 120th anniversary of his birth. Documents and souvenirs. (Warsaw, 1930.)

incorporated in opus 74 by Schlesinger of Berlin in 1872. It was believed at the time to be by Chopin. Arguments have subsequently been advanced against its authenticity, but its expressive quality is Chopinesque, in the manner of the larger dramatic pieces. As an example, the mysterious E flat minor passage may be cited:

EX. 16

The poem is by Wincenty Pol, a soldier-poet and patriot who lived from 1809 to 1876.

| | |
|---|---|
| Leci liście z drzewa, | Leaves are falling from the tree, |
| Co wyrosło wolne! | which grew up free! |
| Znad mogiły śpiewa | Over the grave sings |
| Jakieś ptaszę polne. | some bird of the field. |
| | |
| Nie było, nie było, | It was not, it was not |
| Polsko, dobrze tobie! | well for you, Poland! |
| Wszystko się prześniło, | Everything has vanished into air, |
| A twe dzieci w grobie. | and your children are in the grave. |
| | |
| Popalone sioła, | Burnt-out hamlets, |
| Rozwalone miasta, | ruined cities, |
| A w polu dokoła | and in the field all around |
| zawodzi niewiasta. | laments a woman. |
| | |
| Wszyscy poszli z domu, | Everyone went out from the house, |
| Wzięli z sobą kosy, | they took with them scythes; |
| Robić nie ma komu, | there is no one to work, |
| W polu giną kłosy. | in the field the corn perishes. |
| | |
| Kiedy pod Warszawa | When by Warsaw |
| Dziatwa się zbierała, | a multitude has gathered itself, |
| Zdało się, że z sławą | it may be that with glory |
| Wyjdzie Polska cała. | the whole of Poland will emerge. |

| | |
|---|---|
| Bili zimę całą, | They fought a whole winter, |
| Bili się przez lato, | they fought through the summer, |
| Lecz w jesieni zato | but in the autumn, then |
| I dziatwy nie stało. | the supply of men was not enough. |
| | |
| Skończyły się boje, | The battles have ended, |
| Ale pusta praca, | but in vain was the work, |
| Bo w zagony swoje | because to their furrows |
| Nikt z braci nie wraca. | none of the brotherhood comes back. |
| | |
| Jednych ziemia gniecie, | Some of them the earth crushes, |
| A inni w niewoli, | and others are in slavery, |
| A inni po świecie | and others throughout the world |
| Bez chaty i roli. | are without a hut or land. |
| | |
| Ni pomocy z nieba, | No help from heaven, |
| Ani ludzkiej ręki, | nor from a human hand; |
| Pusta leży gleba, | empty lies the soil, |
| Darmo kwitną wdzięki. | in vain the bloom of youth charms. |
| | |
| Leci liście z drzewa, | Leaves are falling from the tree, |
| Znów leci z drzewa, | again are falling from the tree, |
| | |
| O polska kraino, | O Polish land, |
| gdyby ci rodacy, | if only those fellow-countrymen |
| co za ciebie giną | who perish for you |
| wzięli się do pracy | betook themselves to work |
| | |
| I po garstce ziemi | ⎰and took just a handful of earth |
| Z ojczyzny zabrali, | ⎱from their country, |
| Już by dłońmi swymi | already with their own palms |
| Polskę usypali. | they would raise Poland up. |
| | |
| Lecz wybić się siłą | But to strike out with strength, |
| To dla nas już dziwy, | this for us is already a marvel, |
| Bo zdrajców przybyło, | because there was an influx of traitors, |
| A lud zbyt poczciwy. | and the people are too good-hearted. |

13. *Moja pieszczotka* (*My darling*) op. 74, no. 12. 1837 (Adam Mickiewicz)

This beautifully finished large-scale mazurka has an ABA form with a long coda—more than a third of the length of the Song—in which the vocal line is handled with remarkable flexibility. Ex. 17 shows the beginning of the Song from which everything develops with complete naturalness.

EX. 17

This is in every way the most impressive of the dance-style songs.

| | |
|---|---|
| Moja pieszczotka, gdy w wesołej chwili | When in a gay moment my darling |
| Pocznie szczebiotać i kwilić, i gruchać, | stops chirping and murmuring and cooing, |
| Tak mile grucha, szczebioce i kwili, | so pleasantly she coos, chirps, and murmurs, |
| Że nie chcąc słówka żadnego postradać | so not wanting to lose even one word |
| Nie śmiem przerywać, nie śmiem odpowiadać | I dare not interrupt, I dare not answer back |
| I tylko chciałbym słuchać! | and I'd only want to listen! |
| | |
| Lecz mowy żywość gdy oczki zapali | But when the liveliness of speech lights up little eyes |
| I pocznie mocniej jagody różować, | and starts more strongly to turn cheeks rosy, |
| Perłowe ząbki błysną śród korali; | and pearly little teeth glitter among the coral; |
| Ach! wtenczas śmielej w oczęta poglądam, | ah! then I dare to gaze into her eyes, |
| Usta pomykam i słuchać nie żądam, | I close her mouth and I do not ask to listen, |
| Tylko całować! | only to kiss! |

14. *Wiosna* (*Spring*) op. 74, no. 2. 1838 (Stefan Witwicki)

Chopin himself, as well as Liszt, made a pianotranscription of this Song, and there are five manuscripts of his transcript ion ranging in date from April 1838 to September 1848. But in spite of his obvious enthusiasm for it, it is one of the least interesting songs, with only one chromatic twist in the melody to save it from complete ordinariness.

| | |
|---|---|
| Błyszczą krople rosy, | Dewdrops shine, |
| Mruczy zdrój po błoni, | the brook murmurs in the meadow, |
| Ukryta we wrzosy | hidden in heather |
| Gdzieś jałówka dzwoni. | somewhere a heifer's bell rings. |
| | |
| Piękną, miłą błonią | The beautiful, pleasant meadow |
| Leci wzrok wesoło, | rests on the gaze gaily, |
| Wkoło kwiaty wonią, | all around the flowers are fragrant, |
| Kwitną gaje wkoło. | the groves are flowering all around. |
| | |
| Paś się, błąkaj trzódko, | Graze then, wander, cattle; |
| Ja pod skałą siędę, | I sit under a rock, |
| Piosnkę lubą, słodką | a sweet, pleasant song |
| Śpiewać sobie będę. | I will sing to myself. |
| | |
| Ustroń miła cicha! | The pleasant brook is quiet. |
| Jakiś żal wpamięci, | With some regret in the memory |
| Czegoś serce wzdycha, | the heart sighs a little, |
| Woku łza się kręci. | in the eye a tear wells up. |
| | |
| Łza wybiegła z oka, | The tear has fallen from the eye, |
| Ze mną strumyk śpiewa, | with me the little brook sings, |
| Do mnie się z wysoka | to me from above |
| Skowronek odzywa. | the lark responds. |
| | |
| Lot rozwija chyży, | His swift flight unfolds, |
| Ledwo widny oku, | scarcely visible to the eye, |
| Coraz wyżej, wyżej . . . | gradually higher, higher . . . |
| Zginął już w obłoku. | he is lost already in the sky. |
| | |
| Ponad pola, niwy, | Above ploughland and cornfield |
| Jeszcze pioskę głosi | he still proclaims his song, |
| I śpiew ziemi tkliwy | { and he carries his tender song of |
| W niebo aż zanosi! | { the earth up into the sky. |

15. *Dumka (Elegy)* Complete Edition, No. 19. 1840 (Josef Zaleski)

This tiny Song was discovered by Stanisław Lam in an album that belonged to Witwicki, and it was published in the daily paper *Słowo Polskie* in Lwów in 1910. It is a simple strophic setting of the first and third stanzas of the poem set in full five years later and given below under *Nie ma czego trzeba* (no. 18). It cannot compare in impact with the later version.

The author of the poem, Josef Bohdan Zaleski (1802–86), was dubbed 'the Ukrainian Nightingale' by Mickiewicz, with whom he enjoyed a close friendship in Paris in the 1830s. His poetry has been described as possessing 'the wild charm, the mystic music, of the Steppes'.

16. *Śliczny chłopiec* (*Handsome lad*) op. 74, no. 8. 1841 (Josef Zeleski)
This is another elegant mazurka, with a subtly displaced rhythm in the cadence:

EX. 18

| | |
|---|---|
| Wzniosły, smukły i młody. | Upstanding, slender, and young, |
| O! nie lada urody. | O! no ordinary beauty. |
|   Ślicznyż chłopiec, czego chcieć? |   Handsome lad, what more could you want? |
|   Czarny wąsik, biała płeć! |   Black moustache, white complexion! |
| | |
| Niech się spóźni godzinę, | Let him be an hour late, |
| To mi tęskno, aż ginę. | it makes me long for him fit to die. |
|   Ślicznyż etc. | |
| | |
| Ledwie murugnie oczyma, | If he barely winks with his eyes |
| Radość całą mnie ima. | joy wholly seizes me. |
|   Ślicznyż etc. | |
| | |
| Każde słówko co powie | Every word that is said |
| Lgnie mi w sercu i w głowie. | sticks in my heart and in my head. |
|   Ślicznyż etc. | |
| | |
| Gdy pląsamy we dwoje, | When we dance, we two, |
| Patrzą na nas ócz roje. | they watch us. |
|   Ślicznyż etc. | |

On powiedział mi przecie,         He told me, still,
Żem mu wszystkim na świecie!      that to him I am everything in the
Ślicznyż etc.                     world.


17. *Dwojaki koniec* (*Double ending*) op. 74, no. 11. 1845 (Josef Zaleski)

The melodic elegance of this strophic Song is more than its dull
words deserve. Chopin has turned an indiscriminate moan into a
neatly turned little elegy:


EX. 19

Rok się kochali, a wiek się nie        For a year they loved each other, and
   widzieli,                               for an age they did not see each other,
Zbolały serca, oboje na pościeli.      their hearts ached, both of them, in
                                          their beds.

Leży dziewczyna w komnacie swej        The girl lies in her room on the bed,
   na łożu,
A kozak leży w dąbrowie na             and the cossack lies in a glade at the
   rozdrożu!                              crossroads!
O! nad dziewczyną rodźiny całej        O! over the girl the whole family
   płacze,                                weeps,
A nad kozakiem, och! siwy orzeł        and over the cossack, oh! a grey eagle
   kracze.                                croaks.
Oboje biedni, wnętrzności ogień        Both of them wretched, fire burns
   pali!                                  their entrails!
Cierpieli srodze, cierpieli i          They suffered cruelly, they suffered
   skonali.                               and died.
O! nad dziewczyną po siole dzwony      O! over the girl all around the village
   biją,                                  bells ring,
A nad kozakiem po lesie wilki wyją.    and over the cossack all around the
                                          forest wolves bay.

Kości dziewczyny grób zamknął          The bones of the girl a blessed grave
   poświęcony,                            encloses,
Kości kozaka bieleją na wsze           the bones of the cossack grow white
   strony.                                on all sides.

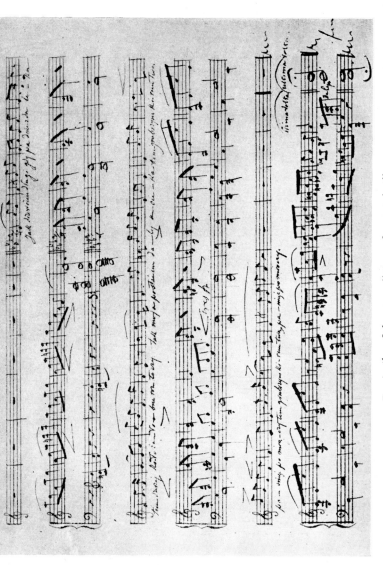

Facsimile of the song "Out of my sight!"
(Maria Wodzinska's Album: State Collection, Warsaw)
Autograph destroyed

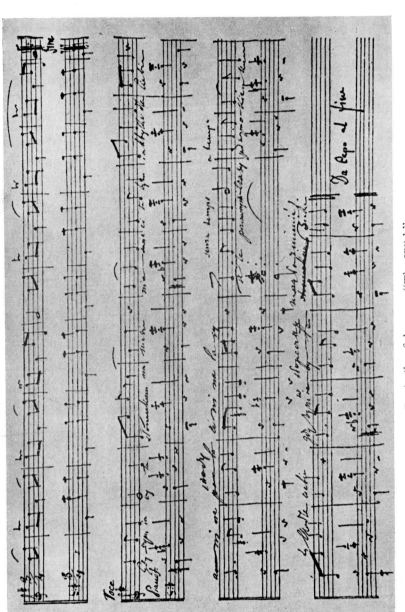

Facsimile of the song "The Wish"
(Maria Wodzinska's Album: State Collection, Warsaw)

18. *Nie ma czego trzeba* (*There is no need*) op. 74, no. 13. 1845 (Josef Zaleski)

(This Song, like the earlier setting of a portion of the same poem, is sometimes called *Dumka*.)

*Nie ma czego trzeba* is perhaps Chopin's most moving song, with an eloquent vocal line set off by a simple and well-spaced accompaniment:

EX. 20

On the last word of each stanza the voice rises to a poignant melisma.

| | |
|---|---|
| Mgła mi do oczu zawiewa z łona, | Mist drifts towards my eyes from my breast, |
| W prawo i w lewo ćmi naokoło; | on the right and on the left darkens all around; |
| Dumka na ustach brząknie i skona! | an elegy on the lips sounds and dies! |
| Niemo, och! niemo, bo niewesoło. | Dumb, oh dumb, because it is not gay. |
| Nie ma bo, nie ma czego potrzeba! | For there is no need! |
| Dawno mi tutaj nudno, niemiło: | A long time I have endured misery and sorrow here: |
| Ni mego słońca! ni mego nieba! | I have no sun, no sky, |
| Ni mego czegoś! czym serce żyło. | nothing by which the heart lives. |
| Kochać i śpiewać było by błogo! | To love and to sing would be blissful! |
| W cudzej tu pustce śniłbym jak w domu: | Here in the foreign desert I dream as at home: |

C–H

| | |
|---|---|
| Kochać, o, kochać! i nie ma kogo! | To love, oh, to love! and there is no one to love! |
| Śpiewać, o, śpiewać! i nie ma komu! | To sing, oh, to sing! and there is no one to sing to! |
| | |
| Niekiedy wzrokiem ku niebu wiercę, | Sometimes with my gaze I penetrate to the heavens, |
| Poświstom wiatru wcale nie łaję: | the whistling wind I scold not at all: |
| Zimno, o! zimno, lecz puka serce, | it's cold, oh cold, but the heart beats, |
| Ze z dumka w insze odlecim kraje! | so with an elegy we'll fly away to other countries! |

### 19. *Melodia* (*Melody*) op. 74, no. 9. 1847 (Zygmunt Kraskiński)

Chopin's last Song forms a worthy conclusion to the series. The composer is hardly likely to have been acquainted with Beethoven's *Fidelio*, but the words of the poem make the similarity of the piano's opening phrase to the accompaniment of the Prisoners' Chorus all the more remarkable:

This through-composed Song is exceptionally free and wide-ranging in melody and harmony, and it ends with a moment of high poetry:

The text is by Count Zygmunt Kraskiński (1812–59), a friend of Mickiewicz. His mysticism acted strongly on Chopin's inspiration here. If *Nie ma czego trzeba* is the most moving of the songs, *Melodia* is the most beautiful.

| | |
|---|---|
| Z gór, gdzie dźwigali str asznych krzyżów brzemię, | From the hills, where they carried the load of nightmarish crosses, |
| Widzieli z dala obiecaną ziemię. | they saw from a distance the promised land. |
| Widzieli światło niebieskich promieni, | They saw light's heavenly rays, |
| Ku którym w dole ciągnęło ich plemię, | towards which in the valley their tribe was dragging its load, |
| A sami do tych nie wejdą przestrzeni! | though some of them will not enter those infinite spaces! |
| Do godów życia nigdy nie zasiędą, | To the comforts of life they will never sit down, |
| I nawet może zapomnieni będą. | and even, perhaps, they will be forgotten. |

The special genius of Chopin's piano music is the way it seems to grow out of the very nature of the instrument. The same cannot be claimed for his vocal music; but the songs, though not fully exploiting the technical resources of a first-class singer, are all gratefully written for the voice. A group of the smaller ones would be a charming addition to many recital programmes, since the emotions they express, though small in scale, are conveyed with sensitive and genuinely musical discernment; and the best ones—pre-eminently *Nie ma czego trzeba* and *Melodia*—are far too good for the neglect they have fallen into. These two songs at least can hold up their heads in the best company there is in the repertoire.

HUMPHREY SEARLE

# Miscellaneous Works

CHOPIN'S 'miscellaneous' works fall into three categories: works for piano and orchestra, chamber music works and works for piano solo. Most of them are early works, written before Chopin decided to confine himself almost entirely to writing for piano alone, but some were written late in his life, and even the early works include many of great interest. Chopin matured very early as a composer, unlike his friend and almost exact contemporary Liszt. He was composing from the age of 7 onwards, and many of the works written in his teens already show surprising accomplishment.

## Piano and Orchestra

All his works for piano and orchestra, including the two concertos, were composed before his arrival in Paris at the age of 21: in those days every pianist-composer was expected to write works for himself to play with orchestra, usually variations on popular operatic themes or folk-songs, and so it is not surprising that Chopin's published op. 2 (though, of course, not his second composition: Arthur Hedley in his study of Chopin lists some twenty-five earlier works) should be a set of brilliant variations for piano and orchestra on 'Là ci darem la mano' from Mozart's *Don Giovanni*. This was written in 1827, when Chopin was 17 and on holiday at a country place near Poznán: he performed it with orchestra at his first concert in Vienna two years later, and it was one of the works which brought him widespread fame. The Viennese music publisher Haslinger quickly brought out the score; Chopin gave numerous successful performances of the work in many European towns, and in 1831 the music critic of the Leipzig *Neue Zeitschrift für Musik*, the 21-year-old Robert Schumann, published the famous article on the work which culminated in the words 'Hats off, gentlemen! A genius!' He also persuaded Clara Wieck to perform it in Leipzig in July 1832.

The work, which is dedicated to Chopin's friend and confidant Titus Woyciechowski, consists of an introduction, five variations and a finale. The slow introduction is mainly based on the first bar of the theme, and gives the solo pianist ample opportunity for display; he also states the theme, here transposed to B flat.[1] This consists of the $\frac{2}{4}$ section of the duet—not the whole of it, which Liszt used as a basis for variations in his *Réminiscences de Don Juan*—and is followed at the end of the theme and of each variation by a short orchestral ritornello. Most of the variations contain an extremely elaborate piano part, and the fifth variation, an Adagio in B flat minor, is highly dramatic. In the finale the theme is transformed into a brilliant Polacca. Schumann in his review attempted to interpret the different variations by reference to various episodes in Mozart's opera, but it seems hardly likely that Chopin was deliberately intending to write a 'programme-piece' in this work, however much he may have been affected by his knowledge of *Don Giovanni* and his love of Mozart. The Variations do not, of course, display the originality of Chopin's later works—one can hardly expect that they should—but they are certainly an enormous improvement on the similar works by his contemporaries Kalkbrenner, Herz and so on, and go a long way to justify Schumann's panegyric.

The same may be said of Chopin's two succeeding works for piano and orchestra, the *Fantaisie sur des airs nationaux polonais*, op. 13, and the *Krakowiak, Grand Rondeau de Concert*, op. 14. These were both written in 1828, a year after the Variations, while Chopin was completing his third and final year under his master Elsner. The Fantasy was first

[1] Mozart's original is in A major. ED.

performed by the composer in Warsaw in 1830, together with the first
performance of his F minor Concerto, and was an immediate success:
it remained one of his most popular works during the early part of his
career. Chopin reported after a concert in Warsaw in 1830: 'This time
I understood myself, the orchestra understood what I was doing, and
the public understood, too. For once the final mazurka called forth
terrific applause. I had to appear four times to bow my thanks.' The
work consists of a slow introduction, again with brilliant passage-work
for the soloist, followed by a melody in $\frac{6}{8}$ time, 'Już miesiąc zaszedl'
('Already the moon had set'), to the words of the pastoral 'Laura and
Filon' by Kurpiński, given as a folk-song by W. Sowiński in 'Les
Musiciens polonais'.

EX. I

This is then subjected to variation, some of it quite brilliant: next
comes a $\frac{2}{4}$ allegretto, described as 'Theme de Charles Kurpiński',[2] in
F sharp minor, somewhat melancholy in character.

EX. 2

This too is varied by the soloist: the final section, the Kujawiak, is
the mazurka referred to by Chopin in his letter, and it is certainly a
brilliant and exciting piece. Here is an account of a member of the
audience at Chopin's Warsaw concert.

> 'His gayest melodies are tinged with a certain melancholy by the
> power of which he draws the listener along with him . . .
> Chopin knows what sounds are heard in our fields and woods, he
> has listened to the songs of the Polish villager, he has made it his
> own, and has united the tunes of his native soil in skilful composi-
> tion and elegant execution.'[3]

[2] Karol Kurpiński (1785–1857), violinist, composer and professor at the Warsaw
Conservatoire.
[3] See Arthur Hedley, op. cit.

This last sentence perhaps gives the clue to Chopin's approach: instead of the direct down-to-earthness of the folk-song arrangements of Bartók (who indeed went so far as to suggest that Chopin had no real contact with the true folk-music of Polish peasants), we have a combination of Chopin's real feeling for Polish folk-music with his innate sensitivity and elegance, which could not help throwing a veil of sophistication over his material, however close he tried to get to the soil. He did indeed aim to 'get to the heart of our national music', as he himself put it: but he used actual Polish folk-songs very rarely in his works, preferring to regard them as a point of departure from which he could embody them in a more sophisticated form.

The *Krakowiak* Rondo was first performed by Chopin at his second concert in Vienna, on 18 August 1829, together with the Variations, op. 2. He had intended to play it at his first concert a week earlier, but the badly written orchestral parts made it impossible to rehearse it in time. It was well received, except by the 'petrified Germans' (Chopin's words) and he repeated it as his second Warsaw concert the following year. It is again primarily a virtuoso piece, beginning with an introduction in $\frac{3}{4}$ time, mainly in the style of a mazurka, before going into the $\frac{2}{4}$ Rondo, based on the rhythms of the popular dance of the Cracow region. This has two main themes which alternate in the normal manner, the first in F major and the second in D minor on its first appearance; they are separated by a good deal of brilliant passage-work.

EX. 3

Chopin's most successful work for piano and orchestra, apart from the two concertos, is the Andante spianato and Grande Polonaise Brillante op. 22, though it is something of a hybrid. The Polonaise was written first, in 1830–1, before Chopin's arrival in Paris: the Andante dates from 1834, and thus belongs to his mature period—by this time he had

written the Studies, op. 10, and the B minor Scherzo, among other
works. Chopin performed the Andante spianato and Polonaise at one of
his last public appearances in Paris, on 26 April 1835, and won great
success with the Polonaise, though he had realized by now that the
Parisian public did not really appreciate his mature music, and there-
after he very rarely performed at large public concerts. The Andante
spianato ('level' or 'even') is for piano solo: as Arthur Hedley rightly
remarks, it is an idyll rather than a nocturne, a quiet rippling piece in
G major, $\frac{6}{8}$, with a more chordal trio in C major, $\frac{3}{4}$, which still keeps the
same quiet atmosphere. After a brief return of the $\frac{6}{8}$ Andante and a
final reference to the Trio, the orchestra enters with a short bridge
passage which modulates to the E flat major tonality of the Polonaise.
This is in Chopin's earlier brilliant style, but is by no means a bad
example of it, and many critics have been unduly harsh to it. The main
melodic interest is, as usual, in the solo piano part, and the opening
theme is very characteristic of Chopin at this period.

EX. 4

The central section, in C minor, has a rather more 'Polish' atmosphere,
and the work has a brilliant and effective ending.

## Chamber Works

Apart from the Cello Sonata, op. 65, Chopin's chamber works were
written in his earlier period, either for his friends to play or for performance at fashionable soirées. Thus the Variations for Flute and
Piano were written as early as 1824, when Chopin was only 14. The
theme is taken from Rossini's opera *La Cenerentola* (the finale 'Della
fortuna istabile', no. 12), and it has been suggested that the Variations
were written either for Chopin's father Nicholas or his friend Jan
Matuszynski to play, though another source suggests that they were
composed for the flautist Cichocki. The theme itself is a simple one, and
so are the four variations, the melodic interest remaining entirely
in the flute part, which is certainly effectively written, while the piano
has only accompanying chords. The piece was not published till 1955.

EX. 5

A more mature and interesting work is the Trio in G minor for piano, violin and cello, op. 8, which was written in 1828–9, and is dedicated to Prince Antoine Radziwill, an admirer of Chopin's who was himself a composer and cellist. Later, in 1830, Chopin wondered whether he should have written it for viola rather than violin, 'as the first string predominates in the violin, and in my trio is hardly used at all. The viola would, I think, accord better with the cello.' It is true that the colouring of the Trio is somewhat dark on the whole, but the work is perfectly effective in performance and is one of the most interesting of Chopin's earlier works. It is written in the usual four movements, with the Scherzo coming second: the piano writing is, of course, very much more elaborate than in the flute variations, but not so much so as to overshadow the other two instruments. The first movement, Allegro con fuoco, is strong and dramatic, and is written in the normal sonata form: the Scherzo, marked Con moto, ma non troppo, is more lyrical in style. It contains a device which Chopin was to use on a larger scale in some of his later works, notably the first movement of the B minor sonata: the 'development' section of the Scherzo begins with its opening theme, but this does not reappear at the beginning of the reprise, which starts with the second phrase. The Trio, in C major, is also lyrical in feeling: the Adagio sostenuto is remarkable for the contrast—one can almost say struggle—between the dramatic opening phrase and the expressive main theme which appears in the fifth bar.

EX. 6

This dramatic phrase dominates the central section of the movement, and at the end it prevents the expected quiet restatement of the main theme by its constant interjections, remaining prominent to the last in the bass of the piano. The finale, Allegretto, is more in Chopin's

Polish style, a kind of *Krakowiak*, brilliant and gay in spite of its G minor tonality: here the piano writing becomes somewhat more elaborate. As a whole the Trio is not only an interesting and fully assured work, but it certainly deserves to take its place in the chamber-music repertoire.

The Introduction and Polonaise Brillante for cello and piano, op. 3, dates from a visit by Chopin to Prince Radziwill's estate at Antonin near Poznán in the autumn of 1829: the Polonaise was written at that time, and the slow introduction followed a few months later. Chopin wrote to his friend Woyciechowski:

> 'It is nothing more than a brilliant drawing-room piece suitable for the ladies. I should like Princess Wanda (Prince Radziwill's daughter) to practise it. I was supposed to give her lessons. She is a beautiful girl of seventeen, and it was charming to direct her delicate fingers.'

Wanda played the work with her father at Antonin, but Chopin actually dedicated the work to the Warsaw cellist Joseph Merk (1795–1852), whose playing he much admired. It is certainly no more than an effective piece, well laid out for the cello and with some brilliant piano writing, though the 'second subject' in F major is more typical of Chopin.

EX. 7

Much the same may be said of the Grand Duo in E major, on themes from Meyerbeer's *Robert le Diable* for piano and cello, which Chopin wrote in 1832 in collaboration with the cellist Auguste Franchomme. (This was also published in a version for piano duet, with Chopin's fingering, as op. 15, a number which properly belongs to the Nocturnes in F major, F sharp major and G minor.) In 1831 Chopin had been dazzled by Meyerbeer's *Robert le Diable*, but by 1849 he could scarcely sit through *Le Prophète*. At any rate, the Duo, of which Schumann also gave an over-favourable review, can scarcely be regarded as anything more than elegant salon music. Franchomme (1808–84) was a cellist in the Paris Opéra Orchestra and later in that of the Théâtre Italien: it seems likely that his contribution to this work was more in the nature of technical advice than actual composition, for the style of the writing is exactly the same as that of Chopin's other salon pieces of the period. However, Chopin greatly appreciated Franchomme, both as cellist and friend: his late Cello Sonata is dedicated 'À son ami A. Franchomme', and Franchomme took part in Chopin's last Paris concert, when the composer was already in failing health, on 16 February 1848. The Duo consists of a slow introduction in C sharp minor, $\frac{3}{4}$, with an elaborate piano part, an Andantino in E major, also in $\frac{3}{4}$, and a $\frac{6}{8}$ Allegretto in A major which is briefly interrupted by a slower Andante cantabile. Among the themes used are the Romanza, Act I, the chorus 'Non pietà', Act I, and the Terzetto 'Le mie cure ancor del cielo', Act V.

As a transition to Chopin's works for solo piano his Rondo in C major for two pianos may be mentioned here. It was indeed originally written for piano solo in the summer of 1828, but was rearranged for two pianos in the same year, and thus belongs to Chopin's student works, in spite of its late opus number, 73; it was not, in fact, published until after Chopin's death. Chopin, writing to Woyciechowski on 9 September 1828, says that he had made the rearrangement during the summer and adds: 'Today I tried it with Ernemann, at Buchholtz, and it came out pretty well.' By arranging the work for two pianos Chopin was able to add a number of effective antiphonal effects, and also to make the texture slightly more elaborate, though nowhere is it thick or heavy. The Rondo, in fact, is a very charming piece and a valuable contribution to the two-piano repertoire, which even today is not as rich as it might be. In spite of its early date it shows great accomplishment and is very much more than a mere salon piece. After a short introduction in $\frac{4}{4}$ time, marked Allegro maestoso, the Rondo itself begins in $\frac{2}{4}$ time with the main theme announced by the first piano and repeated by the second. The Rondo is in the usual A B A C A form, with the second group of themes appearing first in A minor and for the second time in E minor.

### Solo Piano

Chopin's 'miscellaneous' works for solo piano were written in a variety of forms. Among the earliest is the set of variations on the

German national air, *Der Schweizerbub* (The Cattleboy[4]), which appears
to date originally from about 1826, though it may have been revised
later. At any rate, it was among the works which Chopin sent to
the Viennese publisher Haslinger in 1829, together with the 'Là ci
darem' Variations and the Sonata in C minor; however, Haslinger did
not publish it until after Chopin's death. The theme is a Tyrolean
folk-song which was first published in 1822; the variations are dedicated to the wife of General J. Sowiński, and were apparently written
at her house, 'in a few quarter hours'. They begin with a slow introduction, containing some elaborate piano writing; then follows the
theme, a fairly naive tonic-and-dominant affair, four variations and a

EX. 8

final waltz. In the fourth variation, which is in E minor, and the waltz,
Chopin does try to develop the theme into something of musical
interest, but he gets very little support from the melody itself, and the
variations hardly show him at his best.

Various smaller works date from this period. One, a Contredanse in
G flat major, was composed for Titus Woyciechowski, possibly in
1827. It is a slight but charming piece, very simple in style; the very
brief Trio (eight bars) is actually written out in the key of C flat major.
Chopin also wrote some *Écossaises* about this time, or perhaps earlier,
of which three were published after his death as op. 72; these are again
brief and slight, in some ways similar to Beethoven's *Écossaises*. The
only one which vaguely resembles Scottish music is the first.

EX. 9

A more interesting work is the Funeral March in C minor which
was also published posthumously as part of op. 72; it, too, appears to
date from 1827. This exists in two versions, that edited by Fontana and

4 Not 'The Swiss Boy' as the common mis-translation has it. ED.

published by Schlesinger in 1885 and one published in the Oxford Edition of Chopin. Of these the second, though perhaps cruder in some ways, is the more interesting, showing Chopin trying to work out novel keyboard effects which sound almost orchestral at times. The Fontana version, though 'safer', is not so individual. The following examples may serve to illustrate this.

EX. 10

In 1829 Paganini visited Warsaw and gave ten concerts between 23 May and 19 July. Chopin was as impressed by his virtuosity as were Schumann and Liszt, and the first of his studies dates from this period. He also wrote a short piece called 'Souvenir de Paganini' which is a set of variations for piano on *Le Carnaval de Venise*: this was not published till 1881. This, like his later Berceuse, is written over an ostinato bass in $\frac{6}{8}$ quavers, and continues throughout in the same mood, though the writing for the right hand is often elaborate and brilliant. This excerpt gives some idea of the style.

EX. 11

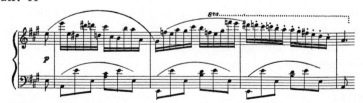

The atmosphere is calm and relaxed—a real Gondoliera—and there are very few forte passages. It is one of the most poetical of Chopin's earlier works.

The set of variations on *Je vends des scapulaires* from Hérold's *Ludovic* dates from 1833. The theme comes from Hérold's last opera, which was left unfinished at his death in 1833 and was completed by Halévy; it was produced in Paris in the same year. Chopin's Variations must have been written very rapidly, for they were published as early as November 1833 as op. 12. Early in 1834 Chopin sent his sister an album containing the Nocturnes, op. 15, which Schlesinger had just published; the album also contains a number of fantasias and variations by Pixis, Hünten and Herz on the same 'rondeau favori' from Hérold's opera. Chopin's variations are no better than these—evidently there was a demand for works of this kind. No wonder Chopin became infuriated with the Parisian public; when one thinks that Hérold and Halévy are known today by the overture to *Zampa* and by portions of *La Juive* respectively one can hardly blame him. Chopin had reached maturity by this time, and this was the last work of the kind which he composed. As usual, the work begins with an introduction which provides some brilliant passage-work for the pianist; then follows a straightforward statement of the simple tune, with a short ritornello at the end. There are three variations, of which the third is in the minor, and a final scherzando treatment of the theme.

However, 1833 also saw the composition of a more interesting work, the Bolero, op. 19. Chopin knew Auber's Spanish opera *Masaniello*, which contains a bolero, very well; it had first been performed in 1828 and was still popular in Paris. At this time Chopin could not have had any first-hand information about Spanish music; this only came later when he knew Pauline Viardot-Garcia. But the work does have a reasonably genuine Spanish atmosphere, which may well have been suggested by Auber's opera. Though it is often described as being in C major, it is only the opening section which is in this key; this is a fast, exciting section in $\frac{3}{8}$ time. With the main Bolero section the music goes into A minor and into $\frac{3}{4}$ time with a very Spanish-seeming theme.

EX. 12

Later there is a new theme in A major, and in the middle section the music modulates through a number of keys before returning to the original A minor theme: but it is the A major theme which ends the work.

From the following year, 1834, dates a short Cantabile in B flat major which is somewhat in the style of a nocturne, though it consists of only fourteen bars in $\frac{6}{8}$ time; it was not published till 1931. Probably from about the same period comes a Largo in E flat major, dated simply 'Paris, 6 juillet'. As Chopin was in Paris in early July in 1832, '34, '38, '40, '47, '49 and perhaps '33 and '36, the date is extremely uncertain. It is a short but solemn piece in $\frac{4}{4}$ time, almost religious in character, and working up to a fortissimo just before the end. It was first published in 1938 from a manuscript in the Paris Conservatoire Library.

Another occasional piece is the variation written for the collection known as 'Hexameron'; this was occasioned by a charity concert given in 1837, and for it six composers, Chopin, Liszt, Thalberg, Pixis, Czerny and Herz, each wrote a variation on the March from Bellini's *I Puritani*. Liszt appears to have been the prime mover in this enterprise. He wrote not only the second variation, but the introduction, the piano arrangement of the theme, the linking passages and the finale; later he often played the work at his concerts, in some cases with orchestral accompaniment, though he did not orchestrate the work himself. Chopin's variation is the sixth and last. Marked 'Largo', it is fairly simple in style and begins and ends quietly, though it does rise to a fortissimo in the middle section.

Chopin's Tarantella dates from 1841. Writing from Nohant to Julian Fontana in Paris that same year he says:

> 'I send you the Tarantella. Please copy it, but first go to Schlesinger, or better still to Troupenas, and see the collection of Rossini's songs published by him. In it there is a Tarantella in A [La Danza]. I do not know whether it is written on $\frac{6}{8}$ or $\frac{12}{8}$ time. As to my composition, it does not matter which way it is written, but I should prefer it to be like Rossini's.'

This question of notation hardly implies that Chopin was copying Rossini in this work: indeed, their personalities could not be more different. Without going as far as Arthur Hedley, who remarks: 'There is no Italian gaiety in the work: the composer is bent on killing or

curing the poor victim of the tarantula's bite!' one can say that Chopin
has clearly imposed his own personality on the dance-form, and the
result is a very interesting and individual piece. This is clear from the
very opening theme, with its chromatic descending bass,

EX. 13

and it continues throughout the piece, with its characteristic use of
subdominant minor harmony in such passages as these:

EX. 14 (a) and (b)

The speed increases even from its opening Presto with the return of the
main theme, and the work ends with a crescendo passage climbing
chromatically upwards to a furious climax.

Another remarkable but little-known work which dates from this
period (1841–2) is a Fugue in A minor, which, however, was not
published till 1898. The Fugue is in two parts only, and is based on this
interesting subject and countersubject:

EX. 15

In the manuscript Chopin wrote 'thème' at the beginning of the Fugue and again at the end of bar 15 in the treble, also at the transition from bar 31 to bar 32 in the bass: at the end of bar 38 and under bar 39 in the bass he wrote 'thème sous-dominante'. Over the first notes in the treble in bars 6–7, at the transition from bar 21 to bar 22 in the bass and at the transition from bar 29 to bar 30 in the treble he wrote 'réponse'. In fact, the music modulates through a variety of keys and shows great ingenuity in the treatment of its limited material. Towards the end there are two long trills on E, one in the treble for two and a half bars and one in the bass for five, followed by a statement of the subject and its inversion simultaneously.

The only other published piano piece of Chopin's which need be mentioned here is the Album Leaf in E major, written in 1843 for Countess Anna Szeremetieff. This consists of twenty bars, Moderato $\frac{4}{4}$ in E major; it is not a very characteristic piece, and was no doubt composed as a piece of politeness. It was first published in 1910.

All the works so far discussed in this chapter have been published in the complete edition of Chopin's works issued by the Chopin Institute of Warsaw. There are in addition a number of unpublished works, of which the most important are the following. Firstly, a Contrabass to a three-part canon in B minor by Mendelssohn, written on 16 April 1832. Mendelssohn called his Canon 'à 3', but his bass part is in strict canon with the three upper parts: Chopin's addition is a kind of parody written in the empty bars of Mendelssohn's bass part. Mendelssohn wrote on the manuscript: 'Contra basso libro composti di Scopino (Chopin). La basso est à vous.' There is also an Andantino in G minor, an arrangement for piano solo of the song 'Wiosna' (Spring), op. 74, no. 2, of which Chopin made no less than five versions between 1838 and

1848, probably as album leaves for friends. A Canon at the octave, probably dating from 1839, is a rough draft of about nineteen bars on this theme:

EX. 16

Finally there are two Bourrées, written down by Chopin, probably in 1846, and given a simple harmonization by him when he was at Nohant. They are supposed to be dance tunes native to Berry and were used by George Sand for the music in her play *Francois le Champi*.[5]

---

[5] For information about these unpublished works and much valuable information elsewhere I am indebted to Maurice J. E. Brown's admirable *Index of Chopin's Works* (London, rev. 1965).

ALAN WALKER

# Chopin and Musical Structure

## An Analytical Approach

I AM not concerned here with the conventional approach to musical analysis. My reasons are twofold. First: conventional analysis is descriptive. It is no part of my aim to identify self-evident 'first' and 'second' subjects, 'expositions' and 'developments'. Useful as these terms are, they are tautological: they only tell you what you hear in the music anyway. Second: I shall, from time to time, address the practising pianist. Musical analysis becomes a dead letter once the performance is forgotten. It is the player who makes music live; the more he knows about the way it hangs together, the more successful he will be in this task.

## Description and Analysis

There is an essential difference between description and analysis. Description tells you *what* is there. Analysis attempts to tell you *why* it is there. If you read that 'the first subject of Chopin's B minor Sonata is a march-like theme in the tonic key which eventually gives way to a contrasting lyrical second subject in the relative major', you have learned nothing that a single hearing of the music does not tell you more directly and more effectively. But once you have discovered *why* Chopin chose those two contrasting themes, *why*, in short, they hang together so satisfactorily, you know something of fundamental interest about the work. At the same time, you are better equipped to perform it.

Why does a great composer choose the contrasting ideas of a masterpiece to share the same framework? Why those *particular* contrasts rather than others? Why, in fact, do particular themes belong to particular movements? Why do particular movements belong to particular works? These questions are worth asking. They force one to abandon simple description; they inspire a truly analytic attitude.

## Backgrounds and Foregrounds

I should like to put forward a hypothesis about great musical structures. *All the contrasts in a masterpiece are foreground projections of a single background idea.* Masterpieces diversify a unity. Behind the shifting, kaleidoscopic variety of a great work's *manifest* music lies its *latent* idea, the inspired, unitive source which makes that variety meaningful. Analysis is a process of moving from the manifest to the latent level of music. It seeks to explain musical *foregrounds* in terms of musical *backgrounds*. In so far as it succeeds it is a reversal of the composing process which needs must move from the level of unity to that of diversity.

Now, what evidence is there to suppose that the *foreground/background* aspect of musical structure is true? Quite simply, our experience of music. There is a perceptible difference between works which hang together and works which do not. Moreover, as soon as you try to exchange different themes from different works you lose the compelling inevitability of the originals. Of course, this butchery may still allow you to retain a semblance of continuity; but this is a poor substitute for an inspired unity. Indeed, I regard the presence or absence of background unity as a criterion which enables us to distinguish between mastery and mediocrity.[1]

[1] Many analysts have never accepted the foreground-background nature of musical structure. In consequence, they often confuse unity with mere identity. For them, a work like Liszt's Sonata in B minor has greater unity than Chopin's own B minor Sonata because Liszt 'metamorphoses' his themes in the manifest foreground. Yet the Chopin Sonata conveys a far stronger sense of unity precisely because it contains greater diversity. There is no unity without contrast. It is *contrast* that is the real challenge to analysis, and without it there is little to explain. Until this fact sinks in analysis represents for many musicians a mere search for identities—a musical game of 'Snap'.

It might well be asked why I should approach Chopin, of all composers, in this way. He composed intuitively, it might be argued. Even his revision was governed by instinct. Is it possible that a composer who wrote his music out of such a profound sense of inner necessity has anything to offer musical analysis? My simple reply is: Yes. The musical intuition of a genius obeys unconscious laws. We are more likely to catch a glimpse of them in Chopin than in many other composers precisely because he worked intuitively. Paradoxically, it is the 'clever' composer, the 'intellectual' composer, who tends to be least interesting from the analytical point of view. At the slightest whiff of an inspiration he brings down the iron curtain of his intelligence and starts thinking instead of feeling. He denies his musical unconscious.

## Unity and the Performer

For the player the problem of unity within diversity is always the same: until he has properly understood the unity he cannot properly interpret the diversity either. The one unmistakable feature of his playing is monotony, which, in a desperate bid for a performance which 'coheres', he is forced to substitute for a unity he has not grasped.

But the player who has experienced a work's unity has the key to its diversity which, in consequence, he may unfold freely and spontaneously. The deeper you experience unity the freer you are to diversify it. The unparalleled mobility of the acrobat is only possible because of the pull of gravity without which, paradoxically, he has no real freedom of movement.

## The Role of Analysis

It is one of the musical intelligentsia's most cherished notions that analysis is the key to musical understanding. I take this idea to be a fallacy.

Everybody has experienced those mysterious moments of revelation when everything, quite unexpectedly, 'clicks' into position. One minute we do not comprehend; the next, we do. It is as if we had arrived, so to speak, via an unconscious 'leap in the dark'. This 'leap in the dark' I regard as a *sine qua non* of all musical understanding. Musical understanding is essentially intuitive, essentially non-conceptual. Whether or not we understand music has nothing whatever to do with how closely we analyse it. If it had, nobody would have any excuse for misunderstanding anything; all music is analysable. We understand *despite*, not because of, analysis. Music is something which is caught rather than taught. To put it simply: Music either communicates, or it does not. Where it does, analysis is unnecessary; where it does not, analysis is helpless.

What then is the role of analysis? The reader has every right to demand why I should embark on an essay of this kind having, apparently, spiked my own guns before they have fired a single shot. My reply is one which, in this day and age, the musical intelligentsia would hardly accept, but it is one which modern psychology readily supports. The role of analysis is to explain what, on an intuitive level, we already know to be true. It rationalises musical experience. It succeeds the 'leap in the dark'. It helps one to understand one's musical understanding.

## Selection of Works

The selection of works caused me some trouble. Three principles governed my final choice. (1) Each work had to represent an analytic challenge. (2) It had to possess characteristics, a discussion of which might interest the player. (3) It had to be well known. Analysis, as I have just observed, is wise after musical experience; it cannot be wise before it. Where you are not already familiar with music, you can hardly corroborate anything you may read about it.

In this respect, I would ask that my music examples be given every consideration; above all, that they be *heard*. They carry the burden of my thesis about musical unity. Moreover, I have constantly checked my findings against the aural experience of colleagues, excluding anything they themselves failed to corroborate. To that extent, then, my examples have been 'objectified'. This does not necessarily prove them true. But where the reader cannot accept them it is now as likely to be his fault as mine.

## Antecedents

I cannot forgo the opportunity of mentioning the inspirational sources of my essay. First, there are the pioneer writings of Heinrich Schenker. He was the first musician to define the *foreground/background* aspect of musical structure. For years his work was ignored. It is only now receiving due recognition. Second, there are the analyses of Schoenberg, which have had more influence on contemporary criticism than those of Schenker. Schoenberg's concept of a dynamic *grundgestalt*, a work's basic idea, has become fundamental to most subsequent developments in musical analysis.[2] One of the most original of these has been Hans Keller's wordless Functional Analysis. Keller recomposes the score in order to bring out its latent unity. Listening to these analyses has provided me with many a stimulating experience. Nor should I forget the work of Hugo Leichtentritt. His *Analyse von Chopins Klavierwerken*[3] is important. At a time when it was still fashionable to regard Chopin as a mere dreamer, a loose musical thinker, Leichtentritt subjected the music to rigorous analysis and demonstrated Chopin's structural mastery to a generation who had not yet heard the news. Lastly, and above all, there remains the work of Freud. Singlehanded he started a revolution in art-analysis which is still going on today. While his lifelong endeavours to interpret the conscious in terms of the unconscious were only once turned specifically towards art (his book on Leonardo da Vinci has since become a classic), they have had extraordinarily fruitful repercussions from which music has not remained immune.[4]

[2] Schoenberg's writings constantly return to the problem of unity. He once expressed himself thus: 'A real composer does not compose merely one or more themes, but a whole piece. In an apple tree's blossoms, even in the bud, the whole future apple is present in all its details—they have only to mature, to grow, to become the apple, the apple tree, and its power of reproduction. Similarly, a real composer's musical conception, like the physical, is one single act, comprising the totality of the product. The form in its outline, characteristics of tempo, dynamics, moods of the main and subordinate ideas, their relation, derivation, their contrasts and deviations—all these are there at once, though in embryonic state. The ultimate formulation of the melodies, themes, rhythms and many details will subsequently develop through the generative power of the germs.' (Essay, 'Folkloristic Symphonies', *Style and Idea*, London, 1951.)

[3] 2 vols., Berlin, 1921–2.

[4] See, for example, *The Haunting Melody*, by Theodor Reik, a pupil of Freud; also *The Psycho-Analysis of Artistic Vision and Hearing*, by Anton Ehrensweig.

By way of introduction, let me give one or two elementary examples of the unity of Chopin's contrasts. The first comes from the Fantaisie-Impromptu,[5] which begins

EX. 1

Compare this idea with the following one, the beginning of the work's central 'episode'.[6]

EX. 2

On the superficially descriptive level, all is diversity. On the deeper, analytical level, however, all is unity. If you really understand these contrasts, you experience the latent drive which generates them. They are, in fact, different aspects of the same basic idea; their respective common backgrounds run

EX. 3

Hear Ex. 3(b) in the minor mode and you remove the last shred of contrast.

[5] The reason why Chopin never published this masterpiece during his lifetime is likely to remain a mystery. It was composed relatively early in 1835 and remained in manuscript for twenty years. I do not accept the view that he regarded it as inferior (see p. 258). Rather am I inclined to agree with Arthur Hedley's suggestion that Chopin was conscious of too close a resemblance with Moscheles's Impromptu in E flat major—a piece he probably knew very well indeed through its having been published in the same volume as his own op. 15 Nocturnes a short time earlier.

[6] A corollary of my argument is that the usual dictionary definition of the term 'episode'—a part of the musical structure in which 'new' ideas are presented—is only superficially true. There are no 'new' ideas in great music; there is only *one* idea, diversified.

My next elementary example comes from the Nocturne in B major, op. 32, no. 1. Its opening idea shows Chopin at his melodically inspired best.

EX. 4

The contrasting second subject (which I transpose) runs

EX. 5

The question is: How do these two ideas hang together? When we move from the manifest notes to the latent unity, from the conscious foreground to the unconscious background, we find that both themes diversify the same basic idea. Ex. 6 brings these two ideas together by showing the basic unconscious drive behind them.

EX. 6

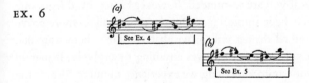

The Waltz in A flat major, op. 42, contains some particularly telling demonstrations of background unity. So powerfully integrated is this miniature masterpiece that it is almost self-analytical. In the following examples I shall let Chopin do my analysing for me. First, listen to this:

EX. 7

And now, to this:

EX. 8

So far, all we hear is diversity. Now, telescope these contrasts—listen to them simultaneously:

EX. 9

Here we have an intriguing instance of the unconscious certainty of a genius's thinking.[7]

One hopes not to be accused of naïvety. You can 'prove the unity' of *any* two themes if you are so-minded, however far removed from one another they may be in musical fact. But the result will no more prove that they *are* unified than it will prove that Chopin's themes are *not*. Analysis neither proves nor disproves anything to anybody. It merely attempts to demonstrate something we experience in music. Where the reader lacks such experience, where he does not know the music, analysis is irrelevant. And where the analyst lacks such experience, his analysis is a sham.

Let us put our theory of unity to a practical test. Let us take a grand-stand view, so to speak, of a complete, large-scale structure. For it is one thing to show that individual ideas express a unity; it is quite another to show that entire works do the same.

The piece I have in mind is the F minor Fantasy. As its title does not imply, it is a full-fledged sonata movement. It contains an astonishing

---

[7] Had anyone pointed out this connexion to Chopin he would probably have been horrified. He might well have considered it to be a criticism of the work. In fact, it is a symptom of its success.

diversity of ideas and, consequently, an equally astonishing degree of unity. The solemn, march-like tread of its introduction contains the kernel of the matter.

EX. 10

Let us push straight to the heart of the problem. What has this theme to do with the rest of the Fantasy? The fact is, it is generated by the same all-embracing idea which inspires every other contrasting theme in the work. Ex. 11 illustrates the lines of force that flow beneath its surface.

EX. 11

Observe the characteristic sequence of falling fourths ('X'), together with the falling sixth ('Y') which is the melodic span, the *thematic boundary* of the idea. Now these same 'lines of force' function throughout the entire structure. I assemble below, for ease of comparison, the remainder of the Fantasy's most important themes. 'X' and 'Y' once more indicate the latent drives.

EX. 12

As we can see, the unity of these contrasts is self-evident. It renders verbal explanation almost tautologous. Ex. 13 shows how even 'subordinate' material (Ex. 13(b)) is integrated (rhythmically and melodically) with the basic idea (Ex. 13(a)).

EX. 13

Incidentally, Klindworth's 'alternative' notation of Ex. 13(b) is worth comparing with Chopin's original. Apart from the fact that it introduces one or two right-sounding (and therefore dangerous) wrong notes (wrong-sounding wrong notes are less lethal: they are immediately identifiable), it robs Chopin's notation of its audacity by substituting enharmonic 'equivalents'. The feeble-looking result makes no difference to the sound, of course; but it does obscure the adventurous manner in which Chopin deliberately juxtaposed remote chromatic harmonies. (See also footnote, p. 239.)

Everything we have observed so far seems to bear out our hypothesis (p. 228). All great music is variations. Chopin shows his unconscious knowledge of the fact on every page of his music. Nowhere is this more apparent than in the A flat major Ballade. The whole of the first page of this splendid work is obsessed with ringing the changes on

EX. 14

Nobody seems to have noticed the simple fact that this passage revolves continuously throughout the texture of the first twenty-four bars with the predictability of a planet in orbit. Chopin disintegrates it and re-expresses it in a variety of ways. But still it returns. Here are two of its disguises.

EX. 15 (a) and (b)

Generations later, Schoenberg was to define this kind of composing as 'developing variation'. There is nothing new under the sun.

All this happens in the foreground: it is manifest development. In the unconscious background, the drives which promote the Ballade's far-flung contrasts

EX. 15 (c)

are present from the outset. They leave no aspect of the structure uninfluenced. Whether we consider the 'second subject' themes

EX. 16

or whether we consider the central 'episode' (which, incidentally, makes a first-rate variation on the works' opening idea)

EX. 17

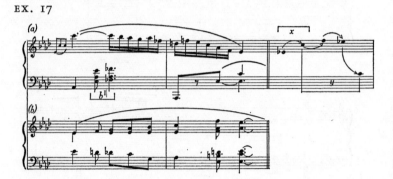

the fact remains that the more closely we observe this Ballade the more surely is the unity behind its variegated structure borne in on us.

Chopin possessed an unrivalled knowledge of the keyboard. Indeed, his music discloses what I should like to call the creative principle of *identity between idea and medium*. Consider a simple question. Why does a great composer choose a particular instrumental medium for particular music? The answer, I submit, lies in the fact that his ideas belong exclusively to that medium; they acquire a degree of distortion once they are expressed through another. The identity projected by a masterpiece between idea and medium is, I maintain, an integral part of its greatness. It is more. It is a criterion whereby we can *demonstrate* its greatness. Transpose a great work from one medium to another and you damage its ideas; you may even destroy them.

I think I can illustrate just how well Chopin understood this principle. In the middle of the C sharp minor Scherzo occurs the following passage.

EX. 18

The lightning switch from chords to filigree finger-work required within bracket 'X' *cannot be rendered in time*. Chopin knows it. There is a split-second delay between beats one and two as the hands skim up the keyboard (a four-octave journey for the left hand). They must then 'prepare', and then commence the downward cascade of quavers. The resultant hesitation, a *built-in* characteristic of the musical structure, guarantees the 'safety' of the idea. For the slight delay is exactly what is interpretatively needed. The point behind this passage is the vivid contrast you get by unrolling each of the four stanzas of the chorale-inspired theme with rhythmic exactitude, while separating each stanza from its fellows with 'time-free' ornamentation. To start this ornamentation precisely in time is musically unthinkable. The fact that it remains technically unthinkable at the same time is a neat illustration of the way Chopin identifies a creative urge with a physical limitation.

I should now like to turn to the analysis of one of Chopin's most ambitious works: the Sonata in B flat minor. Finished in 1839, this noble structure was well in advance of its time. It is interesting how many musicians, some of them eminent, failed at first to comprehend it fully. So extreme are its tension-generating contrasts that for long the sonata was considered not to hang together. Schumann observed that Chopin here 'bound together four of his maddest children'. He considered that the Funeral March (composed two years before the other movements) did not belong to the Sonata at all. Sir Henry Hadow went even further. According to him, the last two movements have nothing whatsoever to do with the first two.[8] Mendelssohn was bewildered by the finale.

The Sonata begins with the following, inspired utterance, which, in one form or another, determines the thematic destiny of the entire work.[9]

[8] *Studies in Modern Music* (Second Series), Sir Henry Hadow.
[9] I cannot agree with Rudolph Reti, who, in his analysis of this Sonata (*The Thematic Process in Music*, pp. 298–310, London, 1961), finds Chopin's unusual notation of the Introduction 'almost bizarre'. Yet Chopin could so easily have avoided the abrupt switch to C sharp minor in bar 2 and notated all four bars in B flat minor. Why didn't he? The fact is, the 'bizarre' notation is highly characteristic of the basic idea's predilection for generating advanced harmonic progressions. It is also characteristic of Chopin's lifelong pursuit in bringing together extreme tonal centres. The 'authentic' Polish Edition attempts to rewrite the history of harmony by notating the Introduction 'properly' in B flat minor. See Ex. 19.

EX. 19

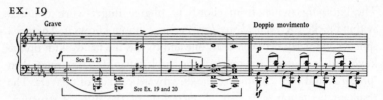

The powerful motif in the bass

EX. 20

reappears in many guises, both in the manifest foreground and in the latent background. Note the crucial mediant degree with which it begins (see Ex. 34 for the full significance of this), the falling diminished seventh and the rising second (the diminished seventh is often expressed in its enharmonic inversion of a minor third. See Ex. 21). These are the cells out of which Chopin's intuitive genius builds one of his most 'spontaneous' works. ('Spontaneity' in art is something of a misnomer. Art is either successful or it is not; where it is, I believe it to have been unconsciously *pre-determined*. Hence the quotation marks.) The first subject proper, strongly contrasted with the introduction though it is, already betrays its origin within its first three notes.[9a]

EX. 21

This mediant-obsessed theme, derived by way of Ex. 21(a), obsesses in its turn the second subject (Ex. 22). It would be difficult to imagine a contrasting idea more extreme than the one Chopin unfolds at the second-subject stage; yet, like all great contrasts it sounds inevitable. Why?

[9a] The symbols 'O', 'I', 'R' and 'RI' which are used in the next, and some subsequent examples, stand for the Original, Inverted, Retrograde and Retrograde Inverted forms of a basic idea.

EX. 22

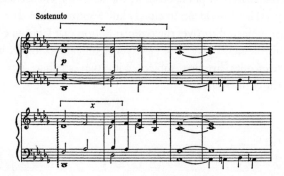

Far from being a 'new' idea, Ex. 22 is a variation on the old one. It expresses the basic motif 'X' in augmentation. (See Ex. 21(b).) Chopin, we may be certain, was hardly conscious of the connexion. Ex. 23, the closing bars of the exposition, displays yet another permutation of the basic idea 'X'.

EX. 23

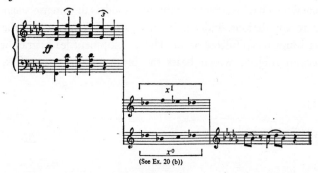

Pianists: observe Chopin's precise injunction 'Doppio movimento' after the 'Grave' introduction. (See Ex. 19.) It means exactly what it says— 'double the speed'—and it is there for a purpose. Far from being something merely 'tacked on' at the beginning, the Grave introduction enjoys a precise tempo-relationship with the first subject, and it becomes the only place to establish the tempo of the entire movement. True, there are several eminent pianists who ignore Chopin's marking. But, then, there are fewer great interpretations of this sonata than there are great pianists.

C–I

From the analytical point of view, the development section (as one might expect) is self-evident. Its closely knit argument, based exclusively on the first subject, disproves the popular notion that Chopin could not develop his themes. I give a solitary, yet significant example, in which Chopin telescopes his first subject with the opening, introductory figure of the entire sonata.

EX. 24

One of Chopin's chief contributions to the history of sonata form, and one which has been widely misunderstood, is the intense *compression* of his recapitulations. Indeed, in this particular movement the first subject is not recapitulated at all. The development leads straight into the second subject, which bears the brunt of the return (Ex. 25).

EX. 25

Modern criticism goes wrong in regarding this procedure as 'structural weakness'.[10] I invite anyone to repair Chopin's 'omission' of his first subject. They will receive a salutary lesson in how not to compose. There are compelling musical reasons that led Chopin to abandon an

[10] A procedure which Chopin was to repeat in the first movement of the Sonata in B minor. There, too, it is the second subject that emerges from the development and ushers in the recapitulation, while the first subject is excluded.

orthodox recapitulation: the first subject generates so much of the development that to recapitulate it as well would be repetitive, less than masterly.[11]

For the rest, I regard structural compression as an unconscious function of creative mastery. Take a bird's-eye-view of sonata form. Its progress is, as it were, telescopic. The divisions between and within its movements gradually collapsed under the creative pressure of every genius from Bach to Schoenberg. What started out as a multi-movement form, with the internal characteristics of those movements sharply defined, had developed two hundred years later into something very greatly compressed. The story of that compression is one of expositions and recapitulations growing ever more developmental; of separate movements being linked and then made to penetrate one another; of every characteristic that it is possible to assemble under the name 'sonata' being scrambled together and served within a single framework. It is the story of musical form from Bach's E major Violin Concerto to Schoenberg's First Chamber Symphony. The creative motive behind this compression is not hard to find. The more you compress, the more you express. Compression is the method *par excellence* of maintaining structural tension which would otherwise be lowered through over-familiarity. To state a complex situation briefly: the composer-listener relationship rests on the music composers and listeners already know. If they did not have much of a common musical past, they could hardly have much of a musical present either, to say nothing of a future; for compressions not only become meaningful when heard against the extended backgrounds over which they were composed: they become *inevitable*. Composers keep on raising the norm of structural tension because listeners keep on lowering it. This is the price of assimilation. Sonata form, inevitably, has always been on the move, and Chopin was one of those who helped to move it.

---

[11] Another notable feature of Chopin's large-scale structures, and one which is likewise misunderstood, is that they often reserve their most extreme, tension-raising contrast until the end. Where other composers 'draw in the threads', Chopin refuses to do so. Consider the codas of the F major Ballade and the F minor Ballade. Far from being the usual summing-up, the music in both cases is a passionate exposition of still further stages of the argument right down to the last bars. Far from being yet another 'structural weakness', this procedure represented a major breakthrough in the development of musical form. It is a truly modern attitude never merely to repeat where one can vary.

Technically, the scherzo makes greater demands than anything else in the sonata.

EX. 26

The minor third, so much in evidence as a background unitive force throughout the sonata, determines the 'direction' in which Ex. 26 unfolds—against a background of rising minor thirds.

EX. 27

Its continuation restores the balance by unfolding against a background of *descending* thirds.

EX. 28

The strongly contrasted trio is subtly integrated by way of the closing bars of the scherzo. Compare Ex. 29(a) with Ex. 29(b).

EX. 29

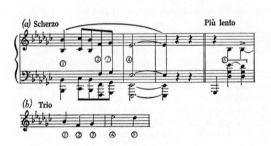

If you do not get the connexion, Ex. 30, their common background, will make it audible. Hear first Ex. 29(b), move on to Ex. 30, then move back to Ex. 29(a).

EX. 30

The trio theme not only looks back to the scherzo: it also looks forward to the 'trio' of the slow movement—the central episode of the *Marche Funèbre*. I place them side by side for comparison.

EX. 31

These themes are integrated by way of the technique of *interversion,* a term first introduced by Rudolph Reti[12] to describe note interchanges within a melodic entity.

The slow movement, the *Marche Funèbre*, poses an interesting structural problem. Composed as a separate piece two years before the remainder of the sonata, Chopin only later placed it within the present context. Following Schumann, critics have often observed that the movement does not 'belong'. Yet in this, as in so many other things, Chopin's musical instincts did not lead him astray. What was it that led his creative unconscious to recognize in this music the sonata's true slow movement?

Rudolph Reti points to the similarity of its melodic outline with that of the first movement's first subject;[13] yet he fails to grasp the *precise*

---

[12] *The Thematic Process in Music*, New York, 1951.
[13] Op. cit., p. 306.

relationship. The melodic contour of the first few bars of the funeral march (a 'grief-motif' that has passed into the unconscious symbolology of music) is, in fact, that of the first movement's first subject *in strict retrograde motion*.

EX. 33

This is creative integrity of a high order.

Pianists: it was Anton Rubinstein who began the tradition of conceiving this movement as the arrival and departure of a funeral cortège, building up the music from pianissimo to fortissimo and back again. Busoni followed this interpretation. So, too, did Rachmaninov, whose recording of the sonata made this approach famous. While it is in flat contradiction to Chopin's own dynamic markings, and while purists consequently condemn it, I personally admit to a secret liking for it. I have not forgotten that this is the age of musicology and that the *urtext* is the thing. But it is high time that our musicologists began to discriminate between textual departures that are musical and those which are not. I have yet to meet the masterpiece that can only be played in one particular way.

I have already indicated that mediant relationships, melodic and harmonic, are important unitive sources in this sonata. So is the mediant degree itself. No fewer than six of the sonata's themes begin on the mediant degree (★).

EX. 34

The finale is without precedent in the entire literature of the keyboard. It is futuristically athematic from beginning to end—no wonder Mendelssohn disliked it—and its continuous whirl of stark-sounding octaves reminded Anton Rubinstein of 'night winds sweeping over church-yard graves'.[14]

EX. 35

Harmonically, the movement is poised on the brink of atonality—an astonishing achievement for a 29-year-old in 1839. (Chopin had already created a number of precedents. The first twenty bars of the C sharp minor Scherzo, for example, are seventy-five years ahead of their time. They are keyless—a fact to which commentators always seem to close their ears in unconscious tribute to Chopin's originality. The extraordinary beginning (Ex. 36) is quite disintegrated tonally. Passages such as this reveal Chopin as one of the 'displaced persons' of musical history—a twentieth-century composer forced by a freak of nature to wander through the nineteenth.

EX. 36

The thunder forked by this kind of lightning reverberated throughout the nineteenth century[15] and had its final outcome in the music of Schoenberg. Nor was this the only way Chopin helped to precipitate

[14] There is a unique dichotomy between the *look* of the printed page and the actual *sound* of the music. I doubt that even the most expert score-reader could reconstruct in his imagination the absolutely individual sound of this movement without first having heard it played.
[15] See p. 264.

the historical process of tonal disintegration. He also deployed his tonal centres in a manner later composers were to call 'progressive tonality'. Witness the Second Ballade. It begins in F major and ends in A minor.)

It would hardly be worthwhile disagreeing with Hadow's view that the finale of the B flat minor Sonata 'is too simple and primitive to justify it as the fitting conclusion of an important work,[16] were it not still possible to hear that view unthinkingly echoed today. The fact is, the movement has no real existence outside the Sonata. The curve of the opening bar betrays the movement's pedigree. It lies squarely across the span of the Sonata's opening idea, the falling seventh and the rising second.

EX. 37

The movement is the most paradoxical in all Chopin—'an enigma wrapped in a mystery'—and it is one of the most difficult to perform well. The music lies a long way behind the notes; few pianists get there. It is a mistake to take it too slowly. I recommend a minimum tempo of m.m♩ =108. But remember speed is not the only way of generating pace. In this connexion the following table is by no means uninteresting.

| Pianist | Duration (excluding last three bars*) | | Record No. |
|---------|------|------|------------|
|         | min. | sec. | HMV |
| Horowitz | I | 10 | DB 21314 |
| Rachmaninov | I | 10 | CAMDEN CDN 1017 |
| Rubinstein | I | 15 | RCA RB 16282 |
| Cortot | I | 16 | HMV DB 2020 |

* The last three bars are, traditionally, played with a great degree of freedom.

[16] Op. cit. p. 156.

Although Rachmaninov and Horowitz take precisely the same time, (1 min. 10 sec.), *Rachmaninov's performance sounds quicker*. Again, Cortot sounds quicker than Rubinstein, although his performance actually takes longer. The lesson is clear. Tempo is not expressed through the stop-watch. Dynamics, note-durations, phrasing pedalling—all these things contribute to the total impression of pace which, as we have seen, may well contradict the clock.[17]

Three questions, predictably, now arise. In the interests of clarity, I shall pose them dialectically.

*Thematic connexions may be unconscious to the composer; therefore, he did not mean them.*

I should say the opposite. Once it is established that a composer created thematic connexions unconsciously, then he meant them beyond a shadow of musical doubt. What is unconscious is, by definition, dynamic and far-reaching in its creative consequences. In my experience, it is often theoreticians and critics, the musical 'outsiders', who refuse to entertain the idea of musical contrasts unconsciously motivated. Composers and performers, on the other hand, the musical 'insiders', seem only too ready to acknowledge it. Is it really necessary in this day and age to stress that, far from being exclusively conscious, artistic creation has deeply unconscious roots?[18]

*Some demonstrations of musical unity are so complex they are inaudible.*

Analysis is only as complex as it has to be. The unity of contrasts is there to be explained, not imposed. As to its 'inaudibility' this raises an interesting point. We usually hear far more than we know. Composers not only compose unconsciously; listeners listen unconsciously, too.[19]

*You can use analysis to create a connexion between any two works.*

By a process of *reductio ad absurdum* you can doubtless 'prove' a

[17] Ever since Leibniz, philosophers have argued that there can be no such thing as a 'time-flow' independent of events. Events do not take place in time; they *express* time. This notion is relevant to musical performance. Whether music sounds 'too quick' or 'too slow' depends ultimately on the way its events are distributed.

[18] There is a mass of evidence from composers (e.g. Mahler, de Falla, Schoenberg, etc.) about their creative processes which strongly supports the fact of an unconscious musical organization. True, there is nothing from Chopin. He had an almost pathological dislike of talking about the way he composed. He rarely missed an opportunity of keeping quiet about it.

[19] See my book, *A Study in Musical Analysis* (Part Four), London, 1962.

connexion between Palestrina's *Missa Brevis* and Gershwin's *I Got Rhythm*. But the result will, in fact, prove no such thing. You cannot create a connexion where none exists. The function of analysis is to explain the experience of music's unity. Where there is no foundation for such experience you can hardly explain it. But what when there is?

Different works *may* sometimes represent a unity. But a unity between works in no wise disproves a unity *within* them. A relationship between A and B does not cease to exist by showing a relationship between A and X. Leopold Godowsky's paraphrases of Chopin's studies telescope various pairs of studies into one another—one plays them simultaneously.[20] This is a remarkable demonstration of the unity of contrasting *works*. Yet the unity of the individual studies themselves remains exactly the same as before. Again, Brahms's *Variations on a theme of Paganini* does not cease to hang together merely because Rachmaninov, Boris Blacher and even Paganini himself all wrote variations on that same theme. Inevitably, overt connexions abound, cutting across the different sets of variations. Yet each set establishes, and maintains, its own unique sense of unity irrespective of the others.

A work which is equally challenging to analysis is Chopin's Sonata in B minor. This mature piece, teeming with contrasts, tells us a great deal about the manner in which Chopin unifies large-scale structures. It contains at least ten sharply differentiated themes which a lesser composer might well have failed to integrate. Without resorting to overt connexions of the Lisztian kind, Chopin here creates a kaleidoscopically varied structure remarkable for its thematic unity.[21]

Even the key is unusual. There is not a single piano sonata by

[20] For example, the two studies in G flat major (the 'Butterfly' Study and the 'Black-Keys' Study).

[21] All the more remarkable at this stage in musical history. The revolution effected by Beethoven and the early Romantics had pushed back the frontiers of musical language so far that major problems of structural integration arose. It is no accident that the 'metamorphosis of themes' and related unifying techniques were developed by the Romantics. These techniques were vital in holding long-range structures together. It is also no accident that the alternative 'solution' fostered by the Romantics was to by-pass the problem entirely by composing miniatures.

Mozart or Beethoven in B minor, and Chopin must have known it. What he could not possibly have known in 1844 was that the key of B minor occurs nowhere in the piano sonatas of Schubert either (to say nothing of Dussek and Hummel) and that both Schumann and Mendelssohn were busily avoiding it—a fact that throws Chopin's sonata into even sharper relief. The question arises: Why should Chopin be one of the first composers to pioneer the key of B minor in a *large-scale, multi-movement* piano work? Possibly because Chopin, more than any previous keyboard composer, was sensitive to the 'lie' of his music and B minor (ostensibly an 'uncomfortable' key and hence usually avoided for *long* works) happens to be, *potentially*, one of the most intrinsically pianistic of all tonal centres.[22] It opens a direct route to the 'flat-finger' keys of B major, D major and F sharp major in which so much of this sonata unfolds. For the rest, the sonata refuses to unfold comfortably in any other key anyway (unlike large numbers of piano works which are physically 'neutral' and will, consequently, transpose happily into several). It is, perhaps, not entirely irrelevant that Liszt, who was a great admirer of the work, began composing his own B minor (*sic*) Sonata a short time afterwards. Liszt actually went to the trouble of making his own manuscript copy of Chopin's piece—a fact which is not generally known. Perhaps I am reading too much into too little; but it strikes me that key-neglect, a fascinating historical pheno-menon, would repay investigation. Some keys were far less composer-prone than others, a fact that our own keyless age tends to forget.

The sonata's motivically inspired beginning contains the essence of the work's unity, and hence of its diversity. Observe 'X', the basic idea.

---

History corroborated itself at the beginning of our own century. After Arnold Schoenberg and his followers had effected a similar 'breakthrough', identical structural problems arose—and they were solved in identical ways: the discovery of twelve-note technique—essentially a technique of unity—and the development of the miniature.

[22] Chopin liked physical contact with the keyboard. The feel of the keys, apparently, stimulated the flow of his musical ideas. There seems to be no authenti-cated case of Chopin ever bringing a work to completion without a piano. Incidentally, most good pianists will testify to the muscular gratification obtained through manipulation of the keyboard. There are powerful libidinal factors involved here.

EX. 38

A programme-note open before me as I write mentions the 'smoothly curving lines' of the second subject. This shattering discovery tells us nothing our ears do not already know after one hearing. It is the *function* of the second subject which poses the really interesting question.

EX. 39

Ex. 39 illustrates the economy of Chopin's thought. Not a single note is wasted. At the foreground level, the theme looks both forwards and backwards. 'X' varies the basic idea (compare Ex. 38), but its characteristic span of a falling ninth (G to F sharp) betrays its origins. Its offshoot 'Y' is a chief motif of the transition section (Ex. 42); 'Z' looks forward to the finale's rondo theme (Ex. 46). If we penetrate to the background, however, the organization of this theme becomes even stricter and its connexion with the first subject is clinched. In Ex. 40 I show the background unitive drives which flow beneath the first and second subjects respectively. They are held together by latent unifying forces which stand in a strict retrograde relation to one another.

EX. 40

Compare Exx. 38 and 39 with Ex. 40 and the underlying connexion becomes apparent.

This second subject disproves the false notion that Chopin was incapable of writing large-scale music. It is conceived on the grandest scale and grows uninterruptedly right up to the last bar of the exposition, and it develops a number of subsidiary themes and their variants en route.[23]

In his discussion of the B minor Sonata, Hugo Leichtentritt observes, with rare insight, that the first and second subjects hang together so closely they can be performed simultaneously with slight textural adjustments. His analytical demonstration can hardly be bettered.[24]

This is the cue for a discussion that is as old as music. Did the unity of these contrasts result from a wide-awake intellectual effort, or did Chopin sleep-walk his way towards it? The 'brain-work' school can have a great time of it arguing with the 'sleep-walking' school, particularly if they distort the truth by oversimplifying it—a condition both sides seem only too ready to fulfil. The none-too-simple truth of the matter is that in musical creation, brain-working and sleep-walking, conscious effort and unconscious inspiration, go hand in hand. The reader will, I feel certain, bear with me if I insist on sparing him the pros and cons of the discussion with which he will have the rest of musical history to become acquainted.

The transition section, out of which the second subject so inevitably grows, is of some interest polyphonically. Soprano and alto unfold canonically over a chromatically rising bass. Note 'Y'.

[23] Why is it that Chopin is so often unthinkingly regarded as a master of the miniature and little else? The answer, I submit, lies in the naive, and widespread, view that equates shortness with smallness. They are not the same thing at all. You measure music according to the size of its paragraphs, not in terms of the stop-watch. Many of Chopin's shorter movements are conceived on an immense scale in that they represent a perpetually developing structure from the first bar to the last.

[24] Op. cit. Vol. 2.

EX. 42

Chopin later uses the continuation to this transition with great originality at the close of the development as a lead-back to the recapitulation. (Compare bars 31–40 with bars 140–8.)

Pianists: structurally the movement is very treacherous. Its 'geometry', superficially so simple, is far more elusive than that of the first movement of the B flat minor sonata. I have only once heard a completely convincing approach, although I am the last person to suggest that only one approach is possible. The difficulty is this. The movement unfolds such an astonishing prodigality of themes, each with its own highly individual propensities, that it can easily degenerate into a shapeless muddle even under experienced hands. It is a ticklish problem to get those themes into the right primary and subordinate relationships to one another—to see the structure *in toto*. The solution is clear yet complex. The movement only takes shape when you have set in motion its long-range, *basic* tempo, the 'pulse behind the pulse' which continues to assert itself even where it is not currently in use, a tempo which may be discarded or resumed at will in order to 'point' the structure, a tempo *against which* the performance may brake and accelerate according to immediate, spontaneous needs. The switch from 'background pulse' to 'foreground pulse' will always dramatise the form. It is one of the great tools of interpretation yet, as I cautioned earlier, there is more than one way of using it. Sooner or later all pianists must come to grips with this most mysterious aspect of interpretation, and this movement represents a splendid challenge to their endeavours.

As in the B flat minor Sonata, Chopin ignores the traditional position of the scherzo and trio and places this movement second, thereby achieving greater contrast and, consequently, greater structural tension. It is by no means uninstructive to compare this movement with Chopin's four independent scherzos. It would never make a successful work in its own right; it is a true *movement* in that it is not musically complete without the remaining movements whose arguments it helps to sustain.

The scherzo is carefully integrated with its trio—especially in the melodic dimension. Ex. 43 ((a) and (b)) is self-explanatory.

EX. 43

The Largo approaches the nocturnes in style. It has a broad melodic canvas. Its opening melody develops a characteristically bel canto line which Chopin almost certainly did not inherit from John Field.[25] Ex. 44 shows its twofold integration.

EX. 44

'Y' is a simple reversion of the initial figure of the first movement's second subject (Ex. 44(b)). 'W', a rising sixth and a falling third, returns to haunt the middle episode where, incidentally, Chopin achieves some remarkable pedal effects.[26]

EX. 45

[25] Field's influence on Chopin is overrated. Chopin had composed the first five of his nocturnes before he came into brief contact with him. On the one fleeting occasion Chopin heard Field play the piano he was rather disappointed. If we must search for a melodic influence, we are far more likely to find it in Bellini.

[26] See p. 126.

The finale is one of the few sonata-rondos in musical history where the main theme returns out of the tonic key. This theme has roots which can be traced back as far as the first movement's first subject (compare 'Z' in Ex. 39 and Ex. 46 respectively). The notation at Ex. 46 is not what Chopin actually wrote, but it is what you actually hear.

EX. 46

Its violently contrasted second subject (Ex. 47(a)) is a masterly blend of at least two other themes heard earlier in the sonata: the 'codetta' theme of the first movement (Ex. 47(b)), and the 'trio' theme of the second movement (Ex. 47(c)).

EX. 47

So much for the structural aspects of Chopin. What of the interpretative? The fact is, there are no aspects of structure that are not, at the same time, aspects of interpretation. Tempo, dynamics, note-duration, agogic accents, rubato, etc.—all these things are *functions of musical structure*. That is the great lesson of musical analysis. A musical structure *contains* the answer to the problem of its own interpretation. A great interpretation is never 'applied' from without; it always emerges from within. The paradox of a successful performance is that it does not really express the music at all; the music expresses it. This may seem a novel view. Yet I think it a true one. The history of piano playing for the past hundred years is full of pianists, with varying degrees of ego-mania, each claiming to give *the* interpretation. Of course, they gave nothing of the kind; the earliest gramophone records show this conclusively. What they *did* give was an interpretation symptomatic only of themselves and their times. History has caught up with them and their performances have dated. It is only the very greatest pianists, perhaps, who actually succeed in cheating history and produce performances which are timelessly true of the music, performances which are *functions* of the structure.

## List of Sources

Ehrensweig, Anton, *The Psycho-Analysis of Artistic Vision and Hearing*, London, 1953.
Keller, Hans, 'Mozart's Chamber Music' (*Mozart Companion*), London, 1956.
Leichtentritt, Hugo, *Analyse von Chopins Klavierwerken*, Berlin, 1921–2.
Reik, Theodor, *The Haunting Melody: Psycho-Analytic Experiences in Life and Music*, New York, 1953.
Reti, Rudolph, *The Thematic Process in Music*, New York, 1951.
Schenker, Heinrich, *Harmony*, Stuttgart, 1906. (Edited & Annotated by Oswald Jonas, Chicago, 1954.)
— *Das Meisterwerk in der Musik*, Munich, 1925–30.
Walker, Alan, *A Study in Musical Analysis*, London, 1962.
Zuckerkandl, Victor, Article on 'Schenker's *Urlinie* and *Ursatz*' (*Harvard Dictionary of Music*), London, 1946.

PAUL BADURA-SKODA

*Chopin's Influence*

ONE of the finest remarks ever made on Chopin is Schumann's famous sentence: 'Chopin's works are guns buried in flowers.' Indeed, Chopin is a truly revolutionary composer. The 'gunpowder' of his bold innovations had the most far-reaching results on the development of music up to the twentieth century. Yet at the same time he used his new musical language with such a classical restraint, with such a unique sense for the balance of form and expression and with such a grace that the 'guns' became invisible and many of his most original inventions could pass unnoticed by the general public. It is true that the works which made Chopin popular are in many cases not his most original ones. In fact, they are often the works which he purposely suppressed as not fulfilling his artistic aims, like the Fantaisie-Impromptu[1] or the E minor Waltz both published posthumously. They became great favourites of the public at large, whereas the works with real explosive power, like his Ballade in F minor, the Barcarolle and many of his mazurkas which never enjoyed as much popularity, were the ones that exercised a strong and lasting influence on many of the great composers from his times up to the present day.

[1] See footnote on p. 232 for a different explanation of why Chopin suppressed publication of this piece. ED.

For obvious reasons an essay on Chopin's influence cannot but give a sketchy account. I shall therefore limit myself to a discussion of his harmonic innovations only, leaving aside many other interesting aspects of his music.

In trying to define the nature of Chopin's harmonic language one might state first that he widened the concept of the term 'consonance' immensely by including in it overtones of the higher order from the row of overtones based on a given fundamental.[1a]

EX. I   'classical' consonance      widened area of consonance

The notes marked with an asterisk are not exactly in the indicated pitch but slightly flat or sharp.

At the end of his E minor Study, op. 25, no. 5, Chopin added F sharp to the E major triad, treating it definitely as a consonance (no. 9 in the hierarchy of overtones) and in the often-discussed ending of the F major Prelude, op. 28, no. 23, the same treatment is given to the seventh (overtone no. 7). It took a long time before other composers dared to follow in his footsteps. The added ninth can hardly be found before the turn of the century; Debussy, Mahler and Scriabin might have been the first to use it. In Mahler, however, it still has the flavour of an unresolved dissonance: the D above the C major triad in the last part of *Das Lied von der Erde* symbolizes somehow a state of infinite longing; the question whether it will finally move downward to C or upward to E is forever left open. The ending of the F major Prelude, on the other hand, is unique. A line can be drawn from here to the 'blue note' frequently used in jazz, which has apparently exactly the same origin. In Chopin it is not the ending with the minor seventh as such (which seems to turn the conclusion into a dominant harmony, speaking in classical harmonic terminology), but the refusal to resolve it, which made it such a bold innovation. At a superficial glance the

[1a] The hypothesis that the rising norm of dissonance is bound up with the character of the harmonic series (itself a kind of progressive 'dissonance ladder') has not so far been proved. Meanwhile, many musicians find the similarity too much of a coincidence not to be true. See the excellent article *Consonance, Dissonance* in the Harvard Dictionary of Music (p. 180) where the rival theories are contrasted and compared. ED.

ending of 'The Entreating Child' from Schumann's *Scenes of Childhood* might seem to be another example of this. Yet there the beginning and ending of the piece in the dominant is explained by the poetical idea of an expectancy which is clearly resolved in the D major triad of the following 'Perfect Happiness' (bars 2 and 4). This one example might well serve to show the difference between the two composers: Schumann, with his gift for writing, was a truly romantic composer whose music was often inspired by literary ideas, whereas Chopin, who had no literary ambition, wrote only absolute music the balance of which is, however, constantly upset by its uniquely expressive 'Romantic harmony'.

In the same category—widening of the concept of consonance— one might include Chopin's frequent use of the tritone above the tonic in his mazurkas. It is, of course, an imitation or rather an elaboration on primitive folk music where apparently the overtone no. 11 (Ex. 1) is included in the primitive scale.[2] Eastern folk music idioms were finding their way into 'serious' music again at the end of the nineteenth century, and later in the work of Kodály and Béla Bartók. An interesting similarity with an early work by Bartók will be shown later.

If the minor seventh can be accepted as a consonance, it follows logically that in more conservative harmonic writing, chords of the seventh might be used with more freedom than before. The emancipation of the chords of the seventh was one of the major trends in the harmonic evolution of the nineteenth century. Chopin, though not the only and not the first composer to use these chords frequently, explored their inherent possibilities in such a way that nearly all the future development in this direction can be traced back to him. The many altered chords of the seventh with added dissonances, as well as chords of the ninth, eleventh, and thirteenth, can be found in Chopin's music. Not only the chords themselves, but the most surprising and yet always convincing combinations of them, show Chopin as a creator whose influence just could not be avoided. If the widening of the concept of consonance was due to a keen observation of accoustical phenomena, Chopin's highly original chord progressions, which offer a never-ending fascination to the music-lover, seem to spring from different roots: a thorough theoretical training of a genius's mind inde-

[2] See p. 74 Ex. 1. ED.

pendent enough to break the existing rules of harmony whenever
necessary, the instinct of the born pianist which by letting his fingers
simply glide over the keys made him discover new sound combinations
which had appeared theoretically unacceptable, and last, but not least,
the creative artistic sense to put them into the right context.

One of the harmonic rules Chopin did not hesitate to break was the
'sacred law' of forbidden parallel fifths and octaves. Long before the
twentieth century he discovered that this rule, originally created for
polyphonic and choral music, was obsolete with regard to a free piano
style, and simply drew the consequences. It is interesting to note that a
hundred years earlier Domenico Scarlatti, the only other great exclusive
keyboard composer, had also purposely broken many theoretical rules,
including this one. As Burney quotes in his *Journeys*, 1772, Scarlatti
admitted that as long as the ear was pleased he had no qualms about
breaking the rules, the aural sense being the only authority he obeyed.

Since the subject of this essay is limited to Chopin's harmonic
influence, there is little to say about his influence on Schumann and
even on Liszt. Both owe a great deal to his pianistic innovations, yet
harmonically they seem to me rather independent. Even if the end of the
first movement of the Schumann Concerto is nearly identical with the
final chords in Chopin's Fourth Ballade, that can hardly have been due
to Chopin's influence, for Schumann wrote this movement one year
earlier. Even when Schumann tried deliberately to imitate him, as he
did in the *Carnaval* Suite, in the movement entitled 'Chopin', the
result was much more Schumann than Chopin. Chopin would hardly
have written a left-hand part with so many *sf*, nor would he have modu-
lated back to the home key of A flat major as fast as Schumann did in
bars 7–8. Only the last five bars might pass for a successful imitation.
Chopin never spoke as highly of Schumann as Schumann did of him.
Yet the slow movement of his Cello Sonata, op. 65, sounds to me like
an *Hommage à Schumann*, showing that he not only gave, but that he
also took. The same might be said about his relationship to Liszt.[3] Liszt's
ornamental passages frequently based on progressions of diminished
seventh chords might well have been inspired by Chopin, e.g. from
the middle section of the E major Study, op. 10, no. 3, or from the last

[3] For this subject, see also my essay, 'Chopin and Liszt' in the *Osterreichische
Musikzeitschrift*, Vienna, February 1962.

movement of the F minor Concerto (the run before recapitulation and the passage thirty-four bars before the end). On the other hand, Liszt's predilection for mediant harmonies, stemming directly from Schubert, probably had some influence on Chopin who, however, used such progressions rarely and comparatively late, as in the C sharp minor Scherzo (bars 94–95), the A flat major Ballade (bars 115–16), the A flat major Polonaise, op. 53 (trio section and third bar from end), in the Barcarolle (bars 23–24), or in the opening of the Polonaise-Fantaisie, op. 61.

Chopin's influence on Brahms has not yet been sufficiently recognized. It is generally known that Brahms made a transcription of Chopin's F minor Study (op. 25, no. 2) and that in his early B minor Ballade (op. 10, no. 3) more than one similarity to Chopin's First and Second Scherzos can be discovered. Strangely enough, it has apparently been overlooked so far that the termination of Brahms's F sharp minor Sonata, op. 2, sounds exactly like a free elaboration on the ending of Chopin's Barcarolle. This can hardly be coincidental. We know from Brahms's correspondence that he knew and admired this piece. Traces of Chopin's influence can be seen also in many of Brahms's later works.[4] One example from the fourth movement of Brahms's Second Piano Concerto may suffice.

EX. 2

The chromatic link between the two dominant harmonies is 'typically Chopin'. The model for this passage could be found either in Chopin's Study in C major, op. 10, no. 7 (bars 17–20), or in the Fourth Ballade (bars 107–11).

[4] The *Klavierstücke*, op. 118, especially, contain several traits of Chopin: the elaborate left-hand part and the canonic imitation in no. 4 (Intermezzo in F minor), and in the middle section of no. 2 (Intermezzo in A major) are similar to the coda of the C sharp minor Mazurka, op. 63, no. 3. (Brahms was co-editor of the Mazurkas for the Complete Edition.) The middle section of no. 5 (Romanze in F major) is a Brahmsian elaboration on the Berceuse.

EX. 3

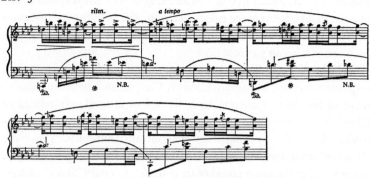

Of course, Brahms was able to assimilate these influences to such a degree that they became his own, even in the Chopinesque parts of his Intermezzi, op. 76 (e.g. no. 3 in A flat major) or in the B major section of his Rhapsody, op. 79, no. 1.

A direct influence of Chopin can be observed on several composers of the Polish and Russian schools on the one hand, and among some of the great French composers on the other. The young Szymanowski often paid tribute to his great countryman, as in his beautiful Study, op. 4, no. 3 (similar in mood to Chopin's op. 25, no. 7) and also in some of his mazurkas. The now-forgotten Russian composer Felix Blumenfeld was once even labelled the 'Russian Chopin'.[5] It is also interesting to see how closely Scriabin followed in Chopin's footsteps in many of his early and even middle works.[5a] His famous Study in D sharp minor, op. 8, no. 12, mirrors closely Chopin's 'Revolutionary' Study. The rhythmical pattern of the melodies is quasi-identical and so also is the excited content of both pieces. One of the starting-points of Scriabin is a combination of altered chords plus added dissonances, such as can be found in Chopin's Second Ballade in the first bar of the coda, bar 169. This bar, taken alone, could well pass for Scriabin.

EX. 4

[5] Felix Blumenfeld (1863–1931) was the teacher of Vladimir Horowitz. ED.
[5a] See Collet, p. 139. ED.

But what to the earlier master was an expression of an exceptional state of anguish later became the rule in Scriabin. The resulting hypertension between feverish excitement and utmost depression would hardly have been one of Chopin's artistic aims.

Tchaikovsky also owed a great deal to Chopin; many passages in his piano concertos are clearly based on Chopin, and the second movement of his Piano Concerto in B flat minor is so closely related to Chopin's Berceuse that one could exchange the melodies or the accompaniments of the opening bars without any difficulty. The piece 'October' from Tschaikovsky's *The Seasons* also show traits of Chopin. Yet it is rather the inner mood of their works, a certain 'Slavic' expression ranging from an immense sadness to a fiery expression of upsurge and triumph which proves an affinity between the two composers, rather than mere idiomatic resemblances in their musical language.

Both Rachmaninov and Prokofiev, although very different from each other, owed not a little to the Polish master. Prokofiev himself said that the Scherzo of his Third Symphony ('The Fiery Angel') was directly inspired by the Finale of Chopin's B flat minor Sonata. This unique piece, which had estranged many contemporaries of Chopin, including Schumann, carries music towards the brink of atonality.[6] Could not the hopeless whirlwind in Alban Berg's 'Lyric' Suite be influenced by it, too? All the Russian composers, however, displayed a massiveness in their style which set them rather apart from Chopin, who abhorred crudeness and exaggeration throughout his life.

The French composers, on the other hand, were more attracted by the refinement and elegance in Chopin's music than by its inherent Slavonic idiom. This can be seen in Fauré, whose barcarolles and nocturnes could not have been written without Chopin's examples. Yet, behind a similar 'dress', what a different expression!

Strong similarities can also be observed between Chopin and César Franck. But even if there are striking resemblances in their harmonic language, it is not at all certain whether one can speak of direct influence. As can be seen also in the case of Wagner and Bruckner, many harmonic inventions of this period may most likely have been made independently of Chopin.

Yet Chopin's claim to have been the originator of a new harmonic

[6] See p. 247. ED.

style remains unchallenged. In his Fantasy, op. 49 (bars 209–11), we find a succession of altered chords of the seventh on a chromatic descending bass line which could have been taken from a Franck Chorale, but was written half a century earlier. One of Franck's many new devices was the use of the submediant minor chord in the minor mode (e.g. in A minor this would mean the introduction of the chord of F minor on the sixth degree; the minor third A flat of the F minor triad is enharmonically identical with the major third G sharp of the dominant E major triad). This 'typically Franckian' harmony which he used, for example, several times in the slow movement of his D minor Symphony, can be found as early as Chopin's E flat minor Polonaise, op. 26 (bars 98–99).

EX. 5

A similar succession of harmonies is found in Chopin's Nocturne in B flat minor, op. 9, no. 1 (bars 7–8).

One generation after Franck it was Ravel who used the same device in his *Scarbo* (bars 94–100).

EX. 6

(The different enharmonic notation with an F double sharp instead of a G natural does not, of course, alter the fact that the second bar is actually in E minor.

Like Brahms, Ravel was especially attracted by Chopin's Barcarolle. He wrote a meaningful poetical evaluation of this piece which clearly reflects his affection for it.[7] No wonder that many roots of Ravel's exquisite harmony can be found there. The striking enharmonic modulation at the end of the middle section (A major V to F sharp major) or the fantastically bold pedal-point in the coda, point clearly to Ravel. Towards the end of this pedal-point the bass note F sharp is topped by the chords of G minor and B flat major (written in enharmonic disguise; see chords marked 'N.B.') treated as passing harmonies, an audacity without precedent in music.

EX. 7

In the last bar of this example Chopin included in the fioritura the suspensions A sharp, C natural, C sharp and E natural to the already rich harmony (an alteration of F sharp major VII):

EX. 8

'Spices' like these can often be found in passages by Ravel.

[7] Quoted in Cortot's edition of the Barcarolle (Salabert).

The Barcarolle also contains another forerunner of the 'Ravel-chord', namely in bar 49:

EX. 9

If one puts the left-hand part an octave higher one gets the 'Ravel-chord' with its typical friction of two minor seconds:

EX. 10

(compare with the opening of *Scarbo*).
Ravel is said, however, to have taken the inspiration of this harmony from the first movement of Beethoven's 'Moonlight' Sonata.

One of the most important 'novelties' in Ravel and in all modern harmony (including Hindemith, Stravinsky, Berg, Schoenberg and others) is what I should like to call 'frozen passing-notes'. These are free dissonances which are no longer resolved. Thus, for example, the succession of these two chords in *Scarbo*

EX. 11

might be imagined as derived from a simple romantic progression with omission of the obvious resolutions of the dissonances.

EX. 12

One starting-point of this 'freezing process' may well be found in Chopin's harmony.

The chromatic Study in A minor, op. 10, no. 2, in itself a simple piece, offers countless opportunities for making 'modern' harmonies, like these:

EX. 13

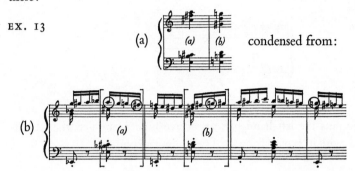

Note also the 'modern' clash between minor and major thirds in the first bar of this study.

This is speculation. Yet Chopin actually did start this 'freezing' process himself. One of his favourite harmonies, used over and over again, contains a dissonance (x) which is not properly resolved, but leaps down by a third instead to the following harmony:[7a]

EX. 14

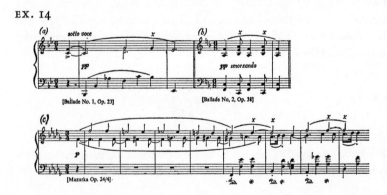

It is interesting that Schumann wrote a similar harmony in the first part of his *Kreisleriana* (bar 13), which is dedicated to Chopin.

[7a] These chords may, of course, be described as dominant thirteenths. Mr Badura-Skoda prefers to exclude them from this harmonic category which he considers separately on pp. 271–2. The thirteenths there resolve 'properly' by step. ED.

In the category of 'frozen dissonances' one might also include the strange chord at the end of the introduction to the First Ballade; the resolving of it comes so late that it is hardly heard as such.[8]

EX. 15

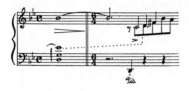

The one composer who might be called Chopin's truest heir was Claude Debussy. No one like him has been able so successfully to amalgamate Chopin's style into a style of his own, extracting all the wonders of the world out of a keyboard. The dedication of his Twelve Studies 'A la Mémoire de Frédéric Chopin' is more than a gesture: it is a sign how deeply he felt himself indebted to his great predecessor. With the exception of his earliest compositions, Debussy's language is in every note unmistakably his own. Yet how many of his stylistic attributes come directly from Chopin! At the beginning of this study we mentioned that the chord of the seventh became 'emancipated' in the nineteenth century. That means that a resolution into a triad was no longer always necessary or desirable. As a result one could move from one chord of the seventh to another without intermediate fundamental triads. This process had begun much earlier in the eighteenth century, but it was Chopin who carried it to the very limit of tonality for the first time in history. One such succession of chords of the seventh can be seen in the F minor Ballade (bars 46–53), where not a single tonic triad is reached in a longer passage; another even more interesting one comes at the end of the C sharp minor Mazurka, op. 30, no. 4 (bars 129–32).[8a]

EX. 16

[8] See Rawsthorne, p. 46. ED.
[8a] An earlier stage of this progression can be seen in the A minor Mazurka, op. 17, no. 4, from bar 9 onward: there, an intermediate chord of the sixth is put between two chords of the seventh.

Schumann when reviewing this mazurka had already remarked on the parallel fifths of this progression, yet the real event is the shifting of whole chords chromatically down through four bars, a motion unthinkable in traditional harmony.[9] This shifting of whole chords became a principle with Debussy: the chords are no longer considered as comprising independent parts, but are treated as self-contained units. Passages of 'forbidden' parallel fifths and octaves occur at the end of the Second Ballade in bars 189–90, and 193–4.

EX. 17

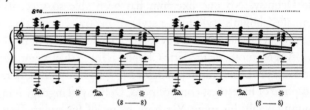

Again this clearly foreshadows Debussy. See for example *Le vent dans la plaine* (bars 9–10, Preludes, Vol. 1), different in expression, but very similar in construction.

EX. 18

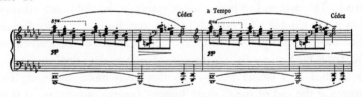

One of the most dramatic passages in all Chopin occurs before the coda of the Fourth Ballade in a truly breathtaking stretto passage (bars 198–201). This is one of Chopin's most powerful 'guns' and this time it is not 'buried in flowers', but exposed. These chords seem to express a state of frenzy—they are like a mad stabbing of a hero, a vision of horror, followed by a long silence.

[9] The only and rare exceptions were chords of the diminished seventh; see Bach's Partita in B flat major (Gigue, bars 34–40), and Mozart's C minor Piano Concerto (1st movement, bars 234–8).

EX. 19

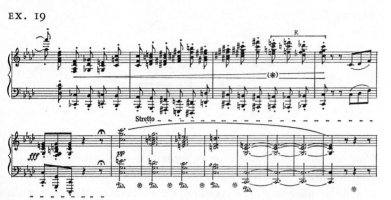

In traditional harmony it would be much simpler if the fourth chord in bar 3(*) was a C major chord instead of the printed harmony. But just here is the turning-point of the passage. Maybe it is also not coincidental that the last four staccato chords of this passage (bracket 'R') form a mirror-reversion of the main motif C-D flat-F-E (See bars 138–40).

To me a similar expression is to be found in the very last bars of the Fourth Act of Debussy's *Pelléas and Mélisande* when the music expresses the horror provoked by the murder of Pelléas. Although these two passages are not really similar, they express the same excitement.

I shall now turn to chords of the higher order, such as chords of the ninth, eleventh and thirteenth. Although Chopin does not use them so frequently, there are quite a few instances where such chords point far into the future either to Wagner or to Debussy.[9a] The latter seems to be evoked in the short middle section of the Study in Thirds, op. 25, no. 6, where the two chords of the ninth based on G and on F with a short intermediate step between hint already at a whole-tone scale.

A beautiful chord of the thirteenth occurs in the third movement of the Sonata in B minor (bar 25, third beat). In the Barcarolle, apart from the opening chord, there are several chords of the ninth and in two instances a chord of the fifteenth (*sic*) where the whole F sharp major scale vibrates together, namely in bar 32 and in bar 92:[10]

[9a] See Collet, p. 132. ED.
[10] This harmony might be explained in a simpler way as passing notes over a chord of the seventh. A genuine chord of the thirteenth is to be found in the penultimate note of bar 102.

EX. 20

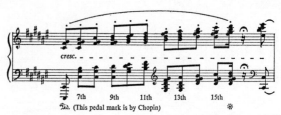

(Another such 'soundcluster' on a chord of the ninth can be seen in the Fourth Ballade, in the fifteenth and seventeenth bars before the end.)

On the other hand, one could call the exuberant pedal-point at the end of the Third Ballade (bars 227–30) more 'Wagnerian', where a chord of the thirteenth is built up gradually. Here, too, in the last bar, Chopin showed no fear of parallel fifths!

EX. 21

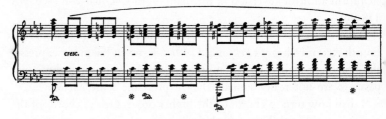

Debussy's *sixte ajouté* has no direct precedent in Chopin's work. But Chopin came close to it in the B major Mazurka, op. 33, no. 1 (bar 24 onward), in the closing passage of the F minor Fantasy, in the penultimate bar of the F sharp major Prelude, and in the penultimate bar of the Romance of the E minor Concerto. Debussy's whole-tone scale is also a novelty hinted at in Chopin's work; in the finale of the F minor Concerto there is a passage, the *bass* notes of which rise by whole tones (bar 221–8).

I hardly feel competent to deal with Chopin's influence on Richard Wagner.[11] Here I would like to mention only that Wagner's highly

---

[11] Good literature on this subject is offered in the books *Chopin the Composer* by Edgar Stillman Kelly, New York, 1913, and *Chopin's Musical Style*, by Gerald Abraham, London, 1960.

expressive musical language owes a great deal to Chopin. The whole
*Tristan* harmony, for example, with its endless chromatic yearning is
already to be found in Chopin. I would like to quote two examples
to show this: namely his last Mazurka, op. 68, no. 4 (bars 9–14), which
contains an almost exact premonition of the *Tristan* harmony in the
last bar:

EX. 22

and the Mazurka, op. 63, no. 3 (bars 164–73), which to me is even more
'Wagnerian' than the previous example.

EX. 23

One could hardly think that a composer like Bruckner has anything
to do with Chopin. Yet, Bruckner's only piano piece, entitled
*Erinnerung*, shows a surprising resemblance to Chopin's C minor
Nocturne, op. 48. Also it is interesting to note that one of Bruckner's
devices of sudden harmonic motion had been found earlier by Chopin,
namely the 'splitting' of one fundamental note into its neighbouring
chromatic notes. This happens, for instance, in the C minor Nocturne
between bars 8 and 9, when the G of bar 8 is split into G flat and A flat,
thus making a sudden switch from G minor to D flat major.[12]

[12] An even more exciting example of 'tone-splitting' can be found in the
Fantasy, op. 49, bars 101–8 and 268–75.

C–K

EX. 24

If we compare bars 18–21 of the first movement of Bruckner's Ninth Symphony, there is only one major difference: namely, that Bruckner continues with a whole-tone step downwards after the first split is made.

EX. 25

The term 'tone-splitting' (in German *Tonspaltung*) was invented by Alfred Orel and is extremely descriptive. Another device Bruckner and Chopin have in common is the joining of two entirely foreign harmonies by chromatic progressions in all parts. Thus, for example, an E major and a C minor triad can be joined together. In Chopin we find an example of such a transition in the A minor Study, op. 25, no. 11 (bars 49 and 50). The harmonic scheme of the progression is:

EX. 26

Another example can be seen in the passage of the first movement of the E minor Concerto, op. 11, starting thirty-seven bars before the end:[13]

EX. 27

---

[13] Exactly the same progression occurs in the last movement of Schumann's Piano Concerto (bars 902–3), possibly a direct influence of Chopin.

Bruckner uses the same principle in the Credo of his F minor Mass between bars 220 and 221. But there are even more affinities between these composers: the solemn, chorale-like ascent so typical of Bruckner (e.g. Adagio of the Eighth Symphony, bars 23–25) has a forerunner in similar passages by Chopin as in the Largo of the B minor Sonata (bars 95–98).[14]

Finally, as mentioned earlier, one aspect of Chopin's connexion with folklore should be dealt with: his harmonization of folk-melodies which are not constructed on our harmonic system. In the trio section of the Mazurka in F major, op. 68, no. 3, Chopin merely underlayed 'bagpipe' fifths, thus imitating peasant dances.[15] But in his Mazurka in B flat major, op. 7, no. 1, he did something more daring. There, the trio section has a melody in B flat minor with an augmented fourth E natural instead of E flat. Chopin, however, instead of harmonizing it in B flat minor, related it to a bass of G flat:

EX. 28

This underlying of a 'wrong' harmony already foreshadows Bartók, who experimented with a new harmonization of primitive folk-music.

First Rumanian Dance (1910)

EX. 29

[14] An astonishing 'Brucknerian' modulation can be seen in the A flat major Mazurka (op. 59, no. 2) twenty-seven bars from the end. There, on the second beats, the chords of the supertonic are reinterpreted as chords of the Neapolitan Sixth (with an added fifth), allowing a modulation from E to C major and then to A flat major (see Bruckner's 'Chorale' in the Fifth Symphony).

[15] See p. 74 Ex. 2. Ed.

I have tried to show some of the important trends that can be seen to derive from the work of Chopin. Because of his enormous popularity he must often have influenced many musicians unconsciously. This essay, as mentioned before, has a very limited scope and many aspects had to be omitted.[16] 'In the history of music Chopin takes a special place, for though he created only for the pianoforte and in smaller forms, he nevertheless exercised a decisive influence on contemporaries and successors.' (Ferruccio Busoni in 1916.)

[16] As, for example, Chopin's influence on the other national schools of the late nineteenth century and on other composers, like Reger, Pfitzner, Strauss, Delius, Elgar, etc.

## List of Sources

Gerald Abraham, *Chopin's Musical Style* (Oxford University Press, London).
Arthur Hedley, *Chopin*, Master Musicians Series (J. M. Dent & Sons Ltd., London).
Edgar Stillman Kelly, *Chopin the Composer (His structural art and its influence on contemporary music)*, Schirmer, New York, 1913.

Many extremely interesting papers were published in *The Book of the First International Musicological Congress de voted to the Works of Frederick Chopin* (Polish Scientific Publishers, Warsaw, 1960), edited by Zofia Lissa, out of which the following articles deal with Chopin's influence:

Boetticher, Wolfgang, 'Über einige Spätstilprobleme bei Chopin'
Borris, Siegfried, 'Chopins Bedeutung für den Chromatismus des XIX Jahrhunderts'
Chailley, Jacques, 'L'importance de Chopin dans l'évolution d'une langue harmonique'
German, Franciszek, 'Chopin im Lichte unbekannter Memoirenquellen gesehen'
Hlawicza, Karol, 'Eigentümliche Merkmale Chopins Rhythmik'
Jiranek, Jaroslav, 'Beitrag zum Vergleich des Klavierstils von Frederyk Chopin und Bedrich Smetana'
Kremlev, Julii, 'La place historique de l'harmonie de Chopin'
Kroo, Gyorgy, 'Einige Probleme des Romantischen bei Chopin und Liszt'
Ladmanova, Milada, 'Chopin und Smetana'
Lehmann, Dieter, 'Satztechnische Besonderheiten in den Klavierwerken von Frederic Chopin und Robert Schumann'
Ottich, Maria, 'Chopin und die Komponisten der nachfolgenden Generationen'
Pischner, Hans, 'Die Bedeutung Chopins für Robert Schumann'
Racek, Jan, 'Les Études faites par Leos Janacek dans les compositions pour piano de Frederic Chopin'
Volek, Jaroslav, 'Die Bedeutung Chopins für die Entwicklung der Alterierten Akkorde in der Musik des XIX Jahrhunderts'

# A Biographical Summary

by

Arthur Hedley

**1810**
*1 March*. Frédéric François Chopin born at Zelazowa Wola, a village near Warsaw. He is the second child and only son of Nicholas Chopin and Tekla-Justyna Chopin (*née* Krzyzanowska), the daughter of a Polish farmer.

In October of this year Nicholas Chopin accepts a post as French teacher at the Warsaw High School and moves with his family to the capital.

**1817**
Frédéric, already a child prodigy, receives piano lessons from Wojciech Zywny. His first little Polonaise (in G minor) is published.

**1818**
Chopin makes his first public appearance as a pianist, playing a concerto by Gyrowetz.

**1822**
He studies composition privately with Joseph Elsner, director of the Warsaw Music School.

**1823**
He becomes a full-time pupil at the High School, where his father teaches, and is given a comprehensive general education.

**1825**
He plays before the Tsar and is rewarded with a diamond ring. His op. 1, the Rondo in C minor, is published.

**1826**
Chopin becomes a regular student under Elsner. Composition of the *Rondo à la Mazur*, op. 5.

**1827**
Composition of the Variations, op. 2, for piano and orchestra; also the first Piano Sonata in C minor, op. 4.

1828
Chopin's first glimpse of the outside world when he visits Berlin. Composition of the Trio, op. 8, the Rondo for Two Pianos, and two further works for piano and orchestra—Fantasia on Polish Airs, op. 13, and the *Krakowiak*, op. 14.

1829
Formal lessons with Elsner ended. He visits Vienna and makes a successful début there. First Studies and F minor Concerto written. He falls in love with a fellow student, Constantia Gladkowska.

1830
In March he plays his F minor Concerto and other works at the National Theatre in Warsaw, and in October the E minor Concerto, before leaving Poland for good on 2 November.

1831
Most of this year is spent in Vienna, where he plays once or twice without attracting notice. He leaves in July and makes his way to Paris via Munich (where he plays) and Stuttgart, where he learns of the capture of Warsaw by the Russians.

1832
He is established in Paris, where he makes his début on 26 February. After a period of uncertainty he settles down as a fashionable piano teacher and composer, making only occasional appearances as a pianist. Friendly contacts with Berlioz, Liszt and Mendelssohn.

1833
Publication of the works brought from Poland (E minor Concerto, etc.) and of the first set of Studies, op. 10.

1834
Visits the Rhineland Music Festival at Mendelssohn's invitation. Popular success with the Waltz in E flat major, op. 18.

1835
In April he makes his last appearance in Paris for several years at a Conservatoire concert. During the summer he visits Germany, where he meets again the girl Maria Wodzińska and sees Mendelssohn and Schumann.

1836
He returns to Dresden and becomes engaged to Maria Wodzińska. Publication of the F minor Concerto, the First Ballade, op. 23, etc. In November he is introduced to George Sand by Liszt.

1837
His engagement to Maria Wodzińska is more or less repudiated by the girl's family owing to Chopin's uncertain state of health. Holiday excur-

sion to London in July. The Studies, op. 25, Scherzo, op. 31, and the Nocturnes, op. 32, are published.

### 1838

In March, Chopin plays his E minor Concerto at Rouen. By the end of June his liaison with George Sand has begun, and in November the pair travel to Majorca, where they are to spend the winter. Chopin soon falls ill and the completion of the Preludes, op. 28, is delayed.

### 1839

After a disastrous winter Chopin and George Sand leave Majorca in February. They spend some weeks at Marseilles (with a trip to Genoa) and the rest of the summer at Nohant, George Sand's country house. In October, Chopin returns to Paris. He meets Moscheles and plays at Court. Opp. 35–41, including the 'Funeral March' Sonata, are completed.

### 1840

A quiet year in Paris. Waltz in A flat major, op. 42, composed.

### 1841

In April, Chopin reappears as a pianist at Pleyel's rooms with brilliant success. Summer at Nohant, where he has ample leisure for composition. Opp. 43–49 completed and published.

### 1842

In February he gives a second private concert in Paris. After the usual vacation at Nohant, Chopin settles into a new home at 9 Place d'Orléans, where he is to remain until a few weeks before his death.

### 1843–6

He continues his secluded life in Paris, teaching and composing, but out of the public eye as a pianist. His routine is fixed: summer at Nohant with George Sand, the rest of the year in Paris. All the time his health is slowly declining as consumption strengthens its hold on him.

### 1847

Family dissensions bring about his separation from George Sand. He completes and publishes his last works, opp. 63–65.

### 1848

A week before revolution breaks out in Paris, Chopin gives his last recital there on 16 February. In April he comes to London for the season. He plays before the Queen (15 May) and gives private concerts on 23 June and 7 July, after which he goes to Scotland. Concerts in Glasgow and Edinburgh. He returns to London at the end of October and makes his final appearance as a pianist at the Guildhall on 16 November. A week later he returns to Paris in a desperate state of health.

1849

After months of suffering and inability to work, Chopin dies on 17 October at 12 Place Vendôme. At his funeral on 30 October, Mozart's Requiem is performed.

1855

The majority of the posthumous works (Fantaisie-Impromptu, etc.) are published.

# GENERAL CATALOGUE OF CHOPIN'S WORKS

(arranged in alphabetical order)

## Pianoforte Solo

| TITLE | OP. NO. | DATE OF COMPOSITION | AGE | DATE OF FIRST PUBLICATION | DEDICATION |
|---|---|---|---|---|---|
| Allegro de Concert in A major | 46 | 1841 (sketched in 1832) | 31 | 1841 | Friederike Müller |
| Andante Spianato in G major | 22 | 1834 | 24 | 1836 | Maria Wodzińska |
| Andantino in G minor (arr. of Chopin's song 'Wiosna' ('Spring')) | 74: 2 | 1838–48 (five versions) | 28–38 | Unpublished | |
| Ballades | | | | | |
| in G minor | 23 | 1835 (sketched in 1831) | 25 | 1836 | Baron Stockhausen |
| in F major | 38 | 1836 (first version) 1839 (final version) | 29 | 1840 | Schumann Mlle Pauline de Noailles |
| in A flat major | 47 | 1841 (sketched in 1840) | 31 | 1842 | |
| in F minor | 52 | 1842 | 32 | 1843 | Baroness Rothschild |
| Barcarolle in F sharp major | 60 | 1845–6 | 36 | 1846 | Baroness Stockhausen |
| Berceuse in D flat major | 57 | 1843 (revised 1844) | 33 | 1845 | Mlle Elise Gavard |
| Bolero | 19 | 1833 | 23 | 1834 | Countess Flahaut |
| Bourrées (two arrangements) | — | 1846 | 36 | Unpublished | |
| Canon at the octave in F minor | — | 1839 | 29 | Unpublished | |
| Cantabile in B flat major | — | 1834 | 24 | 1931 | |
| Contrabass Part (to a three-part Canon in B minor by Mendelssohn) | — | | | 1930 (facsimile) | |
| Contredanse in G flat major | — | 1827 | 17 | 1934 (facsimile) | |

| TITLE | OP. NO. | DATE OF COMPOSITION | AGE | DATE OF FIRST PUBLICATION | DEDICATION |
|---|---|---|---|---|---|
| Écossaises | 72:3 | 1826 | 16 | 1855 | |
| in D major | | | | | |
| in G major | | | | | |
| in D flat major | | | | | |
| Fantasy in F minor | 49 | 1841 | 31 | 1842 | Princess de Souzzo |
| Fantaisie-Impromptu in C sharp minor | 66 | 1835 | 25 | 1855 | Mme d'Esté |
| Fugue in A minor | — | 1841–2 | 31–32 | 1898 | |
| Impromptus | | | | | |
| in A flat major | 29 | 1837 | 27 | 1838 | Countess de Lobau |
| in F sharp major | 36 | 1839 | 29 | 1840 | Countess Esterházy |
| in G flat major | 51 | 1842 | 32 | 1843 | |
| Largo in E flat major | — | 1837 | 27 | 1938 | |
| Marches | | | | | |
| Military March | — | 1817 | 7 | 1817 | |
| Funeral March | 72:2 | 1827 | 17 | 1855 | |
| Funeral March (Sonata in B flat minor) | 35 | 1837 | 27 | 1840 | |
| Mazurkas | | | | | |
| in D major ('Mazurek') | | 1820 | 10 | 1910 (facsimile; not in Chopin's hand) 1955 (facsimile) | |
| in A flat major (first version) | 7:4 | 1824 | 14 | | |
| in A minor | 17:4 | 1824 | 14 | | |
| Two Mazurkas | — | 1826 | 16 | 1826 | |
| in G major | | | | | |
| in B flat major | | | | | |
| in A minor | 68:2 | 1827 | 17 | 1855 | |
| in D major (first version) | | 1829 | 19 | 1875 | |
| in F major | 68:3 | 1829 | 19 | 1855 | |
| in C major | 68:1 | 1829 | 19 | 1855 | |
| in G major | — | 1829 | 19 | 1879 | |
| in A minor | 70:2 | 1829 | 19 | 1902 | |

| TITLE | OP. NO. | DATE OF COMPOSITION | AGE | DATE OF FIRST PUBLICATION | DEDICATION |
|---|---|---|---|---|---|
| Mazurkas (cont.) | | | | | |
| Four Mazurkas | 6 | 1830 | 20 | 1832 | Countess Plater |
| in F sharp minor | | | | | |
| in C sharp minor | | | | | |
| in E major | | | | | |
| in E flat minor | | | | | |
| Five Mazurkas | 7 | 1830–1 | 20–21 | 1832 | M. Johns |
| in B flat major | | | | | |
| in A minor (second version) | | | | | |
| in F minor | | | | | |
| in A flat major (second version) | | | | | |
| in C major | | | | | |
| in D major (second version) | | 1832 | 22 | 1880 | |
| in B flat major | | 1832 | 22 | 1909 | |
| Four Mazurkas | 17 | 1832–3 | 22–23 | 1834 | Mme Lina Freppa |
| in B flat major | | | | | |
| in E minor | | | | | |
| in A flat major | | | | | |
| in A minor | | | | | |
| in C major | — | 1833 | 23 | 1870 | |
| in A flat major | — | 1834 | 24 | 1930 | |
| Four Mazurkas | 24 | 1834–5 | 24–25 | 1836 | Count de Perthuis |
| in G minor | | | | | |
| in C major | | | | | |
| in A flat major | | | | | |
| in B flat minor | | | | | |
| Two Mazurkas | 67 | 1835 | 25 | 1855 | |
| in G major | | | | | |
| in C major | | | | | |

| TITLE | OP. NO. | DATE OF COMPOSITION | AGE | DATE OF FIRST PUBLICATION | DEDICATION |
|---|---|---|---|---|---|
| Mazurkas (cont.) | | | | | |
| Four Mazurkas<br>  in C minor<br>  in B minor<br>  in D flat major ('Minute')<br>  in C sharp minor | 30 | 1836–7 | 26–27 | 1838 | Princess Württemburg |
| Four Mazurkas<br>  in G sharp minor<br>  in D major<br>  in C major<br>  in B minor | 33 | 1837–8 | 27–28 | 1838 | Countess Mostowska |
| in E minor | 41: 2 | 1838 | 28 | 1840 | Stefan Witwicki |
| Three Mazurkas<br>  in C sharp minor<br>  in B major<br>  in A flat major | 41 | 1839 | 29 | 1840 | |
| in A minor (*Notre Temps*) | — | 1840 | 30 | 1842 | Emil Gaillard |
| in A minor | — | 1841 | 31 | 1841 | Leon Szmitowski |
| Three Mazurkas<br>  in G major<br>  in A flat major<br>  in C sharp minor | 50 | 1841–2 | 31–32 | 1842 | |
| Three Mazurkas<br>  in B major<br>  in C major<br>  in C minor | 56 | 1843 | 33 | 1844 | Catherine Maberly |
| Three Mazurkas<br>  in A minor<br>  in A flat major<br>  in F sharp minor | 59 | 1845 | 35 | 1845 | |

| TITLE | OP. NO. | DATE OF COMPOSITION | AGE | DATE OF FIRST PUBLICATION | DEDICATION |
|---|---|---|---|---|---|
| Mazurkas (cont.) | | | | | |
| Three Mazurkas | 63 | 1846 | 36 | 1847 | Countess de Czosnowska |
| in B major | | | | | |
| in F minor | | | | | |
| in C sharp minor | | | | | |
| in A minor (three versions) | 67: 4 | 1846 | 36 | 1835 | |
| in G minor | 67: 2 | 1849 | 39 | 1855 | |
| in F minor | 68: 4 | 1849 | 39 | 1855 | |
| Moderato in E major ('Albumleaf') | — | 1843 | 33 | 1910 | |
| Nocturnes | | | | | |
| in E minor | 72: 1 | 1827 | 17 | 1855 | |
| in C sharp minor (*Lento con gran espressione*) | — | 1830 | 20 | 1875 | |
| Three Nocturnes | 9 | 1830–1 | 20–21 | 1832 | Marie Pleyel |
| in B flat minor | | | | | |
| in E flat major | | | | | |
| in B major | | | | | |
| Two Nocturnes | 15 | 1830–1 | 20–21 | 1833 | Ferdinand Hiller |
| in F major | | | | | |
| in F sharp major | | | | | |
| in G minor | 15 | 1833 | 23 | 1833 | |
| Two Nocturnes | 27 | 1835 | 25 | 1836 | Countess d'Apponyi |
| in C sharp minor | | | | | |
| in D flat major | | | | | |
| Two Nocturnes | 32 | 1836–7 | 26–27 | 1837 | Baroness de Billing |
| in B major | | | | | |
| in A flat major | | | | | |
| in C minor | — | 1837 | 27 | 1938 | |
| Two Nocturnes | 37 | 1838 | 28 | 1840 | |
| in G minor | | 1839 | 29 | 1840 | |
| in G major | | | | | |

| TITLE | OP. NO. | DATE OF COMPOSITION | AGE | DATE OF FIRST PUBLICATION | DEDICATION |
|---|---|---|---|---|---|
| Nocturnes (cont.) | | | | | |
| Two Nocturnes | 48 | 1841 | 31 | 1842 | Mlle Laura Duperré |
| in C minor | | | | | |
| in F sharp minor | | | | | |
| Two Nocturnes | 55 | 1843 | 33 | 1844 | Jane Stirling |
| in F minor | | | | | |
| in E flat major | | | | | |
| Two Nocturnes | 62 | 1846 | 36 | 1846 | Mlle de Könneritz |
| in B major | | | | | |
| in E major | | | | | |
| Polonaises | | | | | |
| in G minor | — | 1817 | 7 | 1817 | Countess Skarbek |
| in B flat major | — | 1817 | 7 | 1934 (facsimile) | |
| in A flat major | — | 1821 | 11 | 1902 | Wojciech Zywny |
| in G sharp minor | — | 1822 | 12 | 1864 | Mme Dupont |
| in D minor | 71: 1 | 1825 | 15 | 1855 | Count Skarbek |
| in B flat minor | | 1826 | 16 | 1826 | |
| in B flat major | 71: 2 | 1828 | 18 | 1855 | |
| in F minor | 71: 3 | 1828 | 18 | 1855 | |
| in G flat major | — | 1829 | 19 | 1870 | |
| Two Polonaises | 26 | 1834–5 | 24–25 | 1836 | Josef Dessauer |
| in C sharp minor | | | | | |
| in E flat minor | | | | | |
| Two Polonaises | 40 | 1838 | 28 | 1840 | Julian Fontana |
| in A major | | | | | |
| in C minor | | | | | |
| in F sharp minor | 44 | 1840–1 | 30–31 | 1841 | Princess de Beauvau |
| in A flat major | 53 | 1842 | 32 | 1843 | Auguste Léo |
| Polonaise-Fantaisie in A flat major | 61 | 1845–6 | 35–36 | 1846 | Mme A. Veyret |

| TITLE | OP. NO. | DATE OF COMPOSITION | AGE | DATE OF FIRST PUBLICATION | DEDICATION |
|---|---|---|---|---|---|
| Preludes (set of twenty-four) | 28 | 1816-9 | 26-29 | 1839 | Camille Pleyel (French Edition) |
| in C major | | | | | J. C. Kessler (German Edition) |
| in A minor | | | | | |
| in G major | | | | | |
| in E minor | | | | | |
| in D major | | | | | |
| in B minor | | | | | |
| in A major | | | | | |
| in F sharp minor | | | | | |
| in E major | | | | | |
| in C sharp minor | | | | | |
| in B major | | | | | |
| in G sharp minor | | | | | |
| in F sharp major | | | | | |
| in E flat minor | | | | | |
| in D flat major ('Raindrop') | | | | | |
| in B flat minor | | | | | |
| in A flat major | | | | | |
| in F minor | | | | | |
| in E flat major | | | | | |
| in C minor | | | | | |
| in B flat major | | | | | |
| in G minor | | | | | |
| in F major | | | | | |
| in D minor | | | | | |
| in A flat major | — | 1834 | 24 | 1918 | Pierre Wolff |
| in C sharp minor | 45 | 1841 | 31 | 1841 | Princess Czernicheff |
| Rondos | | | | | |
| in C minor (see Pianoforte Duets) | 1 | 1825 | 15 | 1825 | Mme Linde |
| Rondo à la Mazur | 5 | 1826 | 16 | 1828 | Countess de Moriolles |
| in C major (see Pianoforte Duets) | 73 | 1828 | 18 | 1954 | |
| in E flat major | 16 | 1832 | 22 | 1834 | Mlle Caroline Hartmann |

| TITLE | OP. NO. | DATE OF COMPOSITION | AGE | DATE OF FIRST PUBLICATION | DEDICATION |
|---|---|---|---|---|---|
| Scherzos | | | | | |
| in B minor | 20 | 1832 | 22 | 1835 | Thomas Albrecht |
| in B flat minor | 31 | 1837 (first version 1831) | 27 | 1838 | Countess de Fürstenstein |
| in C sharp minor | 39 | 1839 | 29 | 1840 | Adolf Gutman |
| in E major | 54 | 1842 | 32 | 1843 | Mlle Jeane de Caraman (German Edition) / Mlle Clothilde de Caraman (French Edition) |
| Sonatas | | | | | |
| in C minor | 4 | 1828 | 18 | 1851 | Josef Elsner |
| in B flat minor | 35 | 1839 | 29 | 1840 | |
| in B minor | 58 | 1844 | 34 | 1845 | Countess de Perthuis |
| Studies (Vol. I: set of twelve) | 10 | 1829–32 | 19–22 | 1833 | Liszt |
| in C major | | | | | |
| in A minor | | | | | |
| in E major | | | | | |
| in C sharp minor | | | | | |
| in G flat major ('Black keys') | | | | | |
| in E flat minor | | | | | |
| in C major | | | | | |
| in F major | | | | | |
| in F minor | | | | | |
| in A flat major | | | | | |
| in E flat major | | | | | |
| in C minor ('Revolutionary') | | | | | |
| Studies (Vol. II: set of twelve) | 25 | 1832–6 | 22–26 | 1837 | Countess d'Agoult |
| in A flat major | | | | | |
| in F minor | | | | | |
| in F major | | | | | |
| in A minor | | | | | |
| in E minor | | | | | |
| in G sharp minor | | | | | |
| in C sharp minor | | | | | |
| in D flat major | | | | | |

| TITLE | OP. NO. | DATE OF COMPOSITION | AGE | DATE OF FIRST PUBLICATION | DEDICATION |
|---|---|---|---|---|---|
| Studies (cont.) | | | | | |
| in G flat major ('Butterfly') | | | | | |
| in B minor | | | | | |
| in A minor ('Winter Wind') | | | | | |
| in C minor | | | | | |
| 'Trois Nouvelles Etudes' | — | 1839 | 29 | 1840 | |
| in F minor | | | | | |
| in A flat major | | | | | |
| in D flat major | | | | | |
| Tarantella in A flat major | 43 | 1841 | 31 | 1841 | |
| Variations | | | | | |
| on *Der Schweizerbub* (German national air) | — | 1826 | 16 | 1851 | Katarina Sowinska |
| on a theme of Paganini ('Souvenir de Paganini') | — | 1829 | 19 | 1881 | |
| on a theme by Hérold ('Ronde' from *Ludovic*) | 12 | 1833 | 23 | 1833 | Emma Horsford |
| for the *Hexameron* (a set of six variations by different composers on the March from Bellini's *Puritani di Scozia*) | — | 1837 | 27 | 1839 | Princess Belgiojoso |
| Waltzes | | | | | |
| in A flat major | | 1827 | 17 | 1902 | |
| in B minor | 69: 2 | 1829 | 19 | 1852 | |
| in A minor (sketch) | | 1829 | 19 | Unpublished | |
| in D flat major | 70: 3 | 1829 | 19 | 1855 | |
| in E major | | 1829 | 19 | 1871 | |
| in E flat major | — | 1929–30 | 19–20 | 1902 | |
| in E minor | | 1830 | 20 | 1868 | |
| in E flat major | 18 | 1831 | 21 | 1834 | Laura Horsford |
| in A minor | 34: 2 | 1831 | 21 | 1838 | Baroness C. d'Ivry |
| in G flat major | 70: 1 | 1835 | 25 | 1855 | |
| in A flat major | 34: 1 | 1835 | 25 | 1838 | Mlle de Thun-Hohenstein |
| in A flat major ('L'Adieu') | 69: 1 | 1835 | 25 | 1855 | Maria Wodzińska |
| in F major | 34: 3 | 1838 | 28 | 1838 | Mlle A. d'Eichtal |

| TITLE | OP. NO. | DATE OF COMPOSITION | AGE | DATE OF FIRST PUBLICATION | DEDICATION |
|---|---|---|---|---|---|
| Waltzes (cont.) | | | | | |
| in A flat major | 42 | 1840 | 30 | 1840 | |
| in E flat major ('Sostenuto') | — | 1840 | 30 | 1955 | |
| in F minor | 70: 2 | 1841 | 31 | 1855 | Mme Charlotte de Rothschild (?) |
| in A minor | — | 1841 | 31 | 1855 | |
| Three Waltzes | 64 | 1846–7 | 36–37 | 1847 | |
| in D flat major ('Minute') | | | | | Countess Potocka |
| in C sharp minor | | | | | Baroness Rothschild |
| in A flat major | | | | | Countess Branicka |
| in B major | — | 1848 | 38 | Unpublished | |
| **Songs** | | | | | |
| Seventeen Polish Songs | 74 | | | 1857 | |
| Życzenie (The Wish) | | 1829 | 19 | | |
| Wiosna (Spring) | | 1838 | 28 | | |
| Smutna Rzeka (Sad River) | | 1831 | 21 | | |
| Hulanka (Drinking Song) | | 1830 | 20 | | |
| Gdzie lubi (What she likes) | | 1829 | 19 | | |
| Precz z moich oczu! (Out of my sight!) | | 1830 | 20 | | |
| Poseł (The Messenger) | | 1830 | 20 | | |
| Śliczny Chłopiec (Handsome lad) | | 1841 | 31 | | |
| Melodia (Melody) | | 1847 | 37 | | |
| Wojak (The Warrior) | | 1830 | 20 | | |
| Dwojaki koniec (Double Ending) | | 1845 | 35 | | |
| Moja pieszczotka (My Darling) | | 1837 | 27 | | |
| Nie ma czego trzeba (There is no need) | | 1845 | 35 | | |
| Pierścień (The Ring) | | 1836 | 26 | | |
| Narzeczony (The Bridegroom) | | 1831 | 21 | | |
| Piosnka Litewska (Lithuanian song) | | 1831 | 21 | | |
| Śpiew grobowy (Hymn from the tomb) | | 1836 | 26 | 1872 | |
| Two Songs | | | | | |
| Czary (Spells) | | 1830 | 20 | 1910 | |
| Dumka (Elegy) | | 1840 | 30 | 1910 | |

| TITLE | OP. NO. | DATE OF COMPOSITION | AGE | DATE OF FIRST PUBLICATION | DEDICATION |
|---|---|---|---|---|---|
| **Pianoforte Duet** | | | | | |
| Rondo in C minor (arr. of the Rondo in C minor for Solo Piano)—1 piano | 1 | | | 1834 | |
| Rondo in C major (arr. of the Rondo in C major for Solo Piano)—2 pianos | 73 | 1828 | 18 | 1855 | |
| **Chamber Music** | | | | | |
| Trio in G minor, for Piano, Violin and Cello | 8 | 1828–9 | 18–19 | 1832 | Princess Radziwill |
| Polonaise in C major, for Piano and Cello | 3 | 1829 | 19 | 1831 | Josef Merk |
| Introduction in C major, for Piano and Cello, to the above Polonaise | — | 1830 | 20 | 1831 | |
| Grand Duo in E major, on themes from Meyerbeer's *Robert le Diable*, for Piano and Cello | — | 1832 | 21 | 1833 | |
| Sonata in G minor, for Piano and Cello | — | 1832 | 21 | 1833 | |
| Variations in E major, for Flute and Piano, on a theme from Rossini's *La Cenerentola* | 65 | 1845–6 | 35–36 | 1848 | Auguste Franchomme |
| | — | 1824 | 14 | 1955 (facsimile) | |
| **Pianoforte and Orchestra** | | | | | |
| Variations on *Là ci darem la mano* from Mozart's *Don Giovanni* | 2 | 1827 | 17 | 1830 | Titus Woyciechowski |
| Grand Fantasia in A major, on Polish Airs | 13 | 1828 | 18 | 1834 | Johann Pixis |
| *Krakowiak*: Grand Concert Rondo in F major | 14 | 1828 | 18 | 1834 | Princess Czartoryska |
| Concerto in F minor | 21 | 1829–30 | 19–20 | 1836 | Countess Potocka |
| Concerto in E minor | 11 | 1830 | 20 | 1833 | Friedrich Kalkbrenner |
| Grand Polonaise in E flat major (the 'Andante Spianato' for solo piano was prefixed to this Polonaise and both were published together) | 22 | 1830–1 | 20–21 | 1836 | Baroness d'Este |

| TITLE | OP. NO. | DATE OF COMPOSITION | AGE | DATE OF FIRST PUBLICATION | DEDICATION |
|---|---|---|---|---|---|
| **Lost Works** | | | | | |
| Variations | — | 1818 | 8 | | |
| Two Polonaises | — | 1818 | 8 | | |
| Polonaise (based on Rossini's *Barber of Seville*) | — | 1825 | 15 | | |
| Variations in F major for Piano Duet | — | 1826 | 16 | | |
| Variations on an Irish National Air, for Piano Duet[1] | — | 1826 | 16 | | |
| Waltz in C major | — | 1826 | 16 | | |
| Écossaise in B flat major | — | 1827 | 17 | | |
| *Andante Dolente* in B flat minor | — | 1827 | 17 | | |
| Waltz in D minor | — | 1828 | 18 | | |
| Waltz in A flat major | — | 1830 | 20 | | |

[1] The manuscript was recently discovered in Cracow.

# CHRONOLOGICAL TABLE
## OF
## CHOPIN'S WORKS

(This Table is based on Maurice Brown's definitive *INDEX* of Chopin's works.[1])

| DATE OF COMPOSITION | AGE | TITLE | OP. NO. | DATE OF FIRST PUBLICATION | DEDICATION |
|---|---|---|---|---|---|
| 1817 | 7 | Polonaise in G minor | | 1817 | Countess Skarbek |
| 1817 | | Military March (lost) | | 1817 | |
| 1817 | | Polonaise in B flat major | | 1934 (facsimile) | |
| 1818 | 8 | Variations (lost) | | | |
| | | Two Polish Dances (lost) | | | |
| 1820(?) | 10 | Mazurka in D major | | 1910 (facsimile; not in Chopin's hand) | |
| 1821 | 11 | Polonaise in A flat major | | 1902 | Wojciech Zywny |
| 1822 | 12 | Polonaise in G sharp minor | | 1864 | Mme Dupont |
| 1824 | 14 | Mazurka in A flat major (first version) | 7: 4 | | |
| 1824(?) | | Variations in E major for Flute and Piano on a theme by Rossini | | 1955 (facsimile) | |
| 1825 | 15 | Rondo in C minor | 1 | 1825 | Mme Linde |
| 1825 | | Polonaise in D minor | 71: 1 | 1855 | Count Skarbek |
| 1826 | 16 | Three Ecossaises | 72: 3 | 1855 | |
| | | D major | | | |
| | | G major | | | |
| | | D flat major | | | |
| 1826 | 16 | Variations in F major for Piano Duet (lost) | | | |
| 1826 | | Variations on an Irish National Air (lost) | | | |
| 1826 | | Waltz in C major (lost) | | | |
| 1826 | | Polonaise in B flat minor | | 1826 | Wilhelm Kolberg |
| 1826 | | Introduction and Variations in E major, on a German National Air (*Der Schweizerbub*) | | 1851 | Katarina Sowinska |
| 1826 | | Rondo à la Mazur, in F major | 5 | 1828 | Countess de Moriolles |
| 1826 | | Two Mazurkas | | 1826 | |
| | | G major | | | |
| | | B flat major | | | |
| 1827(?) | 17 | Contredanse in G flat major | | 1934 (facsimile) | |

[1] London 1960, revised 1965.

| DATE OF COMPO- SITION | AGE | TITLE | OP. NO. | DATE OF FIRST PUBLICATION | DEDICATION |
|---|---|---|---|---|---|
| 1827 | | Ecossaise in B flat major (lost) | | | |
| 1827 | | *Andante Dolente* in B flat minor (lost) | | | |
| 1827 | | Mazurka in A minor | 68: 2 | 1855 | |
| 1827 | | Nocturne in E minor | 72: 1 | 1855 | |
| 1827 | | Funeral March in C minor | 72: 2 | 1855 | |
| 1827 | | Waltz in A flat major | | 1902 | |
| 1827 | | Variations in B flat major (*Là ci darem*) | 2 | 1827 | Titus Woyciechowsk |
| 1828 | 18 | Waltz in D minor (lost) | | | |
| 1828 | | Sonata in C minor | 4 | 1851 | Josef Elsner |
| 1828 | | Polonaise in B flat major | 71: 2 | 1855 | |
| 1828–9 | | Trio in G minor, for Piano, Violin and Cello | | 1832 | Prince Radziwill |
| 1828 | | Rondo in C major for Solo Piano | | 1954 | M. Fuchs |
| 1828 | | Rondo in C major for Two Pianos (an arr. of previous item) | 73 | 1855 | |
| | | Grand Fantasia in A major, on Polish Airs, for Piano and Orchestra | | 1834 | Johann Pixis |
| 1828 | | Krakowiak: Grand Concert Rondo in F major, for Piano and Orchestra | | 1834 | Princess Czartoryska |
| 1828 | | Polonaise in F minor | 71: 3 | 1855 | |
| 1829 | 19 | Mazurka in D major (first version) | | 1875 | |
| 1829 | | Song for Voice and Piano: 'Gdzie lubi' ('What she likes') | 74: 5 | 1857 | |
| 1829 | | Song for Voice and Piano: 'Życzenie' ('The Wish') | 74: 1 | 1856 | |
| 1829 | | Mazurka in F major | 68: 3 | 1855 | |
| 1829 | | Waltz in B minor | 69: 2 | 1852 | |
| 1829 | | Polonaise in G flat major | | 1870 | |
| 1829 | | Variations in A major ('Souvenir de Paganini') | | 1881 | |
| 1829 | | Mazurka in C major | 68: 1 | 1855 | |
| 1829 | | Mazurka in G major | | 1879 | |
| 1829 | | Waltz in D flat major | 70: 3 | 1855 | |
| 1829(?) | | Waltz in A minor (sketch) | | | |
| 1829 | | Polonaise in C major, for Piano and 'Cello | 3 | 1831 | Josef Merk |
| 1829–32 | 19 | Twelve Studies C major A minor E major C sharp minor G flat major E flat minor C major F major F minor A flat major E flat major C minor | 10 | 1833 | Liszt |

| DATE OF COMPO- SITION | AGE | TITLE | OP. NO. | DATE OF FIRST PUBLICATION | DEDICATION |
|---|---|---|---|---|---|
| 1829–30 | | Concerto in F minor for Piano and Orchestra | 21 | 1836 | Countess Potocka |
| 1829 | | Waltz in E major | | 1871 | |
| 1829 | | Mazurka in A minor (first version) | 70: 2 | 1902 | |
| 1829–30 | | Waltz in E flat major | | 1902 | |
| 1830 | 20 | Song for Voice and Piano: 'Wojak' ('The Warrior') | 74: 10 | 1856 | |
| 1830 | | Song for Voice and Piano: 'Precz z moich oczu!' ('Out of my sight!') | 74: 6 | 1857 | |
| 1830 | | Nocturne in C sharp minor (*Lento con gran espressione*) | | 1875 | |
| 1830 | | Two Songs for Voice and Piano: 'Hulanka' ('Drinking Song') 'Poseł' ('The Messenger') | 74: 4 74: 7 | 1857 | |
| 1830 | | Song for Voice and Piano: 'Czary' ('Spells') | | 1910 (facsimile) | |
| 1830 | | Introduction in C major for the Polonaise for Piano and Cello op. 3 | | 1831 | |
| 1830 | | Concerto in E minor, for Piano and Orchestra | 11 | 1833 | Kalkbrenner |
| 1830–1 | | Three Nocturnes B flat minor E flat major B major | 9 | 1832 | Marie Pleyel |
| 1830–1 | | Two Nocturnes F major F sharp major | 15 | 1833 | Ferdinand Hiller |
| 1830 | | Waltz in E minor | | 1868 | |
| 1830 | | Waltz in A flat major (lost) | | | |
| 1830–1 | | Grand Polonaise in E flat major, for Piano and Orchestra | 22 | 1836 | Baroness d'Este |
| 1830 | | Four Mazurkas F sharp minor C sharp minor E major E flat minor | 6 | 1832 | Countess Plater |
| 1830–1 | | Five Mazurkas B flat major A minor (second version) F minor A flat major (second version) C major | 7 | 1832 | M. Johns |
| 1831 | 21 | Waltz in E flat major | 18 | 1834 | Laura Horsford |
| 1831 | | Three Songs for Voice and Piano: 'Smutna Rzeka' ('Sad River') 'Narzeczony' ('The Bridegroom') 'Piosnka Litewska' ('Lithuanian Song') | 74: 3 74: 15 74: 16 | | |
| 1831 | | Waltz in A minor | 34: 2 | 1838 | Baroness d'Ivry |

| DATE OF COMPO- SITION | AGE | TITLE | OP. NO. | DATE OF FIRST PUBLICATION | DEDICATION |
|---|---|---|---|---|---|
| 1831–2 | | Scherzo in B minor | 20 | 1835 | M. Thomas Albrecht |
| 1831–5 | | Ballade in G minor | 23 | 1836 | Baron Stockhausen |
| 1832 | 22 | Contrabass Part to a three-part Canon in B minor by Mendelssohn | | 1930 (facsimile) | |
| 1832 | | Grand Duo in E major, for Piano and Cello, on Themes from Meyerbeer's *Robert le Diable* | | 1833 | |
| 1832 | | Mazurka in D major (second version) | | 1880 | |
| 1832 | | Allegro de Concert (revised in 1841) | 46 | 1841 | Friederike Müller |
| 1832 | | Mazurka in B flat major | | 1909 | Mme A. Wolowska |
| 1832 | | Introduction and Rondo in E flat major | 16 | 1834 | Mme C. Hartmann |
| 1832–3 | | Four Mazurkas B flat major E minor A flat major A minor | 17 | 1834 | Mme L. Freppa |
| 1832–6 | | Twelve Studies A flat major F minor F major A minor E minor G sharp minor C sharp minor D flat major G flat major B minor A minor C minor | 25 | 1837 | Countess d'Agoult |
| 1833 | 23 | Nocturne in G minor | 15: 3 | 1833 | |
| 1833 | | Introduction and Variations in B flat major, on the 'Ronde' from Hérold's *Ludovic* | 12 | 1833 | Mme Emma Horsford |
| 1833 | | Introduction and Bolero in A minor/A major | 19 | 1834 | Countess de Flahault |
| 1833 | | Mazurka in C major | | 1833 | |
| 1833(?) | | Rondo in C minor (an arr. for Piano Duet of op. 1) | | 1834 | |
| 1834 | 24 | Cantabile in B flat major | | 1931 | |
| 1834 | | Mazurka in A flat major | | 1930 | |
| 1834 | | Prelude in A flat | | 1918 | Pierre Wolff |
| 1834–5 | | Four Mazurkas G minor C major A flat major B flat minor | 24 | 1836 | Count Perthuis |
| 1834–5 | | Two Polonaises C sharp minor E flat minor | 26 | 1836 | Josef Dessauer |
| 1835 | 25 | Nocturne in C sharp minor | 27: 1 | 1836 | Countess d'Apponyi |
| 1835(?) | | Waltz in G flat major | 70: 1 | 1835 | |

| DATE OF COMPO- SITION | AGE | TITLE | OP. NO. | DATE OF FIRST PUBLICATION | DEDICATION |
|---|---|---|---|---|---|
| 1835 | | Two Mazurkas | 67 | 1855 | |
| | | G major | 1 | | Mme Mlokosiewicz |
| | | C major | 3 | | Mme Hoffmann |
| 1835 | | Waltz in A flat major | 34: 1 | 1838 | Mlle Thun-Hohenstein |
| 1835 | | Waltz in A flat major | 69: 1 | 1855 | Maria Wodzińska |
| 1835 | | Fantaisie-Impromptu in C sharp minor | 66 | 1855 | Mme d'Este |
| 1835 | | Nocturne in D flat major | 27: 2 | 1836 | Countess d'Apponyi |
| 1836–9 | 26 | Twenty-four Preludes: | 28 | 1839 | Camille Pleyel (Fr. Edition) |
| | | C major | | | J. C. Kessler (Ger. Edition) |
| | | A minor | | | |
| | | G major | | | |
| | | E minor | | | |
| | | D major | | | |
| | | B minor | | | |
| | | A major | | | |
| | | F sharp minor | | | |
| | | E major | | | |
| | | C sharp minor | | | |
| | | B major | | | |
| | | G sharp minor | | | |
| | | F sharp major | | | |
| | | E flat minor | | | |
| | | D flat major ('Raindrop') | | | |
| | | B flat minor | | | |
| | | A flat major | | | |
| | | F minor | | | |
| | | E flat major | | | |
| | | C minor | | | |
| | | B flat major | | | |
| | | G minor | | | |
| | | F major | | | |
| | | D minor | | | |
| 1836 | | Song for Voice and Piano: 'Spiew Grobowy' ('Hymn from the Tomb') | 74: 17 | 1872 | |
| 1836 | | Ballade in F major (revised 1839) | 38 | 1840 | Schumann |
| 1836 | | Song for Voice and Piano: 'Pierścień' ('The Ring') | 74: 14 | 1857 | |
| 1836–7 | | Four Mazurkas | 30 | 1838 | Princess Württemburg |
| | | C minor | | | |
| | | B minor | | | |
| | | D flat major | | | |
| | | C sharp minor | | | |
| 1836–7 | | Two Nocturnes | 32 | 1837 | Baroness Billing |
| | | B major | | | |
| | | A flat major | | | |
| 1837 | 27 | Nocturne in C minor | | 1938 | |
| 1837(?) | | Largo in E flat major | | 1938 | |
| 1837 | | Impromptu in A flat major | 29 | 1838 | Countess Caroline de Lobau |
| 1837 | | Scherzo in B flat minor | 31 | 1838 | Countess Adele de Fürstenstein |
| 1837 | | Song for Voice and Piano: 'Moja pieszczotka' ('My Darling') | 74: 12 | 1857 | |

| DATE OF COMPO-SITION | AGE | TITLE | OP. NO. | DATE OF FIRST PUBLICATION | DEDICATION |
|---|---|---|---|---|---|
| 1837 | | Variation movement no. 6 of the *Hexameron* | | 1839 | Princess Belgiojoso |
| 1837 | | Funeral March Sonata in B flat minor | 35 | 1840 | |
| 1837–8 | | Four Mazurkas G sharp minor D major C major B minor | 33 | 1838 | Countess Mostowsk |
| 1838 | 28 | Song for Voice and Piano: 'Wiosna' ('Spring') | 74: 2 | 1857 | |
| 1838 | | Andantino in G minor, a piano arr. of the song 'Wiosna' ('Spring'). See previous item | | Unpublished | |
| 1838 | | Waltz in F major | 34: 3 | 1838 | Mlle A. d'Eichtal |
| 1838 | | Nocturne in G minor | 37: 1 | 1840 | |
| 1838 | | Polonaise in A major | 40: 1 | 1840 | Julian Fontana |
| 1838–9 | | Polonaise in C minor | 40: 2 | 1840 | Julian Fontana |
| 1838 | | Mazurka in E minor | 41: 2 | 1840 | Stefan Witwicki |
| 1839 | 29 | Scherzo in C sharp minor | 39 | 1840 | Adolf Gutman |
| 1839 | | Three Mazurkas C sharp minor B major A flat major | 41 | 1840 | Stefan Witwicki |
| 1839 | | Nocturne in G major | 37: 2 | 1840 | |
| 1839 | | Sonata in B flat minor | 35 | 1840 | |
| 1839 | | Impromptu in F sharp major | 36 | 1840 | |
| 1839(?) | | Canon at the octave in F minor | | Unpublished | |
| 1839 | | Trois Nouvelles Etudes F minor A flat major D flat major | | 1840 | |
| 1840 | 30 | Waltz in A flat major | 42 | 1840 | |
| 1840 | | Song for Voice and Piano: 'Dumka' ('Elegy') | | 1910 | |
| 1840 | | Waltz ('*Sostenuto*') in E flat major | | 1955 | |
| 1840 | | Mazurka in A minor (Notre Temps) | | 1842 | |
| 1840–1 | | Polonaise in F sharp minor | 44 | 1841 | Princess Beauvau |
| 1840–1 | | Ballade in A flat major | 47 | 1842 | Mlle Pauline Noaille |
| 1841 | 31 | Fantasy in F minor | 49 | 1842 | Princess Souzzo |
| 1841 | | Waltz in F minor | 70: 2 | 1855 | |
| 1841 | | Tarantella in A flat major | 43 | 1841 | |
| 1841 | | Mazurka in A minor | | 1841 | Emil Gaillard |
| 1841 | | Prelude in C sharp minor | 45 | 1841 | Princess Czernichefi |
| 1841 | | Two Nocturnes C minor F sharp minor | 48 | 1842 | Laura Duperré |
| 1841 | | Song for Voice and Piano: 'Śliczny chłopiec' ('Handsome Lad') | 74: 8 | 1857 | |
| 1841–2 | | Fugue in A minor | | 1898 | |
| 1841–2 | | Three Mazurkas G major A flat major C sharp minor | 50 | 1842 | Leon Szmitowski |

| DATE OF COMPOSITION | AGE | TITLE | OP. NO. | DATE OF FIRST PUBLICATION | DEDICATION |
|---|---|---|---|---|---|
| 1842 | 32 | Ballade in F minor | 52 | 1843 | Baroness Rothschild |
| 1842 | | Polonaise in A flat major | 53 | 1843 | Auguste Léo |
| 1842 | | Scherzo in E major | 54 | 1843 | Mlle Jeanne Caraman (Ger. Edition) Mlle Clothilde Caraman (Fr. Edition) |
| 1842 | | Impromptu in G flat major | 51 | 1843 | Countess Esterházy |
| 1843(?) | 33 | Waltz in A minor | | 1955 | |
| 1843 | | Moderato in E major ('Albumblatt') | | 1910 | |
| 1843 | | Two Nocturnes F minor E flat major | 55 | 1844 | Jane Stirling |
| 1843 | | Three Mazurkas B major C major C minor | 56 | 1844 | Catherine Maberly |
| 1843 | | Berceuse in D flat major (revised 1844) | 57 | 1845 | |
| 1844 | 34 | Sonata in B minor | 58 | 1845 | Countess Perthuis |
| 1845 | 35 | Two Songs for Voice and Piano: 'Dwajaki koniec' ('Double Ending') 'Nie ma czego trzeba' ('There is no need') | 74   11    13 | 1857 | |
| 1845 | | Three Mazurkas A minor A flat major F sharp minor | 59 | 1845 | |
| 1845–6 | | Barcarolle in F sharp major | 60 | 1846 | Baroness Stockhausen |
| 1845–6 | | Polonaise-Fantaisie in A flat major | 61 | 1846 | Mme A. Veyret |
| 1845–6 | | Sonata in G minor for 'Cello and Piano | 65 | 1848 | Auguste Franchomme |
| 1846 | 36 | Two Bourrées (arr. by Chopin) G major A major | | Unpublished | |
| 1846 | | Two Nocturnes B major E major | 62 | 1846 | Mlle R. Könneritz |
| 1846 | | Three Mazurkas B major F minor C sharp minor | 63 | 1847 | Countess Czosnowska |
| 1846 | | Mazurka in A minor | 67: 4 | 1855 | |
| 1846–7 | | Three Waltzes D flat major C sharp minor A flat major | 64 | 1847 | Countess Potocka Baroness Rothschild Countess Branicka |
| 1847 | 37 | Song for Voice and Piano: 'Melodia' ('Melody') | 74: 9 | 1857 | |
| 1848 | 38 | Waltz in B major | | Unpublished | |
| 1849 | 39 | Mazurka in G minor | 67: 2 | 1855 | |
| 1849 | | Mazurka in F minor | 68: 4 | 1852 | |

# DISCOGRAPHY

To attempt a complete discography of Chopin's works is unrealistic.
For one thing, record companies all over the world continue to issue a
steady stream of his discs and a 'complete' catalogue would be out of
date before it was even published. For another, such a catalogue would
be enormously bulky and out of all proportion to the size of this book.
As it is, this discography runs to some twenty pages and is likely to meet
the needs of most musicians.

Many of these discs are now deleted and can only be obtained from
the larger record libraries. I thought it worth while to include them,
however, because some of them are of outstanding historical interest
and shed a fascinating light on the way in which the interpretation of
Chopin has changed within two generations.[1]

The catalogue runs in strict alphabetical order and falls under the
following headings.

Section I:   Solo Piano, pp. 301–314.
Section II:  Piano and Orchestra, pp. 314–317.
Section III: Chamber Music, pp. 317–18.
Section IV: Songs, pp. 318–21.

Asterisks (*) indicate 78 r.p.m.; daggers (†) indicate 45 r.p.m.
The word 'or' before a number means a *different* performance by
the same artist; the word 'and' before a number means the *same*
performance re-issued on a new label.

My thanks are due to the staff of the B.B.C. Gramophone Department for so kindly placing their unrivalled facilities at my disposal. *A.W.*

*Section I: Piano Solo*

ALLEGRO de CONCERT (op. 46)
   Claudio Arrau                   COL 33CX 1443

ANDANTE SPIANATO and GRAND POLONAISE BRILLANTE (op. 22)
   Brailowsky, Alexander       PHILIPS ABL 5313
   Cortot, Alfred (recorded from 1910
      piano roll)               ADES MS 30 LA 519

[1] For lists of currently available gramophone records readers are referred to the
latest issues of the Long Playing Classical Record Catalogue, published by the
*Gramophone.*

| | |
|---|---|
| Gheorghiu, Valentin | HMV XLP 20021 |
| Gimpel, Jakob | HMV DLP 1187 |
| Horowitz, Vladimir | HMV BLP 1079 |
| Hofmann, Josef | COL ML 4929 |
| Kempff, Wilhelm | DECCA LXT 5445 |
| | and Stereo SXL 2081 |
| Kentner, Louis | COL DX 895–6★ |
| Siki, Bela | PARLOPHONE PW 8004–5★ |
| | and PMA 1022 |
| Stefanska, Halina | DGG DGM 19083 |
| Rubinstein, Artur | HMV DB 2499–500★ |
| | or HMV BLP 1027 |

### BALLADE NO. 1 in G MINOR (op. 23)

| | |
|---|---|
| Anda, Geza | COL 33CX 1459 |
| Arrau, Claudio | BRUNSWICK AXTL 1043 |
| Backhaus, Wilhelm | DECCA LX 3044 |
| Barère, Simon | REMINGTON R 19917 |
| Brailowsky, Alexander | DECCA CA 8155★ |
| Casadesus, Robert | COL 9609★ |
| Cortot, Alfred | HMV DB 1343★ |
| | or HMV DB 2023★ |
| Doyen, Ginette | NIXA WLP 5169 |
| François, Samson | DECCA K 1398★ |
| Frankl, Peter | VOX PL 12620 |
| Fiorentino, Sergio | DELTA TQD 3014 |
| | and Stereo SQD 107 |
| Frugoni, Orazio | VOX PL 10490 |
| Gheorghiu, Valentin | HMV XLP 20021 |
| Groot, Cor de | PHILIPS NBR 6025 |
| Gulda, Friedrich | DECCA LW 5156 |
| Hofmann, Josef | COL ML 4929★ |
| Horowitz, Vladimir | HMV ALP 1087 |
| Joyce, Eileen | COL DX 1084★ |
| Jambor, Agi | CAPITOL P 8403 |
| Kartun, Louis | PARLOPHONE E 10960★ |
| Kentner, Louis | COL DX 1391★ |
| Karolyi, Julian | DGG DG 16025 |
| Lythgoe, Clive | SOCIETY SOC 962 |
| Malcuzyinski, Witold | COL 33CX 1864★ |
| Rubinstein, Artur | RCA RB 16206 |
| Moiseiwitsch, Benno | HMV C 3101★ |
| Siki, Bela | PARLOPHONE PMA 1008 |
| Stefanska, Halina | DGG DGM 19083 |
| | and HELIODOR 478410 |
| | HMV C 4061★ |
| | and 7p 130† |
| Slenczynska, Ruth | BRUNSWICK AXTL 1096 |
| Ts'ong, Fou | WESTMINSTER XWN 18956 |
| | WORLD RECORD CLUB T 48 |

### BALLADE NO. 2 in F MAJOR (op. 38)

| | |
|---|---|
| Arrau, Claudio | BRUNSWICK AXTL 1043 |
| Ashkenazy, Vladimir | COL 33CX 1563 |
| | or MK 203 B1 |
| Casadesus, Robert | COL LFX 166★ |
| | PHILIPS SBF 260 |
| Cherkassky, Shura | HMV ALP 1489 |
| | and 7ER 5088† |

| Cortot, Alfred | HMV DB 1344★ |
| | HMV DB 2024★ |
| Doyen, Ginette | NIXA WLP 5169 |
| Fiorentino, Sergio | DELTA TQD 3014 |
| | and Stereo SQD 107 |
| Frankl, Peter | VOX PL 12620 |
| Frugoni, Orazio | VOX PL 10490 |
| Groot, Cor de | PHILIPS NBR 6025 |
| | and ABE 10061† |
| Gulda, Friedrich | DECCA LW 5156 |
| Jambor, Agi | CAPITOL P 8403 |
| Jenkins, Philip | CLASSICS CLUB X530 |
| Karolyi, Julian | DGG DG 16025 |
| | and EPL 30030† |
| Kitain, Anatole | COL DX 874★ |
| Malcuzynski, Witold | COL 33CX 1338 |
| | and SEL 1561† |
| | or COL 33CX 1864 |
| Merrick, Frank | MERRICK 3 |
| Mildner, Poldi | TELEFUNKEN LGM 65025 |
| Moiseiwitsch, Benno | HMV C 3685★ |
| Perlemuter, Vlado | CONCERT HALL AM 2223 |
| Rubinstein, Artur | RCA RB 16206 |
| Slenczynska, Ruth | BRUNSWICK AXTL 1096 |
| Siki, Bela | PARLOPHONE PMA 1008 |
| Ts'ong, Fou | WESTMINSTER XWN 18956 |
| | and WORLD RECORD CLUB T 48 |

## BALLADE NO. 3 in A FLAT MAJOR (op. 47)

| Arrau, Claudio | PARLOPHONE R 20443★ |
| | or BRUNSWICK AXTL 1043 |
| Bertram, George | PARLOPHONE E 10572★ |
| Casadesus, Robert | PHILIPS SBF 261 |
| Cherkassky, Shura | HMV 7ER 5120† |
| Cliburn, Van | RCA RB 16273 |
| Cortot, Alfred | HMV DB 1345★ |
| | HMV DB 2025★ |
| Dennery, Jean | PARLOPHONE E 11199★ |
| Doyen, Ginette | NIXA WLP 5169 |
| Entremont, Philippe | PHILIPS ABE 10024† |
| Fiorentino, Sergio | DELTA TQD 3014 |
| | and Stereo SQD 107 |
| Frankl, Peter | VOX PL 12620 |
| Friedman, Ignaz | COL DX 466★ |
| Frugoni, Orazio | VOX PL 10490 |
| Godowsky, Leopold | ALLEGRO AL 31 |
| Groot, Cor de | PHILIPS NBR 6025 |
| | or ABE 10061† |
| Gulda, Friedrich | DECCA LW 5156 |
| Harasiewicz, Adam | FONTANA CFE 15024 |
| Horowitz, Vladimir | HMV ALP 1111 |
| Jambor, Agi | CAPITOL P 8403 |
| Joyce, Eileen | COL DX 976★ |
| Katchen, Julius | DECCA LX 3079 |
| Karolyi, Julian | DGG DG 16025 |
| Kempff, Wilhelm | DECCA LXT 5445 |
| | or Stereo SXL 2081 |
| Kitain, Anatole | COL DX 788★ |
| Levitzki, Mischa | HMV EW 64★ |
| Malcuzynski, Witold | COL 33CX 1864 |

Moiseiwitsch, Benno                    HMV CLP 1282★
                                       or 7EP 7096†
                                       and HMV C3100★

Murdoch, William                       COL 9367★
Niedzielski, Stanislas                 LONDON TW 91147
Pachman, Vladimir de                   HMV D 262★
Paderewski, Ignace                     CLASSICS RECORD LIBRARY
                                       WV 6633–6

Richter, Sviatoslav                    DGG LPM 18766
Rubinstein, Artur                      RCA RB 16206
Siki, Bela                             PARLOPHONE PMA 1008
Slenczynska, Ruth                      BRUNSWICK AXTL 1096
Ts'ong, Fou                            WESTMINSTER XWN 18956
                                       and WORLD RECORD CLUB

## BALLADE NO. 4 in F MINOR (op. 52)

Arrau, Claudio                         BRUNSWICK AXTL 1044
Bishop, Stephen                        HMV CLP 1655
Bruchollerie, Monique de la            HMV DB 6731★
Casadesus, Robert                      PHILIPS SBF 262
Cortot, Alfred                         HMV DB 1346★
                                       or HMV DB 2026★
Doyen, Ginette                         NIXA WLP 5169
Fiorentino, Sergio                     DELTA TQD 3014
                                       and Stereo SQD 107
Frankl, Peter                          VOX PL 12620
Frugoni, Orazio                        VOX PL 10490
Groot, Cor de                          PHILIPS NBR 6025
Gulda, Friedrich                       DECCA LW 5156
Horowitz, Vladimir                     HMV ALP 1111
Jambor, Agi                            CAPITOL P 8403
Karolyi, Julian                        DGG DG 16025
Malcuzynski, Witold                    COL 33CX 1864
Moiseiwitsch, Benno                    HMV CLP 1282
                                       and Stereosonic Tape
                                       SCT 1508
Richter, Sviatoslav                    DGG LPM 18849
Rubinstein, Artur                      RCA RB 16206
Siki, Bela                             PARLOPHONE PMA 1008
Slenczynska, Ruth                      BRUNSWICK AXTL 1096
Solomon                                HMV C 3403★
Stefanska, Halina                      HELIODOR 478410
                                       and DGG DGM 19083
Ts'ong, Fou                            WESTMINSTER XWN 18956
                                       WORLD RECORD CLUB T 48

## BARCAROLLE IN F SHARP MAJOR (op. 60)

Argerich, Martha                       DGG LPM 18672
Arrau, Claudio                         BRUNSWICK AXTL 1043–4
Ashkenazy, Vladimir                    COL 33CX 1621
Bachauer, Gina                         HMV CLP 1057
Badura-Skoda, Paul                     HMV CLP 1784
Banhalmi, George                       VOX PL 10370
Bishop, Stephen                        HMV CLP 1655
Cortot, Alfred                         HMV DB 2030★
Cherkassky, Shura                      WORLD RECORD CLUB T 247
Firkusny, Rudolf                       CAPITOL P 8428
Gieseking, Walter                      COL 33CX 1526
                                       or LX 859★
Gmeiner, Luise                         TELEFUNKEN E 2191

| Horowitz, Vladimir | RCA RB 16064 |
|---|---|
| Kempff, Wilhelm | DECCA LXT 5451 |
| | and Stereo SXL 2024 |
| Karolyi, Julian | DGG DGM 18068 |
| | and EPL 30030† |
| Kentner, Louis | SAGA XID 5233 |
| | or COL DX 1112★ |
| Lipatti, Dinu | COL LX 1437★ |
| | or 33CX 1386 |
| Long, Marguerite | COL LFX 325★ |
| Merrick, Frank | MERRICK 9 |
| Moiseiwitsch, Benno | HMV C 3229★ |
| | or HMV CLP 1072★ |
| Novaes, Guiomar | BRUNSWICK AXA 4519 |
| Palenicek, Josef | SUPRAPHON H 22600 |
| Pennario, Leonard | CAPITOL CCL 7523 |
| Perlemuter, Vlado | CONCERT HALL AM 2223 |
| Pouishnoff, Leff | SAGA XID 5013 |
| Reisenberg, Nadia | WHITEHALL WH 20061 |
| Rowlands, Alan | CLASSICS CLUB X 523 |
| Rubinstein, Artur | HMV DB 1161★ |
| | and HMV DB 21613★ |
| Smith, Cyril | COL DX 1747★ |
| Sandor, Gyorgy | COL LCX 148★ |
| Uninsky, Alexander | PHILIPS GBL 5535 |

## BERCEUSE in D FLAT MAJOR (op. 57)

| Backhaus, Wilhelm | HMV DB 1131★ |
|---|---|
| Badura-Skoda, Paul | HMV CLP 1784 |
| Brailowsky, Alexander | HMV DB 6715★ |
| Christiansen, Karen Lund | HMV Z 347★ |
| Cortot, Alfred | HMV DB 167★ |
| | or HMV DB 1145★ |
| | HMV ALP 1197 |
| | or DB 21175★ |
| Forge, Frank la | VICTOR 55031 |
| Friedman, Ignaz | COL L 2260★ |
| Frugoni, Orazio | VOX PL 10510 |
| Gieseking, Walter | COL 33CX 1761 |
| Groot, Cor de | PHILIPS GBL 5595 |
| Gulda, Friedrich | DECCA K 2167★ |
| Hambourg, Mark | HMV C 1730★ |
| Hofmann, Josef | COL L 1392★ |
| | or COL ML 4929 |
| Johannesen, Grant | HMV CLP 1243 or BR 3032 |
| Joyce, Eileen | PARLOPHONE E 11432★ |
| Karolyi, Julian | DGG DGM 18068 |
| Katin, Peter | DECCA LXT 5516 |
| Kempff, Wilhelm | DECCA LXT 5451 |
| | and Stereo SXL 2024 |
| Koczalski, Raoul | DECCA LY 6146★ |
| Magaloff, Nikita | DECCA LXT 5037 |
| Maggiar, Wilfrid | NIXA LPY 112 |
| Merrick, Frank | MERRICK 9 |
| Michelangeli, Arturo Benedetti | TELEFUNKEN GX 61018 |
| Moiseiwitsch, Benno | HMV D 57★ |
| Novaes, Guiomar | VOX PL 7810 |
| Paderewski, Ignace | HMV DB 601★ |
| Palenicek, Josef | SUPRAPHON H 22602 |

C–L

| | |
|---|---|
| Perlemuter, Vlado | CONCERT HALL AM 2223 |
| Pugno, Raoul | DELTA TQD 3037 |
| Pouishnoff, Leff | SAGA XID 5013 |
| Quinnell, Ivan | QUALITON BLP 11465 |
| Rosenthal, Moritz | ULTRAPHON F 469 |
| Rubinstein, Artur | HMV DB 2149 |
| Ts'ong, Fou | WESTMINSTER XWN L 8956 |
| | and WORLD RECORD CLUB T 48 |
| Worden, Wilfred | DECCA K 707* |

BOLERO (op. 19)

| | |
|---|---|
| Banhalmi, George | VOX PL 10370 |
| Dymont, Lily | DECCA LY 6064* |
| Kentner, Louis | COL DX 1640* |
| Maggiar, Wilfrid | NIXA LPY 112 |

ECOSSAISES (3) (op. 72, no. 3)

| | |
|---|---|
| Bachauer, Gina | HMV CLP 1057 |
| Brailowsky, Alexander | HMV DB 3706* |
| Dorfmann, Ania | COL DX 449* |
| Fiorentino, Sergio | SAGA XID 5016 |
| Frugoni, Orazio | VOX PL 10510 |
| Koczalski, Raoul | HMV DA 4430* |
| Maggiar, Wilfrid | NIXA LPY 112 |
| Nemes, Katalin | QUALITON LPX 1083 |
| Vitebsky, Bernard | CONCERT ARTIST |
| | SPA 9002 and MPO 5008 |

STUDIES (op. 10, op. 25, and *Trois Nouvelles Etudes*)
    (complete recordings)

| | |
|---|---|
| Arrau, Claudio | COL 33CX 1443-4* |
| Ashkenazy, Vladimir (opp. 10 and 25 only) | MK 203 B 1-2 |
| Backhaus, Wilhelm (opp. 10 and 25 only) | HMV DB 1132-4* |
| | or DB 1178-80* |
| Cherkassky, Shura | HMV ALP 1310-1 |
| Cortot, Alfred | HMV DB 2027-9* |
| | and DB 2308-10* |
| Cziffra, György (opp. 10 and 25 only) | PHILIPS AL 3427 |
| Elinson, Iso (opp. 10 and 25 only) | PYE CCT 31002-3 |
| Goldsand, Robert | NIXA CLP 1132-3 |
| Haas, Werner (opp. 10 and 25 only) | FONTANA EFL 2516 |
| Koczalski, Raoul | DECCA LY 6115-21* |
| Kyriakou, Rena (op. 10 only) | VOX GBY 12710 |
| Leimar, Kurt (opp. 10 and 25 only) | HELIODOR 478031 |
| Novaes, Guiomar | VOX PL 9070 |
| Slenczynska, Ruth (opp. 10 and 25 only) | BRUNSWICK AXTL 1084-5 |
| Uninsky, Alexander | PHILIPS A 00405 L |

FANTAISIE-IMPROMPTU (op. 66) (see Impromptus)

FANTASY IN F MINOR (op. 49)

| | |
|---|---|
| Arrau, Claudio | COL 33CX 1755* |
| Badura-Skoda, Paul | HMV CLP 1784 |
| Cherkassky, Shura | HMV BLP 1013 |
| | or DB 9599-9600* |
| Ciccolini, Aldo | COL 33FCX 726 |
| Cliburn, Van | RCA RB 16273 |
| Cortot, Alfred | HMV DB 2031-2* |
| Cziffra, György | HMV ALP 1713 |

| | |
|---|---|
| Frankl, Peter | VOX PL 12620 |
| Gheorghiu, Valentin | HMV XLP 20021 |
| Harasiewicz, Adam | FONTANA CFL 1052 |
| Karolyi, Julian | DGG DGM 18068 |
| Katchen, Julius | DECCA LX 3079 |
| Kempff, Wilhelm | DECCA LXT 5445 |
| | and Stereo SXL 2081 |
| Malcuzynski, Witold | COL 33CX 1695 |
| | or COL 33CX 1066 |
| | and COL LX 1211–2 |
| Merrick, Frank | MERRICK 9 |
| Novaes, Guiomar | VOX PL 7810 |
| Perlemuter, Vlado | CONCERT HALL AM 2223 |
| Solomon | COL DX 668–9★ |
| Ts'ong, Fou | PATHÉ DTX 173 |
| Uninsky, Alexander | PHILIPS GBR 6514 |

FUGUE IN A MINOR

| | |
|---|---|
| Janotha, Nathalie | HMV GL 5561 |
| Vitebsky, Bernard | CONCERT ARTIST MPO 5008 |

FUNERAL MARCH in C MINOR

| | |
|---|---|
| Maggiar, Wilfred | NIXA LPY 112 |
| Vitebsky, Bernard | CONCERT ARTIST MPO 5008 |

IMPROMPTUS (4) (complete recordings)

| | |
|---|---|
| Arrau, Claudio | BRUNSWICK AXTL 1044 |
| Cortot, Alfred | HMV DB 2021–2★ |
| Frugoni, Orazio | VOX PL 10490 |
| Horszowski, Mieczyslaw | VOX PL 7870 |
| Jambor, Agi | CAPITOL P 8403 |
| Karolyi, Julian | DGG DGM 18068 |
| | and EPL 30127† |
| Kempff, Wilhelm | DECCA LXT 5451 |
| | and Stereo SXL 2024 |
| Kyriakon, Rena | VOX GBY 12710 |
| Magaloff, Nikita | DECCA LXT 5037 |
| Slenczynskya, Ruth | BRUNSWICK AXTL 1084–5 |

MAZURKAS (complete recordings)

| | |
|---|---|
| Frugoni, Orazio | VOX VUX 2017/1–2 |
| Magaloff, Nikita | DECCA LXT 5318–20 |
| Rubinstein, Artur | HMV DB 3802–8★ |
| | DB 3839–45★ |
| | or ALP 1398–1400 |

NOCTURNES (complete recordings)

| | |
|---|---|
| Askenase, Stefan | DGG DGM 18262–3 |
| | and HELIODOR 478147 |
| Brailowsky, Alexander (1–19) | RCA 16050–3 |
| Haebler, Ingrid | VOX VUX 2007–1/2 |
| Katin, Peter | DECCA LXT 5122 |
| Lympany, Moura (1–19) | HMV CLP 1424–5 |
| Novaes, Guiomar | VOX PL 9632–1/2 |
| Rubinstein, Artur (1–19) | HMV DB 3186–96★ |
| | or ALP 1701–2 |
| | HMV ALP 1157 and 1170 |

POLONAISE NO. 1 in C SHARP MINOR (op. 26, no. 1)

| | |
|---|---|
| Askenase, Stefan | DGG DGM 19064 |
| | and HELIODOR 478424 |
| Boukoff, Yuri | HMV CLP 1706 |
| Brailowsky, Alexander | CBS BRG 72015 |
| Cziffra, György | PHILIPS AL 3425 |
| Harasiewicz, Adam | FONTANA EFR 2025 |
| | and CFL 1052 |
| Johannesen, Grant | VOX VUX 2003-1 |
| Malcuzynski, Witold | COL 33CX 1690 |
| Pachmann, Vladimir de | HMV DB 931* |
| Rubinstein, Artur | HMV DB 2493* |
| | or HMV ALP 1028 |
| | or RB 16111 |

POLONAISE NO. 2 in E FLAT MINOR (op. 26, no. 2)

| | |
|---|---|
| Askenase, Stefan | DGG DGM 19064 |
| | and HELIODOR 47824 |
| Boukoff, Yuri | HMV CLP 1706 |
| Brailowsky, Alexander | CBS BRG 72015 |
| Cziffra, György | PHILIPS AL 3425 |
| Johannsen, Grant | VOX VUX 2003-1 |
| Malcuzynski, Witold | COL 33CX 1690 |
| | and SEL 1688† |
| | COL LX 1416* |
| | or 33CX 1138 |
| | and SEL 1514† |
| Paderewski, Ignace | HMV DB 5897* |
| Rubinstein, Artur | HMV DB 2494* |
| | HMV ALP 1028 |
| | and 7ER 5048† |
| | or RCA RB 16111 |

POLONAISE NO. 3 in A MAJOR (op. 40, no. 1)

| | |
|---|---|
| Askenase, Stefan | DGG LPM 18791 |
| | DGG EPL 30040 |
| Atwell, Winifred | PYE NPL 18082 |
| Boukoff, Yuri | HMV CLP 1706 |
| | WHITEHALL WH 20061 |
| Cziffra, György | PHILIPS AL 3425 |
| Dennery, Jean | PARLOPHONE E 11207* |
| Entremont, Philippe | PHILIPS ABE 10024† |
| | and SBF 252 |
| Fiorentino, Sergio | SUMMIT LSE 2031 |
| Ganz, Rudlph | PATHÉ FRÈRES 5151 |
| Gorodnitzki, Sascha | CAPITOL P 8374 |
| Godowsky, Leopold | BRUNSWICK 50015* |
| Hambourg, Mark | HMV C 1292* |
| Hofmann, Josef | COL L 1092* |
| Kentner, Louis | COL DX 1083* |
| Loveridge, Iris | COL DX 1239* |
| Magaloff, Nikita | DECCA LX 3076 |
| Paderewski, Ignace (acoustic recording 1911) | HMV DB 590* |
| Paderewski, Ignace (acoustic recording 1914) | HMV DB 375* |
| Rubinstein, Artur | HMV DB 2495* |
| | and HMV ALP 1028 |
| | and 7ER 5005† |
| | or RCA RB 16111 |

Solomon   COL DX 441*
Turner, Mary Jo   DECCA F 2863*

POLONAISE NO. 4 in C MINOR (op. 40, no. 2)

Askenase, Stefan   DGG DGM 19064
   and HELIODOR 478424
Boukoff, Yuri   HMV CLP 1706
Brailowsky, Alexander   CBS BRG 72015
Cziffra, György   PHILIPS AL 3425
Firkusny, Rudolf   CAPITOL P 8428
Johannesen, Grant   VOX VUX 2003-1
Magaloff, Nikita   DECCA LX 3076*
Malcuzynski, Witold   COL 33CX 1690
   and SEL 1695†
   or COL SEL 1561†
Rubinstein, Artur   HMV DB 2495*
   or HMV ALP 1028
   and 7ER 5030†
Stefanska, Halina   SUPRAPHON LPV 299
   and SUA 10012
   HMV C 4100*

POLONAISE NO. 5 in F SHARP MINOR (op. 44)

Askenase, Stefan   DGG DGM 19064
   or HELIODOR 478424
Boukoff, Yuri   HMV CLP 1706
Brailowsky, Alexander   CBS BRG 72015
Cziffra, György   PHILIPS AL 3425
Johannesen, Grant   VOX VUX 2003-1
Malcuzynski, Witold   COL 33CX 1138
   or COL 33CX 1690
Pollini, Maurizio   DGG LPEM 19218
Rubinstein, Artur   HMV DB 2496*
   HMV ALP 1028
   or RCA RB 16111

POLONAISE NO. 6 in A FLAT MAJOR (op. 53)

Anda, Geza   DGG LPM 18604
Askenase, Stefan   DGG LPM 18791
   DGG EPL 30040
Block, Michel   DGG LPE 17215
Boukoff, Yuri   Whitehall WH 20061
   HMV CLP 1706
Brailowsky, Alexander   CBS BRG 72015
   DECCA DE 7029
   UNITED NATIONS UN.M.02
Cherkassky, Shura   HMV 7ER 5120†
Cortot, Alfred   HMV DB 2014*
Cliburn, Van   RCA RB 16273
Cziffra, György   PHILIPS AL 3425
Ellegaard, France   DECCA K 1600*
Farrell, Richard   PYE CEC 32010†
Friedman, Ignaz   COL L 1990*
Fiorentino, Sergio   SUMMIT LSE 2031
Harasiewicz, Adam   FONTANA EFL 2504
Iturbi, José   HMV DB 6288*
   COL SEB 3510†
   and SEL 1673†
   or 33CX 1368*

| | |
|---|---|
| Johannesen, Grant | VOX VIP 45240 |
| | and VUX 2003-1 |
| Katchen, Julius | DECCA K 2293* |
| | DECCA LXT 5656 |
| | or CEP 5523† |
| Kentner, Louis | COL DX 1502* |
| Koczalski, Raoul | HMV DA 4431* |
| Levitzski, Mischa | HMV DA 1316 |
| Malcuzynski, Witold | COL LX 982* |
| | COL 33CX 1138 |
| | and SEL 1514† |
| | or COL 33CX 1690 |
| | and SEL 1695† |
| Niedzielski, Stanislas | LONDON TW 91147 |
| Paderewski, Ignace | HMV DB 3134* |
| Pennario, Leonard | CAPITOL CTL 7102 |
| | and P 8312 |
| | and CCL 7510 |
| Rubinstein, Artur | HMV DB 2497* |
| | RCA RB 16111 |
| Solomon | COL LX 314* |
| Uninsky, Alexander | PHILIPS SBF 110 |
| Verne, Adela | COL L 1213* |
| Worden, Wilfred | DECCA F 3598* |

## POLONAISE—FANTAISIE (op. 61)

| | |
|---|---|
| Askenase, Stefan | DGG DGM 19064 |
| | and HELIODOR 478424 |
| Boukoff, Yuri | HMV CLP 1706 |
| Fiorentino, Sergio | SAGA STM 6021 |
| Horowitz, Vladimir | RCA RB 16019 |
| Johannesen, Grant | VOX VUX 2003-2 |
| Kempff, Wilhelm | DECCA LXT 5445 |
| | and Stereo SXL 2081 |
| Kentner, Louis | COL DX 1146-7* |
| Pouishnoff, Leff | SAGA XID 5013 |
| Rehberg, Walter | DECCA PO 5071-2* |
| Richter, Sviatoslav | DGG LPE 18849† |
| Rubinstein, Artur | HMV DB 2498-9* |
| | or HMV BLP 1027 |
| Zarickaja, Irina | DGG LPEM 19219 |

## POLONAISE NO. 8 in D MINOR (op. posth.)

| | |
|---|---|
| Boukoff, Yuri | HMV CLP 1707 |
| Johannesen, Grant | VOX VUX 2003-2 |
| Stefanska, Halina | HMV C 4076* |
| | SUPRAPHON SUEC 825 |
| | and SUA 10012 |
| | and LPV 299 |

## POLONAISE NO. 9 in B FLAT MAJOR (op. posth.)

| | |
|---|---|
| Askenase, Stefan | DGG DGM 19064 |
| | and EPL 30263 |
| | and HELIODOR 478424 |
| Boukoff, Yuri | HMV CLP 1707 |
| Brailowsky, Alexander | CBS BRG 72015 |
| Friedman, Ignaz | COL L 2339* |
| Hambourg, Mark | HMV C 2579* |
| Johannesen, Grant | VOX VUX 2003-2 |

| | |
|---|---|
| Moiseiwitsch, Benno | HMV D 1280★ |
| | or C 3485★ |
| Nemes, Katalin | QUALITON LPX 1083 |

POLONAISE NO. 10 in F MINOR (op. posth.)
| | |
|---|---|
| Boukoff, Yuri | HMV CLP 1707 |
| Johannesen, Grant | VOX VUX 2003–2 |

POLONAISE NO. 11 in G MINOR (1817)
| | |
|---|---|
| Boukoff, Yuri | HMV CLP 1707 |

POLONAISE NO. 12 in B FLAT MINOR (1817)
| | |
|---|---|
| Boukoff, Yuri | HMV CLP 1707 |

POLONAISE NO. 14 in G SHARP MINOR (1822)
| | |
|---|---|
| Boukoff, Yuri | HMV CLP 1707 |
| Johannesen, Grant | VOX VUX 2003–2 |

POLONAISE NO. 15 in B FLAT MINOR (1826)
| | |
|---|---|
| Boukoff, Yuri | HMV CLP 1707 |
| Johannesen, Grant | VOX VUX 2003–2 |

POLONAISE NO. 16 in G FLAT MAJOR (1829)
| | |
|---|---|
| Boukoff, Yuri | HMV CLP 1707 |

PRELUDES (op. 28) (complete)
| | |
|---|---|
| Anda, Geza | DGG LPM 18604 |
| Arrau, Claudio | PHILIPS GBL 5503 |
| | and ABE 10202–4† |
| Askenase, Stefan | DGG DGM 19002 |
| Brailowsky, Alexander | PHILIPS ABL 3312 |
| Cortot, Alfred | HMV DB 957–60★ |
| | or DB 2015–8★ |
| Elinson, Iso | PYE CCL 30112 |
| Fiorentino, Sergio | SAGA STM 6021 |
| François, Samson | COL 33CX 1877 |
| Groot, Cor de | PHILIPS ABR 4042 |
| Gulda, Friedrich | DECCA LXT 2837 |
| Lympany, Moura | HMV CLP 1051 |
| | and 7EP 7070, 7074, 7079† |
| Moiseiwitsch, Benno | HMV 3905–8★ |
| Novaes, Guiomar | VOX PL 6170 |
| Pennario, Leonard | CAPITOL P 8561 |
| Perlemuter, Vlado | GUILDE INTERNATIONALE MMS 2207 |
| Rubinstein, Artur | HMV DB 9529–32★ |
| | and ALP 1192 or RCA RB 16110 |
| Vondrovic, Otakar | SUPRAPHON SUA 10198 |

PRELUDE in C SHARP MINOR (op. 45)
| | |
|---|---|
| Banhalmi, George | VOX PL 10370 |
| Brailowsky, Alexander | PHILIPS ABL 3313 |
| Cortot, Alfred | HMV DB 21018★ |
| Fiorentino, Sergio | SAGA XID 5076 |
| Harasiewicz, Adam | FONTANA EFL 2504 |
| Koczalski, Raoul | DGG 67509 |
| Perlemuter, Vlado | GUILDE INTERNATIONALE MMS 2207 |
| Ts'ong, Fou | WESTMINSTER XWN 18956 |
| Vásáry, Tamás | DGG LPM 374 |

PRELUDE in A FLAT MAJOR (op. posth.)
    Banhalmi, George             VOX PL 10370
    Fiorentino, Sergio            SAGA XID 5076
    Koczalski, Raoul             DGG 67509
    Ts'ong, Fou                 WESTMINSTER XWN 18956

RONDO in E FLAT MAJOR (op. 16)
    Banhalmi, George             VOX PL 10370
    Kitain, Anatole              COL DX 839*
    Pouishnoff, Leff              SAGA XID 5013

SCHERZOS (4) (complete recordings)
    Arrau, Claudio              BRUNSWICK AXTL 1043-4
    Badura-Skoda, Paul         HMV CLP 1784
    Frugoni, Orazio             VOX PL 10510
    Kentner, Louis              COL 33SX 1033
    Moiseiwitsch, Benno        HMV C3981, D1065, C4011, C4036*
    Pennario, Leonard         CAPITOL P 8486
    Rubinstein, Artur          RCA RB 16222
                             HMV DB 1915-18*
                               or ALP 1136
    Siki, Bela                 PARLOPHONE PMA 1011
    Slenczynska, Ruth          BRUNSWICK AXTL 1091
    Vásáry, Tamás            DGG LPEM 19451

SONATA NO. 1 in C MINOR (op. 4)
    Goldsand, Robert           NIXA CLP 1150
    Kedra, Wladyslaw         HMV CLP 1716

SONATA NO. 2 in B FLAT MINOR (op. 35)
    Askenase, Stefan           DGG DGM 18349
                             and HELIODOR 478436
    Backhaus, Wilhelm         DECCA LXT 2535
    Brailowsky, Alexander     HMV ALP 1401
    Block, Michel               DGG LPEM 19218
    Contestabile, Emma        HMV DB 11327-9*
    Cortot, Alfred              HMV DB 2019-20*
    Donska, Maria             SAGA XID 5120
    Flier, Jacob                MK 1549
    Gilels, Emil                COL 33CX 1364
    Godowsky, Leopold        COL LX 124-6*
    Harasiewicz, Adam        FONTANA CFL 1041
    Horowitz, Vladimir        HMV DB 21312-4*
                             and ALP 1087
                             CBS BRG 72067
    Janis, Byron               RCA RB 16028
    Jenner, Alexander         ORIOLE RM 146
    Katchen, Julius            DECCA LXT 5093
    Katz, Mindru             PYE CCL 30157
    Kedra, Wladyslaw         HMV CLP 1716
    Kempff, Wilhelm          DECCA LXT 5452
    Kilenyi, Edward           COL LX 691-3*
    Malcuzinski, Witold       COL LX 1119-21*
                             COL 33CX 1797
                             COL 33CX 1639
    Novaes, Guiomar          VOX PL 7360
    Pennario, Leonard         CAPITOL P 8457
    Rachmaninov, Sergei      HMV DA 1186-9*
                             and CAMDEN CDN 1017

Rubinstein, Artur      HMV ALP 1477
                             RCA RB 16282
Schioler, Victor       HMV ALP 1243
Vásáry, Tamás        DGG LPEM 19450

## SONATA NO. 3 in B MINOR (op. 58)

| | |
|---|---|
| Ashkenazy, Vladimir | COL 33CX 1621 |
| Askenase, Stefan | DGG DGM 18349 |
| | and HELIODOR 478436 |
| Arrau, Claudio | COL 33CX 1755 |
| Brailowsky, Alexander | HMV ALP 1401 |
| | or HMV DB 3700–2★ |
| | or PHILIPS ABL 3313 |
| Cortot, Alfred | HMV DA 1333–6★ |
| Donska, Maria | SAGA XID 5120 |
| Firkusny, Rudolf | CAPITOL P 8526 |
| Grainger, Percy | COL L 1695–7★ |
| Jenner, Alexander | ORIOLE RM 146 |
| Johannesen, Grant | HMV CLP 1208 |
| Katchen, Julius | DECCA LXT 5093 |
| Kedra, Wladyslaw | HMV CLP 1716 |
| Kempff, Wilhelm | DECCA LXT 5452 |
| | and Stereo SXL 2025 |
| Lipatti, Dinu | COL LX 994–6★ |
| | or 33CX 1337 |
| Malcuzynski, Witold | COL 33C 1005 |
| | COL 33CX 1797 |
| Magaloff, Nikita | DECCA LXT 5037 |
| Novaes, Guiomar | VOX PL 7360 |
| Rubinstein, Artur | RCA RB 16282 |
| Schiöler, Victor | HMV ALP 1243 |
| Ts'ong, Fou | WORLD RECORD T 34 |
| Vásáry, Tamás | DGG LPEM 19450 |

## TARANTELLA in A FLAT MAJOR (op. 43)

| | |
|---|---|
| Arrau, Claudio | PARLOPHONE R 2588★ |
| Banhalmi, George | VOX PL 10370 |
| Cortot, Alfred | HMV DA 1213★ |
| | HMV DB 2023★ |
| | HMV DA 2071★ |
| | or HMV ALP 1197 |
| Dorfmann, Ania | COL DB 1724★ |
| Entremont, Philippe | PHILIPS ABE 10024† |
| | or SBE 252 |
| Maggiar, Wilfred | NIXA PLP 112 |
| Mewton-Wood, Noel | DECCA K 1064★ |
| Perlemuter, Vlado | CONCERT HALL AM 2223 |

## *VARIATIONS BRILLANTES* (op. 12)

| | |
|---|---|
| Banhalmi, George | VOX PL 10370 |
| Gimpel, Jakob | HMV DLP 1187 |
| Goldsand, Robert | NIXA CLP 1133 |
| Maggiar, Wilfrid | PATHÉ PDT 101 |

## VARIATIONS ON A SWISS AIR *DER SCHWEIZERBUB* ('The Cattleboy') (op. posth.)

| | |
|---|---|
| Banhalmi, George | VOX PL 10370 |
| Goldsand, Robert | NIXA CL 1150 |

VARIATIONS ON MOZART'S 'LÀ CI DAREM LA MANO' (op. 2)

| | |
|---|---|
| Cherkassky, Shura | HMV ALP 1489 |
| Goldsand, Robert | NIXA CLP 1150 |

WALTZES (15) (complete recordings)

| | |
|---|---|
| Askenase, Stefan (1–14) | DGG DGM 19060 |
| | and HELIODOR 478416 |
| | DGG LPEM 19397 |
| Brailowsky, Alexander (1–14) | PHILIPS ABL 3311 |
| Cortot, Alfred (1–14) | HMV DB 2311–6* |
| | and COLH 32 |
| Cziffra, György (1–14) | PHILIPS AL 3426 |
| Fiorentino, Sergio | SAGA XID 5016 |
| | DELTA TQD 3015 |
| | and Stereo SQD 108 |
| Haebler, Ingrid | VOX GBY 11970 |
| Hess-Bukowska, Barbara (1–14) | WHITEHALL WH 20034 |
| Lipatti, Dinu (1–14) | COL LX 1341–6* |
| | or 33CX 1032 |
| Lympany, Moura (1–14) | HMV CLP 1349 |
| Malcuzynski, Witold (1–14) | COL 33CX 1685 |
| Novaes, Guiomar | VOX PL 8170 |
| Rauch, František (1–14) | SUPRAPHON SUA 10168 |
| Rubinstein, Artur (1–14) | RCA VICTOR RB 6600 |
| | HMV ALP 1333 |
| | or RCA RB 16150 |
| Rev, Livia | LONDON DTL 93088 |
| Uninsky, Alexander (1–14) | PHILIPS ABL 3216 |

## Section II: Piano and Orchestra

CONCERTO NO. 1 in E MINOR (op. 11)

Anda, Geza
  with Philharmonia Orchestra conducted by
  Alceo Galliera — COL 33C 1057

Askenase, Stefan
  with Hague Philharmonic Orchestra conducted
  by Willem van Otterloo — DGG LPM 18605

Badura-Skoda, Paul
  with Vienna State Opera Orchestra conducted
  by Artur Rodzinski — NIXA WLP 5308

Brailowsky, Alexander
  with Berlin Philharmonic Orchestra conducted
  by Julius Prüwer — DECCA CA 8009–12*

Brailowsky, Alexander
  with Victor Symphony Orchestra conducted by
  William Steinberg — HMV ALP 1015

Cziffra, György
  with French National Radio Orchestra conducted
  by Manuel Rosenthal — PHILIPS AL 3450

François, Samson
  with Paris Conservatoire Orchestra conducted
  by Georges Tzipine — COL 33CX 1238

Frankl, Peter
  with Innsbruck Symphony Orchestra conducted
  by Robert Wagner — VOX GBY 12640

Frugoni, Orazio
  with Vienna Volksoper Opera Orchestra conducted by Michael Gielen — VOX PL/D 11460

Gulda, Friedrich
  with London Philharmonic Orchestra conducted
  by Sir Adrian Boult
    DECCA LXT 2925
    and ACE OF CLUBS ACL 94

Harasiewiez, Adam
  with Vienna Symphony Orchestra conducted by
  Heinrich Hollreiser
    FONTANA Stereo SCFL 101

Horszowski, Mieczyslaw
  with Vienna State Opera Orchestra conducted by
  Hans Swarowsky
    VOX PL 7870

Magaloff, Nikita
  with Lamoureux Orchestra, Paris conducted by
  Roberto Benzi
    PHILIPS GL 5657

Mewton-Wood, Noel
  with Netherlands Philharmonic Orchestra conducted by Walter Goehr
    NIXA CLP 1153
    and MUSICAL MASTER-
    WORKS MMS 35

Musalin, Branka
  with South German Radio Orchestra, Stuttgart
  conducted by Hans Müller-Kray
    NIXA PLP 574

Pollini, Maurizio
  with Philharmonia Orchestra conducted by
  Paul Kletzki
    HMV ALP 1794

Rosenthal, Moritz
  with Berlin State Opera Orchestra conducted by
  Dr Weissmann
    PARLOPHONE R 902–4
    and E 11113–4

Rubinstein, Artur
  with London Symphony Orchestra conducted
  by Sir John Barbirolli
    HMV DB 3201–4*
  with Los Angeles Philharmonic Orchestra conducted by Alfred Wallenstein
    HMV ALP 1250
  with New Symphony Orchestra, London conducted by Stanislaw Skrowaczewski
    RCA RB 16275

Simon, Abbey
  with Royal Philharmonic Orchestra conducted
  by Sir Eugene Goossens
    HMV ALP 1580

Stefanska, Halina
  with Czech Philharmonic Orchestra conducted
  by Václav Smetáček
    DGG DGM 18394

Ts'ong, Fou
  with Warsaw Philharmonic Orchestra conducted
  by Zdzislaw Gorzynski
    PATHÉ DTX 173

Uninsky, Alexander
  with Hague Philharmonic Orchestra conducted
  by Willem van Otterloo
    PHILIPS GBR 6500

Wild, Earl
  with Royal Philharmonic Orchestra conducted
  by Sir Malcolm Sargent
    READERS DIGEST RDM 1020

PIANO CONCERTO NO. 2 in F MINOR (op. 21)

Ashkenazy, Vladimir
  with Warsaw Philharmonic Orchestra conducted
  by Zdzislaw Gorzynski
    COL 33CX 1563

Askenase, Stefan
  with Berlin Philharmonic Orchestra conducted
  by Leopold Ludwig
    DGG LPM 18791

with Berlin Philharmonic Orchestra conducted
by Fritz Lehmann

DGG DGM 18040
and HELIODOR 478086

Badura-Skoda, Paul
with Vienna State Opera Orchestra conducted
by Artur Rodzinski

NIXA WLP 5308

Ballon, Ellen
with London Symphony Orchestra conducted
by Ernest Ansermet

DECCA LX 3035

Brailowsky, Alexander
with Boston Symphony Orchestra conducted by
Charles Munch

HMV ALP 1321

Cortot, Alfred
with unidentified orchestra conducted by Sir
John Barbirolli

HMV DB 2612–5*

François, Samson
with French National Radio Orchestra conducted
by Paul Kletzki

HMV XLP 20017

Frugoni, Orazio
with Vienna Volksoper Orchestra conducted by
Michael Gielen

VOX PL/D 11460

Harasiewicz, Adam
with Vienna Symphony Orchestra conducted by
Heinrich Hollreiser

FONTANA CFL 1040

Haskil, Clara
with Lamoureux Orchestra, Paris conducted by
Igor Markevitch

PHILIPS ABL 3340

Long, Marguerite
with Orchestre des Concerts du Conservatoire
conducted by Philippe Gaubert

COL D 15236–9*
or LX 4–7*

Malcuzynski, Witold
with Philharmonia Orchestra conducted by
Paul Kletzki
with London Symphony Orchestra conducted by
Walter Süsskind

COL LX 1013–6*
and 33CX 1066
or COL 33CX 1695

Mewton-Wood, Noel
with Zurich Radio Orchestra conducted by
Walter Goehr

MUSICAL MASTERWORKS
MMS 4

Musalin, Branka
with South German Radio Orchestra, Stuttgart
conducted by Hans Müller-Kray

NIXA PLP 574

Novaes, Guiomar
with Vienna Symphony Orchestra conducted by
Klemperer

VOX PL 7100

Pennario, Leonard
with Concert Arts Orchestra conducted by
Vladimir Golschmann

CAPITOL P 8366

Rubinstein, Artur
with London Symphony Orchestra conducted by
Sir John Barbirolli
with NBC Symphony Orchestra conducted by
William Steinberg
with Symphony of the Air conducted by Alfred
Wallenstein

HMV DB 1494–7*

HMV ALP 1465

RCA RB 16183

Simon, Abbey
with Royal Philharmonic Orchestra conducted
by Sir Eugene Goossens

HMV ALP 1580

Slezarjeva, Marina
  with Prague Symphony Orchestra conducted by
  Vacláv Smetacék                                    SUPRAPHON ALPV 82
Uninsky, Alexander
  with Hague Philharmonic Orchestra conducted
  by Willem van Otterloo                             PHILIPS GBL 5535
Vásáry, Tamás
  with Berlin Philharmonic Orchestra conducted
  by Janos Kulka                                     DGG LPEM 19452
Vitos, Carmen
  with Vienna Festival Orchestra conducted by
  Hans Swarowsky                                     WORLD RECORD CLUB SC 8
*KRAKOWIAK* 'CONCERT RONDO' (op. 14)
Askenase, Stefan
  with Hague Philharmonic Orchestra conducted
  by Willem van Otterloo                             DGG LPM 18605
Frankl, Peter
  with Innsbruck Symphony Orchestra conducted
  by Robert Wagner                                   VOX GBY 12500
*ANDANTE SPIANATO AND GRANDE POLONAISE* (op. 22)
Arau, Claudio
  with the Little Orchestra Society conducted by
  Thomas Scherman                                    COL LX 1267–8
Frankl, Peter
  with Innsbruck Symphony Orchestra conducted
  by Robert Wagner                                   VOX GBY 12500
Rubinstein, Artur
  with Symphony of the Air conducted by
  Alfred Wallenstein                                 RCA 16183
Stefanska, Halina
  with the Czech Philharmonic Orchestra
  conducted by Václav Smétaček                       SUPRAPHON LPM 429
Vásáry, Tamás
  with Berlin Philharmonic Orchestra conducted
  by Janos Kulka                                     DGG LPEM 19452

## Section III: Chamber Music

INTRODUCTION AND POLONAISE FOR CELLO AND PIANO IN C MAJOR
  (op. 3)
Fournier, Pierre
  with Gerald Moore                                  COL 33CX 1606
Hoelscher, Ludwig
  with M. Raucheisen                                 TELEFUNKEN LGX 66061
Navarra, André
  with Jeanne-Marie Darré                            SAGA XID 5166
Pleeth, William
  with Margaret Good                                 DECCA K 922*
Rostropovich, Mstislav
  with Alexander Dedyukhin                           HELIODOR 479018
Vectomov, Sasa
  with Vladimir Topinka                              SUPRAPHON FUA 10150

GRAND DUO ON THEMES FROM *ROBERT LE DIABLE* BY MEYERBEER
Navarra, André
  with Jeanne-Marie Darré                            SAGA XID 5166

SONATA FOR CELLO AND PIANO in G MINOR (op. 65)
Navarra, André
  with Jeanne-Marie Darré                            SAGA XID 5166

Parisot, Aldo
  with Leopold Mittman      OVERTONE 17
Starker, János
  with György Sebök      PHILIPS AL 3460
Stork, Klaus
  with Daniela Ballek      DGG LPEM 19196
Vectomov, Sasa
  with Vladimir Topinka      SUPRAPHON SUA 10150
TRIO in G MINOR (op. 8)
Trio di Bolzano      VOX PL 8480

RONDO in C MAJOR FOR TWO PIANOS (op. 73)
  Bauer, Kurt, and Bung, Heidi      DGG LPEM 19158
  Babin, Victor, and Vronsky, Vitya      BRUNSWICK AXA 4508

VARIATIONS ON A THEME FROM ROSSINI'S *LA CENERENTOLA* FOR FLUTE AND PIANO
Rampal, Jean-Pierre,
  with Veyron-Lacroix      DISCOPHILES FRANCAIS DF 730019

## Section IV: Songs

SEVENTEEN POLISH SONGS (op. 74) (complete recordings)
  Kurenko, Maria (sop.)      CONCERT ARTIST
    with Robert Hufstader      LPA 1040
  Slobodskaya, Oda (sop.)
    with Frederick Stone      DELTA DEL 12006
  Zareska, Eugenia (mezzo-sop.)
    with Giorgio Favaretto      COL 33CX 1607

## Individual Songs

1. *Życzenie* ('The Wish')
  Kurenko, Maria (sop.)      CONCERT ARTIST
    with Robert Hufstader      LPA 1040
  Sembrich, Marcella
    accompanying herself      MUZA XL 0109
  Slobodskaya, Oda (sop.)
    with Frederick Stone      DELTA DEL 12006
  Zareska, Eugenia (mezzo-sop.)
    with Giorgio Favaretto      COL 33CX 1607

2. *Wiosna* ('Spring')
  Kurenko, Maria (sop.)      CONCERT ARTIST
    with Robert Hufstader      LPA 1040
  Slobodskaya, Oda (sop.)
    with Frederick Stone      DELTA DEL 12006
  Zareska, Eugenia
    with Giorgio Favaretto      COL 33CX 1607

3. *Smutna Rzeka* ('Sad River')
  Bolechowska, Alnia (sop.)
    with Serguisz Nadgrizowski      DGG Stereo SLPE 133004
  Conrad, Doda (bass)
    with Irene Aitoff      HMV DB 11199*
  Kurenko, Maria (sop.)      CONCERT ARTIST
    with Robert Hufstader      LPA 1040
  Slobodskaya, Oda (sop.)
    with Frederick Stone      DELTA DEL 12006

Zareska, Eugenia (mezzo-sop.)
  with Giorgio Favaretto — COL 33CX 1607

4. *Hulanka* ('Drinking Song')
  Conrad, Doda (bass)
    with Irene Aitoff — HMV DB 11199*
  Kurenko, Maria (sop.)
    with Robert Hufstader — CONCERT ARTIST LPA 1040
  Slobodskaya, Oda (sop.)
    with Frederick Stone — DELTA DEL 12006
  Witt, Janina de (sop.)
    with Alberto Semprini — FONITOPIA 8080
  Zareska, Eugenia (mezzo-sop.)
    with Giorgio Favaretto — COL 33CX 1607

5. *Gdzie Lubi* ('What she likes')
  Bolechowska, Alina (sop.)
    with Serguisz Nadgrizowski — DGG Stereo SLPE 133004
  Kurenko, Maria (sop.)
    with Robert Hufstader — CONCERT ARTIST LPA 1040
  Slobodskaya, Oda (sop.)
    with Frederick Stone — DELTA DEL 12006

6. *Precz z Moich Oczu!* ('Out of my sight!')
  Bolechowska, Alina (sop.)
    with Serguisz Nadgrizowski — DGG Stereo SLPE 133004
  Conrad, Doda (bar.)
    with Irene Aitoff — HMV DB 11199*
  Korolkiewicz, Josef (bar.)
    with Jerzy Lefeld — MUZA 1119
  Kurenko, Maria (sop.)
    with Robert Hufstader — CONCERT ARTIST LPA 1040
  Slobodskaya, Oda (sop.)
    with Frederick Stone — DELTA DEL 12006
  Zareska, Eugenia (mezzo-sop.)
    with Giorgio Favaretto — COL 33CX 1607

7. *Poseł* ('The Messenger')
  Bolechowska, Alina (sop.)
    with Serguisz Nadgrizowski — DGG Stereo SLPE 133004
  Kurenko, Maria (sop.)
    with Robert Hufstader — CONCERT ARTIST LPA 1040
  Slobodskaya, Oda (sop.)
    with Frederick Stone — DELTA DEL 12006
  Zareska, Eugenia (mezzo-sop.)
    with Giorgio Faveretti — COL 33CX 1607

8. *Śliczny Chłopiec* ('Handsome Lad')
  Kurenko, Maria (sop.)
    with Robert Hufstader — CONCERT ARTIST LPA 1040
  Slobodskaya, Oda (sop.)
    with Frederick Stone — DELTA DEL 12006
  Zareska, Eugenia (mezzo-sop.)
    with Giorgio Favaretto — COL 33CX 1607

9. *Melodia* ('Melody')
  Bolechowska, Alina (sop.)
    with Serguisz Nadgrizowski — DGG Stereo SLPE 133004
  Slobodskaya, Oda (sop.)
    with Frederick Stone — DELTA DEL 12006 / CONCERT ARTIST LPA 1040
  Kurenko, Maria (sop.)
    with Robert Hufstader
  Zareska, Eugenia (mezzo-sop.)
    with Giorgio Favaretto — COL 33CX 1607

10. *Wojak* ('The Warrior')
   Kurenko, Maria (sop.)
      with Robert Hufstader               CONCERT ARTIST
                                         LPA 1040
   Slobodskaya, Oda (sop.)
      with Frederick Stone                 DELTA DEL 12006
   Zareska, Eugenia
      with Giorgio Favaretto              COL 33CX 1607

11. *Dwojaki Koniec* ('Double Ending')
   Bolechowska, Alina (sop.)
      with Serguisz Nadrizowski       DGG Stereo SLPE 133004
   Kurenko, Maria (sop.)                CONCERT ARTIST
      with Robert Hufstader               LPA 1040
   Slobodskaya, Oda (sop.)
      with Frederick Stone                 DELTA DEL 12006
   Zareska, Eugenia (mezzo-sop.)
      with Giorgio Favaretto              COL 33CX 1607

12. *Moja Pieszczotka* ('My Darling')
   Bolechowska, Alina (sop.)
      with Serguisz Nadgrizowski      DGG Stereo SLPE 133004
   Kurenko, Maria (sop.)                CONCERT ARTIST
      with Robert Hufstader               LPA 1040
   Poplawski, Janusz (tenor)
      with Jerzy Lefeld                    MUZA 1119
   Witt, Janina de (sop.)
      with unidentified pianist           FONITOPIA 8391
   Slobodskaya, Oda (sop.)
      with Frederick Stone                 DELTA DEL 12006
   Zareska, Eugenia (mezzo-sop.)
      with Giorgio Favaretto              COL 33CX 1607

13. *Nie ma Czego Trzeba* ('There is no need')
   Bolechowska, Alina (sop.)
      with Serguisz Nadgrizowski      DGG Stereo SLPE 133004
   Kurenko, Maria (sop.)                CONCERT ARTIST
      with Robert Hufstader               LPA 1040
   Slobodskaya, Oda (sop.)
      with Frederick Stone                 DELTA DEL 12006
   Zareska, Eugenia (mezzo-sop.)
      with Giorgio Favaretto              COL 33CX 1607

14. *Pierścień* ('The Ring')
   Bolechowska, Alina (sop.)
      with Serguisz Nadgrizowski      DGG stereo SLPE 133004
   Kurenko, Maria (sop.)                CONCERT ARTIST
      with Robert Hufstader               LPA 1040
   Slobodskaya, Oda (sop.)
      with Frederick Stone                 DELTA DEL 12006
   Zareska, Eugenia (mezzo-sop.)
      with Giorgio Favaretto              COL 33CX 1607

15. *Narzeczony* ('The Bridegroom')
   Bolechowska, Alina (sop.)
      with Serguisz Nadgrizowski      DGG Stereo SLPE 133004
   Kurenko, Maria (sop.)                CONCERT ARTIST
      with Robert Hufstader               LPA 1040
   Slobodskaya, Oda (sop.)
      with Frederick Stone                 DELTA DEL 12006
   Zareska, Eugenia (mezzo-sop.)
      with Giorgio Favaretto              COL 33CX 1607

16. *Piośnka Litewska* ('Lithuanian Song')
   Kurenko, Maria (sop.)                CONCERT ARTIST
      with Robert Hufstader               LPA 1040

Witt, Janina de (sop.)
    with Alberto Semprini         FONITOPIA 8080
Slobodskaya, Oda (sop.)
    with Frederick Stone         DELTA DEL 12006
Zareska, Eugenia (mezzo-sop.)
    with Giorgio Favaretto         COL 33CX 1607

17. *Śpiew Grobowy* ('Hymn from the Tomb')
    Bolechowska, Alina (sop.)
        with Serguisz Nadgrizowski     DGG Stereo SLPE 133004
    Kurenko, Maria (sop.)         CONCERT ARTIST
        with Robert Hufstader         LPA 1040
    Slobodskaya, Oda (sop.)
        with Frederick Stone         DELTA DEL 12006
    Zareska, Eugenia (mezzo-sop.)
        with Giorgio Favaretto         COL 33CX 1607

# BIBLIOGRAPHY

*Abraham, Gerald*   Chopin's Musical Style   (London, 1939)
*Audley, Mme A.*   Frédéric Chopin: sa vie et ses oeuvres   (Paris, 1880)
*Barbedette, H.*   Frédéric Chopin   (Paris, 1861)
*Barbag, S.*   Study of Chopin's Songs   (Léopol, 1927)
*Bennett, Joseph*   Frédéric Chopin   (London)
*Bidou, Henri*   Chopin   (Paris, 1925; London, 1927)
*Binental, Leopold*   Chopin (Documents and Souvenirs)   (Warsaw, 1930)
—— Chopin   (Paris, 1934)
—— Chopin: Life and Art   (Warsaw, 1937)
*Bory, Robert*   La Vie de Frédéric Chopin
*Boucourechliev, A.*   Chopin: A Pictorial Biography   (London, 1963)
*Bronarski, Ludwik*   Chopin's Harmony   (Warsaw, 1935)
—— Chopin Studies, 2 vols.   (Lausanne, 1946)
*Brookshaw, Susanna*   Chopin in Manchester (London, 1938)
*Brown, Maurice J. E.*   Chopin: an Index of his works in chronological order   (London, 1960)
*Chantavoine, Jean*   L'Italianisme de Chopin   (Paris, 1912)
*Cherbuliez, A.-E.*   Fryderyck Chopin: Leben und Werk   (Zurich, 1948)
*Cortot, Alfred*   Aspects de Chopin   (Paris, 1949)
   (Translated as *In Search of Chopin*; New York, 1952)
*Davison, J. W.*   Essay on the Works of F. Chopin   (London, 1843)
*Delacroix, Eugène*   Journal   (Paris, 1893–5)
*Dunn, J. P.*   Ornamentation in the works of Frederick Chopin   (London, 1921)
*Egert, Paul*   Friedrich Chopin   (Potsdam, 1936)
*Finck, Henry T.*   Chopin and other Musical Essays   (New York, 1899)
*Ganche, Édouard*   Frédéric Chopin: sa vie et ses ouvres   (Paris, 1921)
—— Dans le souvenir de Frédéric Chopin   (Paris, 1925)
—— Voyages avec Frédéric Chopin   (Paris, 1934)
—— Souffrances de Frédéric Chopin   (Paris, 1935)
*Gide, André*   Notes sur Chopin   (Paris, 1949; New York, 1949)
*Hadden, J. C.*   Chopin   (London, 1903)
*Hadow, Sir Henry*   Studies in Modern Music, vol. 2   (London, 1926)
*Hedley, Arthur*   Chopin   (Master Musician Series, London, 1964)
—— Selected Correspondence of Fryderyck Chopin   (London, 1962)
*Hipkins, E. J.*   How Chopin Played   (London, 1937)
*Hoesick, Ferdynand*   Chopin: his Life and Work   (Warsaw, 1904–11)
—— Chopiniana   (Warsaw, 1912)
*Huneker, J.*   Chopin: the Man and his Music   (London, 1901)
*Heine, H.*   Lutèce   (Paris, 1855)
*Jachimecki, Z.*   Frédéric Chopin et son oeuvre   (Paris, 1930)
*Jonson, E. Ashton*   Handbook to Chopin's Works   (London, 1905)
*Karenine, Wladimir*   George Sand: sa vie et ses oeuvres   (Paris, 1899–1926)
*Karasowski, Moritz*   Life and Letters of Chopin   (German, 1877; English, 1879)
*Karlowicz, M.*   Souvenirs inédits de Chopin   (Paris, 1904)
*Kelly, E. S.*   Chopin the Composer   (New York, 1913)
*Kleczynski, J.*   Chopin's Greater Works   (Leipzig, 1898)
*Koczalski, R.*   F. Chopin: Betrachtungen   (Cologne, 1935)
*Leichtentritt, Hugo*   Analyse von Chopins Klavierwerken   (Berlin, 1921)
—— Friedrich Chopin   (Berlin, 1905)

*Lenz, Wilhelm v.* The Great Piano Virtuosos of our Time (German, 1872)
*Liszt, Franz* Frederick Chopin (London, 1877)
*Maine, Basil* Chopin (London, 1933)
*Mariotti, G.* Chopin (Florence, 1933)
*Maurois, André* Frédéric Chopin (New York, 1942)
*Meister, E.* Style-elements and the Historical Basis of Chopin's Piano Works (Hamburg, 1936)
*Miketta, Janusz* Analysis of Chopin's Mazurkas (Cracow, 1949)
*Mirska, Maria* Szlakiem Chopina (Essays) (Warsaw, 1949)
*Morgan-Brown, Humphrey* Frédéric François Chopin The Heritage of Music, vol 2 (Oxford, 1934)
*Murdoch, William* Chopin: his Life (London, 1934)
*Niecks, Frederick* Fredrick Chopin as Man and Musician (London, 1888)
*Opienski, Henryck* Collected Letters of Chopin (Warsaw, 1937; London, 1932)
—— Chopin (Lwów, 1909)
*Ottlich, M.* Chopin's Klavierornamentik (German, 1938)
*Osborne, G. A.* Reminiscences of Frederick Chopin (Proc. Mus. Ass., vol. VI, 1880)
*Paderewski, I.* Chopin—a Discourse (London, 1911)
*Poirée, E.* Chopin (Paris, 1907)
*Porte, J. F.* Chopin: the Composer and his Music (London, 1935)
*Pourtalès, Guy de* Chopin ou le Poète (Paris, 1927)
  (Translated as *Frederick Chopin: a Man of Solitude*; London, 1920)
*Revue Musicale, La* Special Chopin Number (Paris, 1931)
*Rocheblave, Samuel* George Sand et sa Fille (Paris, 1905)
*Sand, George* Histoire de ma vie (Vol. X, 1856)
—— Correspondence (Paris, 1882–4)
—— Un hiver à Majorque
—— Lucrezia Floriani
*Scharlitt, B.* Chopin (Leipzig, 1919)
—— Friedrich Chopins gesammelte Briefe (Leipzig, 1911)
*Schumann, Robert* Music and Musicians (London, 1880)
*Seguel, M.* Chopin's Tempo Rubato (1928)
*Sikorski, R.* Souvenirs of Chopin (Polish, 1849)
*Slonimsky, Nicolas* Chopiniana: some materials for a biography (*Musical Quarterly*, 1948)
*Sydow, B. E.* Um Chopins Geburtsdatum (Die Musikforschung, III)
—— *Bibliografia* F. F. Chopin
*Szymanowski, Karol* Fryderyk Chopin (Warsaw, 1925)
*Tarnowski, Count* Chopin: as revealed by Extracts from his Diary (London, 1899)
*Thuguttowna, Wanda* Introduction to Chopin's Mazurkas (Warsaw, 1927)
*Tovey, Sir Donald* Essays in Musical Analysis: Chamber Music (Oxford, 1944)
*Uminska and Kennedy* Chopin, the Child and the Lad (London, 1925)
*Valetta, I.* Chopin: la vita, le opera (Turin, 1910)
*Volkmann, H.* Chopin in Dresden (Dresden, 1933; Supplement, 1936)
*Vuillermoz, É.* La vie amoureuse de Chopin (Paris, 1927)
*Weinstock, Herbert* Chopin: the Man and his Music (New York, 1949)
*Wierzynski, Casimir* The Life and Death of Chopin (New York, 1949)
*Willeby, C.* Frédéric François Chopin (London, 1892)
*Windakiewiczowa, E.* Basic Forms of Polish Popular Music in Chopin's Mazurkas (Warsaw, 1927)
*Wodzinski, Count* Les Trois Romans de Frédéric Chopin (Paris, 1886)
*Wójcik-Keuprulian B.* Chopin's Melody (Lwów, 1930)
*Zukowski, O.* Chopin in the Light of Polish Poetry (Lwów, 1910)

# INDEXES

# INDEX OF MUSIC EXAMPLES

## Works by Chopin

Sonatas
  in C minor (op. 4), 145–7
  in B flat minor (op. 35), 159–60, 240–2, 244–8
  in B minor (op. 58), 126, 161–5, 252–6
  for cello and piano (op. 65), 165–7
Songs (op. 74)
  The Wish, 191
  What she likes, 192–3
  Drinking Song, 193
  Out of my sight!, 194
  The Messenger, 189
  The Warrior, 196
  Spells, 197
  Sad River, 189–90, 199
  The Bridegroom, 200
  The Ring, 202
  Hymn from the tomb, 203
  My Darling, 205
  Elegy, 207
  Double Ending, 208
  There is no need, 209
  Melody, 210
Studies (op. 10)
  in A minor (no. 2), 268
  in C major (no. 1), 130
  in E flat minor (no. 6), 132
  in F minor (no. 9), 133

Studies (op. 25)
  in A flat major (no. 1), 134
  in F minor (no. 2), 19
  in G sharp minor (no. 6), 135
  in C sharp minor (no. 7), 136, 157
  in A minor (no. 11), 137, 274

Trois Nouvelles Études
  in F minor, 137
  in D flat major, 138
Tarantella (op. 43), 224
Trio in G minor (op. 8), 217

Variations
  for flute and piano (1824), 217
  *Der Schweizerbub* (1826) (The Cattleboy), 220
  *Le Carnaval de Venise* (1829), 221

Waltzes
  in A flat major (op. 34, no. 1), 90
  in A minor (op. 34, no. 2), 92–94
  in A flat major (op. 42), 90, 233–4
  in C sharp minor (op. 64, no. 2), 90, 92
  in E minor (op. posth.), 87–89

## Works by Other Composers

Bach, Six Little Preludes (no. 2), 116
Bartók, First Rumanian Dance, 275
Brahms, Piano Concerto in B flat major, 262
Bruckner, Symphony No. 9, in D minor, 274

Clementi, Study in B flat minor, 118
Cramer, Study in D minor, 117; Study in E flat minor, 118

Debussy, *Le vent dans la plaine*, 270

Folk songs: 'Juz miesiac zaszedł', 214; 'Oj Magdalino', 74

Liszt, Transcendental study in A minor, 123

Ravel, *Scarbo*, 265, 267

Schubert, *Trockne Blumen*, 189

# GENERAL INDEX

Abraham, Gerald, 66, 75, 80, 99, 100, 106, 272
d'Agoult, Marie, 36, 122
Albert Hall performances, 23
Album Leaf in E major (1843), 225
Alkan, Charles, 121, 123
Allegro de Concert, op. 46, 149, 150, **155–8**
Analysis: backgrounds and foregrounds in musical structure, 228; nature of, 229–30; relation to performance, 256–7; *Urform*, 91–92; unity, **227–57**, 228–9, 231
Andante spianato, op. 22, 95, **215–16**
Andantino in G minor (1838–48) (piano arrangement of the song *Wiosna* (Spring)), 225
Auber, Daniel, *Masaniello*, 222

Bach, C. P. E., 130
Bach, J. S., 10, 41, 64, 86, 116, 132, 138, 139, 166, 168, 243; 'Forty-eight', 116, 130, 138; Partita in B flat major, 270; 'Short Preludes', 138; Violin Concerto in E major, 243
Bach, J. C., 25
Badura-Skoda, Paul, 46, 139, 132
Balakirev, Mily, 149
Baldick, Robert, 41
Ballades (general), 42–45
  in G minor, op. 23, **46–50**, 269, 278
  in F major, op. 38, 16, 43, **50–53**, 195, 243, 263 (similarity to Scriabin), 270
  in A flat major, op. 47, 43, 45, **53–55**, 60, 106, 158, **236–8**
  in F minor, op. 52, **55–59**, 114, 137, 243, 258, 262, 269, 270–1
Balzac, Honoré de, 25, 36
Barcarolle, op. 60, 17, 106, 114, 157, 163, **184–6**, 258, 262, 267, 271
Bartók, Béla, 73, 124, 215, 260, 275; First Rumanian Dance, 275
Baudelaire, Charles, 140
Beethoven, Ludwig van, 24, 25, 29, 30, 31, 34, 57, 62, 68, 69, 82, 115, 116, 119, 121, 122, 123, 125, 127, 128, 133–4, 139, 147, 148, 151, 159, 166, 250, 251
  Bagatelles, 77, 139
  *Fidelio*, 210
  *Écossaises*, 220
  Quartet in C sharp minor, op. 131, 53

*Sonatas*
  Appassionata, op. 57, 134
  Moonlight, op. 27, No. 2, 267
  Spring, op. 24, 62
  'Waldstein', op. 53, 125
  in A flat major, op. 26, 115
  in F major, op. 54, 115
*Symphonies*
  Eroica, op. 55, 69
  Pastoral, op. 68, 69
Bellini, Vincenzo, 39, 164, 255; *La Sonnambula*, 39; *I Puritani*, 39, 223; *Norma*, 39
Berlioz, Hector, 8, 24, 27, 28, 35, 187, 278
Bennett, Sterndale, 50
Berceuse, op. 57, **183–4**, 221
Berg, Alban, 264, 267; 'Lyric' Suite, 264
Birkbeck, Morris, 28
Binental, Leopold, 202
Blacher, Boris, 250
Bloch, Ernest, 73
Blumenfeld, Felix, 263; Chopin's influence, 263
Brahms, Johannes, 32, 166; Chopin's influence, 262–3
  Ballade in B minor, op. 10, No. 3, 262; Intermezzo in E minor, op. 116, No. 5, 55; *Klavierstücke*, op. 118, 262; Piano Concerto in B flat major, op. 83, 262; Rhapsody op. 79, No. 1, 263; Sonata in F sharp minor, op. 2, 262; *Variations on a theme of Paganini*, op. 35, 115, 250
Broadwood, Thomas, 36
Brown, Maurice, J. E., 73, 172, 201, 226
Bolero, op. 19, 164, 222
Bruckner, Anton, 264, 274, 275; Chopin's influence, 275, 273
  *Erinnerung*, 273; Mass in F minor, 275
  *Symphonies*: in B flat major (no. 5) 275; in C minor (No. 8) 275; in D minor (No. 9) 274
Bourrées (1846), 226
Bülow, Hans von, 19, 36
Burney, Dr. Charles, 29, 261; *Journeys* (1772), 261
Busoni, Ferruccio, 43, 52, 121, 246, 276; *Études de travail*, 124

Canon at the octave (1839), 226
Cantabile in B flat major (1834), 223

Carlyle, Thomas, 11
Chopin, Frédéric
  *works indexed separately*
  admiration for Bach, 10, 24, 83, 116, 139
  admiration for Mozart, 24
  as a pianist, 13, **14–16**, 21, **36–37**, 38, 120, 170, 214
  as a teacher, 40, 135
  attitude to Liszt, **15**, 37, 149
  comparison with Liszt, 121–2, 228
  illness, 7
  place in history, 1, 2, 23
  personality, **2–3**, 5–6, **7–9**
  national idioms, 26, 73–74, 214–15, 260, 275
  misconceptions of his music, **17–18**, 49–50
  patriotism, 10–11
  *Interpretation* (general), 3, **13–23**, 254, 256
    fingering, 133
    pedalling, **125–7**
    tempo rubato, 59, 77–78, **254**
    metronome markings, 19, **127–8**
  *Composing techniques*
    athematicism, 247
    atonality, 80, 247, 264
    chromaticism, 274
    dance-models, 86
    economy of means, 8–9
    'frozen' passing notes, 267–9
    introversion, 245
    identity between idea and medium, **238–9**
    metrical originality, 22, 57, 146–7, 171–2
    modality, 74, 79, 82
    notation, 159, 168, **236**, **239**
    orchestration, 149
    parallel fifths and octaves, 261, 270, 272
    phrase structure, 51, 56, 74, 89–90
    polyphony, 116, 132, 224–5
    progressive tonality, 248
    refrains, 90–91
    serialism, 70
    structural compression, **242–3**
    thematic unity, 47, 65, 158
    'tone-splitting', **273–4**
    tonality, 79, 110–11, 145–6, 152–3, 154–5, 161
    word-setting, 188–90
  *Form*
    introductions, 43–45, 103, 136, 159
    canon, 83, 84, 85
    codas, 48, 58–59, 83–84, 177–8, 243
    developments, 52, 151
    'lead-backs', 85, 254
    recapitulations, 48, 145–6, 161, 176, 217, **242**
Chopin, Justyna (mother), 5, 278
Chopin, Louise (sister), 171, 191

Chopin, Nicholas (father), 4, 216, 278
Cichocki, Josef, 216
Clementi, Muzio, 118; *Gradus ad Parnassum*, 117, 118, 119
Collet, Robert, 159, 271
Concerto in E minor, op. 11, 3, 25, 35, 131, 146, **147–9**, **152–5**, 274, 278, 279
Concerto in F minor, op. 21, 21–22, **149–52**, 171, 214, 278
Conrad, Joseph, 50
Contrabass to a 3-part canon by Mendelssohn, 225
Cortot, Alfred, 122, 141, 248, 249, 266
Couperin, François, 121, 130; *L'art de toucher le clavecin*, 115, 117
Cramer, Johann, 117–19
Czerny, Karl, 119, 130, 223; 'Forty Daily Studies', 118; 'School of the Virtuoso', 118

Dannreuther, Edward, 121
Debussy, Claude, 132, 139, 171, 259; Chopin's influence, 269–72
  Twelve Studies, 124, 269; *Le vent dans la pleine*, 270; *Pelléas and Mélisande*, 271
Delacroix, Eugène, 3, 25, 36, 140
Dickens, Charles, 40
Döhler, Theodor, 22
Donizetti, Gaetano, 132
Dussek, Jan, 251
Dvořák, Anton, 73

*Écossaises*, op. 72, 220
Ehrensweig, Anton, 231; *The Psycho-Analysis of Artistic Vision and Hearing*, 231, 257
Elsner, Joseph, 13–14, 141, 144, 213, 278
Encyclopaedia Britannica, 41
Érard, Sébastien, 36
Ernemann, 219

Falla, Manuel de, 249
Fantaisie-Impromptu (see Impromptus)
*Fantaisie sur des airs nationaux polonaise*, op 13, **213–14**, 278
Fantasy in F minor, op 49, **60–62**, 113, 114, 149, 158, **234–6**, 272
Fauré, Gabriel, 28, 171, 185; Chopin's influence, 264
Field, John, 39, 119, 170, 172; Chopin's reaction to him, 255
Filtsch, Karl, 14, 40
Folk Songs (Polish): 'Oj Magdalino', 73; 'Lulajze Jezuniu', 65
Fontana, Julian, 3, 4, 10, 21, 87, 148, 155, 158, 172, 191, 198, 202, 220, 221, 223
Franchomme, August, 36, 165, **218–19**
Franck, César, 264; Chopin's influence, 265; Symphony in D minor, 265
Freud, Sigmund, 231; *Leonardo da Vinci*, 231